The Rhetoric of
Donald Trump

The Rhetoric of Donald Trump

NATIONALIST POPULISM AND

AMERICAN DEMOCRACY

Robert C. Rowland

University Press of Kansas

Published by the University Press of Kansas (Lawrence, Kansas 66045), which was
organized by the Kansas Board of Regents and is operated and funded by Emporia State
University, Fort Hays State University, Kansas State University, Pittsburg State University,
the University of Kansas, and Wichita State University.

Library of Congress Cataloging-in-Publication Data

Names: Rowland, Robert C., 1954– author.
Title: The rhetoric of Donald Trump : nationalist populism and American democracy /
    Robert C. Rowland.
Other titles: Nationalist populism and American democracy
Description: Lawrence, Kansas : University Press of Kansas, 2021 |
    Includes bibliographical references and index.
Identifiers: LCCN 2020040366
    ISBN 9780700631964 (cloth)
    ISBN 9780700631971 (epub)
Subjects: LCSH: Trump, Donald, 1946– —Language. | Presidents—United States—
    Election—2016. | Rhetoric—Political aspects—United States—History—21st century.
    | Communication in politics—United States—History—21st century. | Presidents—
    United States—Election—2016. | Populism—United States—History—21st century.
    | Democracy—United States—History—21st century. | United States—Politics and
    government—2017–
Classification: LCC E911 .R69 2021 | DDC 973.933092—dc23
LC record available at https://lccn.loc.gov/2020040366.

British Library Cataloguing-in-Publication Data is available.

Printed in the United States of America

10 9 8 7 6 5 4 3 2 1

The paper used in this publication is acid free and meets the minimum requirements of
the American National Standard for Permanence of Paper for Printed Library Materials
Z39.48-1992.

CONTENTS

ACKNOWLEDGMENTS

My approach to rhetoric has been shaped by my teachers, including, especially, Lee Griffin, Tom Goodnight, and David Zarefsky at Northwestern and Wil Linkugel, Karlyn Kohrs Campbell, and Donn W. Parson at the University of Kansas (KU). I also have learned a great deal from the graduate students I worked with first at Baylor and now for more than three decades at KU. The debaters I worked with at both schools also influenced my thinking. I also want to thank Stephen H. Browne from Penn State and Denise Bostdorff from the College of Wooster for their extremely insightful commentary and Melanie Stafford for her particularly careful and graceful copyedit. I owe a particular debt to one of the best editors I know, Dennis Gouran, for his invaluable suggestions and to Donn W. Parson for a lifetime of teaching about Kenneth Burke, public argument, and life. Most of all, I am thankful for Donna.

INTRODUCTION: DONALD TRUMP—

A RHETORICAL ENIGMA

When Donald Trump announced his candidacy, almost no one believed he would be a serious contender for the Republican nomination for president. Yet, he won the nomination easily, crushing what was labeled a strong field of potential candidates that included the former governor of Florida, Jeb Bush—who happened to be the brother of one former president and the son of another—as well as rising star Senator Marco Rubio and darling of the right Senator Ted Cruz.

When Trump won the Republican nomination, almost no one believed he would defeat Hillary Clinton, a former US senator from New York, US secretary of state, and wife of a former president widely believed to be the shrewdest political tactician of his age; she had the strong support of a transformational and charismatic two-term Democratic president, Barack Obama. Yet, Trump won the presidency.

The puzzle becomes still more confusing given the unconventional campaign Trump ran and the many gaffes he committed. He was running for the highest office in the land but lacked any experience in public office. Moreover, although he had been a successful business owner, he also had multiple bankruptcies, had been accused of not paying his contractor bills and even bilking students who attended Trump University, and had lived a colorful personal life accumulating three wives and being accused of infidelity and a host of other sins.[1] His personal background was particularly problematic given that conservative Christians were among the most important groups supporting the Republican Party. And yet Trump won.

His personal life and business career were not the only issues that dogged him throughout the primary and general election campaigns in 2016. Again and again during the campaign, critics said that the latest gaffe would doom his campaign, but it never did. They said this when he attacked Mexican immigrants in his announcement speech, when he denigrated Senator John McCain's military service in the Vietnam War, when he insulted a Gold Star family, and on a host of other occasions.[2] In fact, *Politico* counted "The 37 Fatal

Gaffes That Didn't Kill Donald Trump," which had occurred by late September 2016, just before the presidential debates began.[3] Of course, more gaffes occurred after the debates, including the release of a tape in which Trump seemed to brag about committing sexual assault. After this incident, Michael Gerson, *Washington Post* columnist and former speechwriter for President George W. Bush, concluded, "Trump is sickeningly cruel, boorish, bonkers, subversive, conspiratorial, obsessive, authoritarian, and reckless with the reputation of American democracy."[4] And yet Trump won.

In retrospect, there is some reason to believe that what the press saw as "gaffes" might have reinforced his message with core supporters. Joshua Green noted of Trump's constant violation of campaign norms, "Republican voters thrilled to his provocations and rewarded him."[5] In this way, Trump's use of rhetoric to create outrage was similar to that of George Wallace, who, like Trump, "gave voice to the angst of millions of Americans who felt forgotten, displaced, disrespected, and ignored."[6] Yet, when Wallace made outrageous statements for the purpose of "riling up the disaffected," he was perceived only as a protest or a regional candidate.[7] In contrast, Trump's creation of outrage not only activated the "disaffected" but won his national party's nomination and then the presidency, a result reflecting a major change in American rhetorical practice.

Trump's campaign was extraordinary not only for the gaffes the candidate inexplicably survived but also because it succeeded even as it "violated every norm."[8] He had hardly any campaign aside from tweets and rallies, and yet he won.[9] In addition, he lacked a coherent platform and made little effort to generate policy proposals, instead substituting phrases such as the "Great Border Wall" for a more formal set of planks. As Lilliana Mason observed, "Donald Trump's campaign was relatively devoid of coherent policy proscriptions and was described by Trump's own pollster as being 'post ideological.'"[10] Green added, "Trump didn't even feign interest in the policy details that are the ammunition of most candidate debates."[11] Trump's violation of campaign norms was so serious that few thought he could win, but "it turned out many people didn't notice or didn't care."[12]

Moreover, the debates were a disaster for him. Although presidential debates usually have had a modest influence on the outcome of the campaign, there is consensus that debates can make a significant difference if a candidate makes a major gaffe or fails to demonstrate the capacity to fulfill the presidency. In contrast, a challenger can gain ground by demonstrating knowledge of the issues and an appropriate temperament to serve as pres-ident.[13] Trump's performance in the 2016 debates violated every aspect of what scholars thought they knew about debates. There is consensus that Trump did very badly in the 2016 debates, whereas Clinton demonstrated a mastery of the issues.[14] Jonathan Capehart nicely summarized the consen-sus view that Trump "did what was once unthinkable: show up unprepared for a globally televised job interview."[15] In addition, Trump violated conven-tional standards of decorum and was widely criticized for "loudly talking over Mrs. Clinton and hectoring her with interruptions."[16] In 2000, when Al Gore much more mildly violated normal rules of demeanor, it substantially hurt him.[17] Conservative columnist Charles Krauthammer summed up the consensus of scholars and commentators about the Trump/Clinton debate: "By conventional measures—poise, logic, command of the facts—she won the debate handily. But when it comes to moving the needle, conventional measures don't apply this year."[18] Everything scholars thought they knew about presidential debates from John F. Kennedy/Richard M. Nixon in 1960 through Mitt Romney/Barack Obama in 2012 suggested that Trump's perfor-mance would hurt him badly and that it would be viewed as disqualifying by a substantial percentage of the electorate. That did not happen.

Trump had no political experience and lacked a large or experienced cam-paign staff. He did not have a developed agenda, performed badly in the presidential debates, and committed gaffe after gaffe. And yet he won. Gerson was on target when he wrote that the successful campaign was "the single strangest development in American history."[19] It is inexplicable that Trump won.

It is also confusing that although Trump was able to break political norms without harming his campaign, and perhaps even helping it, those same norms seemed still to apply to other candidates. Notably, when Senator Ru-bio attempted to counter Trump with the latter's own weapons of name-calling and ridicule, public reaction was quite negative.[20] Similarly, Clinton's campaign was seriously damaged by a controversy over keeping emails from her service as secretary of state on her personal server and by the allegation that she had failed to act to protect the security of US diplomats in Libya, although in both cases extensive examination found no wrongdoing on her part.[21] It is confusing that norm violations and alleged scandal seriously damaged the campaigns of Rubio, Clinton, and others but had little effect on that of Trump.

The situation did not become any clearer after Trump was elected. In the presidency, he continued to make intemperate statements, use Twitter as a weapon, reference his opponents with unflattering nicknames, and hold rallies as if the campaign had not ended. Because he continued to act and talk as he had during the campaign, his presidency was defined by one gaffe or crisis after another.[22] At the same time, with the exception of the State of the Union Address, required by the Constitution, he largely avoided the major policy addresses previous presidents used to support their agenda.[23] Yet, despite the gaffes and crises, the Twitter wars and outrageous comments, not to mention the failure to lay out a clear policy agenda and the fact that many citizens viewed him as acting in an entirely unpresidential manner, his core supporters remained loyal and his poll standing showed little variability.[24] Trump did not speak or act like any previous president, but his supporters did not care.

Before Trump's election, the greatest Republican hero of the previous forty years was Ronald Reagan, noted for his eloquence, his empowering vision of the American dream, and his faith in democratic norms. In both personal behavior and the vision of the nation expressed in rhetoric, Trump is the very antithesis of Reagan. And yet with few exceptions, such as Senators John McCain and Jeff Flake (both of Arizona) and Governor John Kasich of Ohio, Republican stalwarts who had idolized Reagan for a generation happily supported Trump as the Republican Party became the party of Trump. The journey from Reagan's vision of a "shining city on a hill" to Trump's description in his Inaugural Address of "American carnage" is inexplicable.

Scholars and commentators agree that Trump's successful campaign for the presidency and then his behavior as president were fundamentally unlike that of any previous campaign or presidency.[25] Americans were not the only ones confused by Trump's election. Many people in Europe and elsewhere found it an incomprehensible development. Social psychologists Stephen Reicher and Alexander Haslam wrote,

> His ascendancy to the White House also seemed to be a defeat for civility, for decency, for truth, for reason. How could a man who celebrated the assault of women, who encouraged attacks on his opponents, who encouraged bizarre conspiracy theories, and who spoke without regard for the evidence ascend to the most powerful office on earth? How could over 60 million people vote for him? What does this say about politics, about society, and about the human psyche?[26]

The questions Reicher and Haslam and so many others raised were particularly important because Trump's campaign and behavior as president seemed similar to political developments occurring across Europe. Declan Walsh observed that in Europe "many see Mr. Trump's campaign as an extension of the political tides that have buffeted their own countries. The French see shades of the hard-right nationalist Marine Le Pen. Britons see parallels with supporters of Brexit."[27] David Frum called the situation a democratic "crisis" for the United States and the world.[28]

Trump was not a leader of an interest group or wing of the Republican Party. Yet, he again and again mobilized support in the form of anger in his base of supporters.[29] Trump's primary weapon was rhetoric in the form of interviews with friendly media reporters, speeches at rallies, and a stream of tweets numbering in the tens of thousands attacking opponents and praising himself. It is essential to explain how Trump used rhetoric as his sword and shield and to consider what this says about US politics and the status of democracy in the United States and around the world.

Conclusion

The key to explaining the Trump phenomenon is to identify the elements of his rhetoric that created a strong bond with supporters. In Chapter 1, I describe four key components that defined Trump's rhetoric and appeal—a message containing strident nationalism, a populist attack on elites, a celebrity outsider persona that over time took on characteristics of a strongman, and a vernacular style that broke with rhetorical norms. I define each element and distinguish Trump's nationalist populist message from that of progressive populists throughout US history. I also explain how Trump used this message to create a strong bond with supporters, and I illustrate the potency of the message by discussing the speech announcing his candidacy for the presidency.

In the next several chapters, I show that Trump's rhetoric as a whole contained all the elements of nationalist populism and the celebrity outsider persona and that this general rhetorical pattern evolved over time in response first to the changing campaign situation and then to the requirements of being president. I first focus on the 2016 campaign and demonstrate that the characteristics of nationalist populism were present in campaign speeches, primary debates, the convention acceptance address, and the general election debates. I then show that the same pattern dominated his Inaugural Address despite generic constraints calling for an optimistic and inclusive message stating basic ideological principles.

Next, I demonstrate that with some significant evolution, a variant of the same pattern was present in Trump's presidential rhetoric, although it was a particularly bad fit for major policy speeches such as the State of the Union Address and those given on ceremonial occasions. This pattern largely explains why in comparison with other presidents he spoke so rarely in these contexts and why his rhetoric on those rare occasions had so little impact or import. In rallies, interviews, and other contexts in which he essentially continued the campaign, his message did evolve. With Republicans in charge of all of the branches of the government for the first two years of his term, it became more difficult for him to blame Democrats and elites for their failure to pass a major infrastructure plan, immigration reform, a health-care plan to replace the Affordable Care Act (known as Obamacare), and so forth. This led Trump to a greater focus on the media as "the enemy of the people," a tactic that escalated as the media investigated Trump and his family. Trump also faced the problem that he had run on promises of immediate action that would produce near-magical progress on jobs, immigration, infrastructure, and other issues but that behind these grandiose promises there were no plans, only a claim that his celebrity leadership would produce immediate change. This dilemma also influenced his rhetoric. One consequence was that the role he played evolved from celebrity outsider to presidential strongman, and he began claiming credit for the almost straight-line continuation of economic trends that during the Obama administration he had attacked as "fake news" and a near-depression-level economic crisis.

I next turn to Trump's use of Twitter during his campaigns and his presidency and then explain why this rhetorical pattern created such a strong emotional bond with core supporters and simultaneously produced a powerful negative reaction from his opponents. I conclude by building a sustained argument that Trump's nationalist populist message threatens to undermine US democracy itself.

The Elements of Trump's Rhetoric

Identifying the elements in Trump's message is not a mystery. There was little subtlety or artistry in his speeches, interviews, and debate performances. He constantly attacked the media and other elites; claimed the nation was threatened by undocumented immigrants, Islamic terrorists, and various other groups who were not white Americans; and relied on his background as a celebrity businessman to create a persona as an authentic outsider. The puzzle is to explain how and why Trump's message resonated strongly enough to win election to the presidency via the Electoral College (although Hillary Clinton won the popular vote), as well as to maintain his popularity with core supporters, and what this tells us about American rhetorical practice and democracy itself.

Katy Tur, the first national television correspondent assigned to the Trump campaign, provides a clue about how this happened. She observed of the multiple times in which Trump's campaign was proclaimed "dead" that "the more Mr. Trump's candidacy was said to flatline, the more life I saw in his crowds." She concluded that his "supporters were tired—of Washington, of the media, of waiting. And that fatigue allowed them to overlook a lot. They knew he was flawed, but at least they thought he was on their side."[1] Similarly, Amanda Taub noted during the primary campaign, "What's scariest is . . . the extent and fervor of his support."[2] Lilliana Mason echoed this conclusion: "Despite very little policy content, the campaign generated antagonistic and angry reactions that divided family members and friends on a social level."[3] The response of pro-Trump crowds suggests that the key to understanding his victory in the campaign and continuing popularity with his base is to explain the emotional connection Trump created with core supporters.[4] On the importance of emotion in politics, Karen Stenner presciently wrote in 2005, "We fail to recognize that there are politics other than the politics of ideas, and that a great deal of political 'reasoning' might be rather less reasoned than we like to imagine."[5] The emotional bond Trump created with his supporters through his rhetoric produced the sense that he was on their side and helped him become president and maintain his popularity.

We can draw a second clue about the resonance of Trump's message from the core audience Trump appealed to and the common themes he used to appeal to that audience. Trump's base was initially the white working class, and this group was crucial to his victory, with "twice as many of these voters cast[ing] their ballots" for Trump than for Clinton.[6] In the primaries, many in the Republican establishment initially opposed his candidacy. Thus, the keys to solving the puzzle about the Trump presidency are how he used rhetoric to create a strong emotional bond with the white working class and then how he won over the Republican establishment.

Affective Rhetoric

In recent years, rhetorical theorists and critics have focused a great deal of attention on affect as well as emotion, or pathos, as Aristotle referred to it.[7] For example, Jamie Landau and Bethany Keeler-Jonker analyzed affective circulation in the case of Barack Obama's Tucson eulogy for the victims murdered in an unsuccessful attempt to assassinate US Representative Gabby Giffords (D-AZ). These authors "conceptualize[d] emotion as symbolized affect," claimed that "one important role of the contemporary president is to be a conductor of public feelings," and explained how Obama transformed "anger and pain to social (civic) love." Notably, they added, "Trump could be considered a prototype of a conductor of public feelings of anger."[8] In the past, the conventional wisdom has been that expressing anger, except in rare cases such as in wartime, has not been perceived as appropriate presidential leadership. Examining how Trump effectively produced anger and fear to create an emotional bond is essential to understanding his appeal.

One means for a speaker or writer to create strong emotion is to focus attention on some problem or injustice to generate pity or righteous anger in an audience. Rhetorical critics have explained, for example, how "Doonesbury" cartoons about the impact of the wars in Afghanistan and Iraq on soldiers and the community created strong emotional connections.[9] Similarly, Erin Rand argued that Larry Kramer, a gay artist, used the formal qualities of the polemic in order to create anger. She concluded, "Kramer always presents his expressions of emotion as a natural and legitimate reaction to a truth or to the violation of a truth."[10] Unlike Kramer, who relied on reasoned argument to create righteous anger, Trump drew on irrational fears of dangerous Others who in fact were not very threatening. Catherine Chaput observed of irrational emotional responses, "Affect, in the form of something as taken for granted as a gut sense, exerts pressure on our decision making and does not crumble under the deliberative weight of better arguments or more information."[11] Chaput's point is particularly important in explaining the effectiveness of Trump's rhetoric. Fact checkers again and again demonstrated that much of what he said was false, but this denial of the truth of his message had little or no impact on his bond with core supporters. In fact, there is some evidence that media reporting of the many errors and false statements in his rhetoric indirectly reinforced Trump's attack on the press as elitist and out of touch, thereby making supporters "more loyal, not less."[12]

Theoretical treatments of affect or emotion demonstrate the importance of explicating the power of Trump's strong emotional bond with core supporters, but they do not directly address the critical puzzle of explaining how he nurtured that relationship. At this point, it is important to recognize that Trump's emotional connection to members of his base was reflected both in their strong attraction to the candidate and to their expression of negative emotions such as fear, anger, and hatred against perceived elites and "dangerous" groups such as immigrants and refugees. It is therefore crucial to consider the tactic of inciting strongly negative emotions in creating group solidarity. There is considerable evidence that strong negative emotions often play a crucial role in creating group identity.[13] Celeste Condit noted that "emotions" function as "relational signals for co-orienting people" and explained that the "inherently relational quality of emotions constitutes a predisposition toward partisanship, or what is often called a 'we/they' orientation"—an orientation clearly present among Trump supporters. In an analysis of Robert Welch's rhetoric in *The Blue Book of the John Birch Society,* Condit concluded that a speaker or writer can generate anger "by showing an enemy that has violated perceived justice, status hierarchies, or morality" and that this strategy can be a "powerfully effective" means of creating "identifi-cation" within a group.[14] Condit also observed, "Emotions can be developed through narratives that are not determined by an ideology," which speaks to Trump's connection to his supporters; he rarely presented developed ideo-logical positions.[15] Condit's analysis of how the construction of a scapegoat can create anger and therefore group solidarity points to the importance of identifying the characteristics of Trump's rhetoric that contributed to both aims. Similarly, Emily Winderman focused on the way "angry rhetoric can be a collectivizing moral emotion when it binds bodies together in relationship to other bodies and objects deemed harmful or unjust for the purposes of actionable redress."[16] She explained how Margaret Sanger used "formal ele-ments," including "*perspective by incongruity*," to create shared identity with supporters, an identity that produced a form of "*emotional adherence.*"[17] Winderman's research implicitly makes the point that creation of anger can serve several rhetorical functions. In the case of Sanger, anger was not in-consistent with strong argument but the result of it. In that way, Sanger's use of anger was quite similar to the policy-oriented rhetoric of progressive populism, including that of contemporary leaders such as Senators Bernie Sanders and Elizabeth Warren. Unlike Sanger, Sanders, and Warren, how-ever, Trump used a fundamentally false narrative to create fear of and anger toward groups that in fact were not inherently threatening. There is little mystery about why true stories of injustice produce anger and create a sense of group solidarity; explaining how Trump's false narrative did so is critically important.

In this book, I argue that Trump created an affective genre based in na-tionalist populism and a celebrity outsider persona that over time, especially after he assumed the presidency, evolved to take on characteristics of the strongman along with an associated vernacular style. He used this rhetori-cal pattern to create commitment from core supporters and anger, fear, and hatred toward groups of "dangerous" Others, along with elites he depicted as corrupt and unwilling to confront the Others. This rhetoric tapped into many white working-class people's alienation and sense that they had lost their country and created a strong emotional bond with Trump.

Although the key elements in Trump's message might seem obvious, the way those elements are developed and how they function to create a pow-erful emotional connection merit explanation. Trump's narrative of a na-tion threatened by Others, including immigrants, refugees, Islamic terrorists,

Black protesters, and "nasty women," served three important emotional functions for core supporters. First, Trump's narrative created a sense of shared identity among supporters by providing enemies to blame for their own misfortune. The fact that undocumented immigrants and the other groups Trump demonized were not in fact especially dangerous or responsible for the economic decline experienced by the white working class did not diminish the power of his nationalist narrative. Second, in Trump's narrative, he was the hero who through force of will would take the nation back to an entirely imaginary idyllic past filled with opportunity. The role of heroic protector strengthened Trump's affective bond with his supporters and therefore their commitment to him. Third, Trump's narrative created a sense of group identity by depicting his core supporters as the "real Americans" compared with the elites who looked down on them and compared with the dangerous Others such as immigrants and refugees who threatened their way of life. In that way, Trump's narrative produced both anger and solidarity, strong emotions that bonded his core supporters to him and helped immunize him from criticism within this group. This rhetorical pattern strongly tapped into white working-class people's perceived loss of economic and political power. It also fostered a growing strain of authoritarianism in the United States. The first step in understanding these developments is to recognize the two dominant forms of populist rhetoric.

Populist Rhetoric

Populism, as Michael Lee noted, has been "a fixture of U.S. democratic deliberation," but its nature is difficult to define because "it lacks stable content" and, therefore, possesses "chameleonic qualities."[18] Similarly, Mark Rolfe commented that many scholars "see it as a slippery term with no fixed meaning or ideology," and Cas and Cristóbal Rovira Kaltwasser added that this "broad usage . . . creates confusion and frustration."[19] Jan-Werner Müller argued that the varying usages reflect a "lack" of "coherent criteria" for distinguishing populist from nonpopulist political leaders.[20] One of the major scholars to study populism, Michael Kazin, said that the key to understanding how populism functions is to recognize that "populism is not an ideology. It's an impulse, it's a form of impression, it's rhetoric, which includes imagery. The enemies are a tiny elite, and the people on your side are the vast majority; the vast majority are moral people who are being betrayed by the elite."[21]

Rather than particular content, Lee identified "interrelated and mutually reinforcing themes" in what he labeled the populist "argumentative frame": a description of the people "as heroic defenders of 'traditional' values" fighting against enemies who are "tangibly different in race, class, or geographical location" and who threaten "the destruction of traditional values," a description of the economic and political system as fundamentally corrupt, and a call for "apocalyptic confrontation" in service of "revolutionary change."[22] The perceived combination of the threat to the people from the alien Other and the utter corruption of the political system justifies "radical means . . . to prevent the enemy's impending victory" and explains the "disdain toward traditional forms of democratic deliberation and republican representation" often expressed by populists.[23]

Lee is clearly right that populist rhetoric can take many forms and be expressed by conservative, liberal, or radical movements; as a consequence, the description of characteristics of a populist argumentative frame by itself provides little guidance for explaining the resonance or lack of resonance of a given populist movement. Moreover, although many populist movements might reflect the characteristics identified by Lee and other scholars, movement-specific themes also can be important. For example, Kristy Maddux noted "the significance of religion within the populist argumentative frame" in the discourse of William Jennings Bryan, an indication that the heroes and enemies in populist discourse can take many forms.[24]

Two Forms of Populism

The confusion about the nature of populism can be resolved by distinguishing between progressive and nationalist variants. Some researchers claim, "There can't be such a thing as left-wing populism by definition" because populism "isn't about policy content" but rather about the "core claim" that "only some of the people are really the people."[25] A more compelling case can be made, however, that there are two primary variants of populism: a progressive populism focused on policy reforms and a nationalist variant focused on emotional release rather than policy change. Howard Erlich hinted at this distinction when he noted that populism has been "linked to McCarthyism" and labeled an "American fascist creed," but other variants have focused on progressive change, including "the attempt to obliterate the color line and develop a political alliance between Southern white and black farmers" and support for other policies manifesting "humane tendencies."[26]

In the most influential history of American populist movements, for instance, Kazin noted that a clear distinction can be drawn between progressive populist movements such as the People's Party of the 1890s, which "brandished a lengthy blueprint for reform," and conservative variants. Kazin observed greater similarity between the populism of Trump, which he labels "a brilliant specimen of performance art," and "the Know-Nothing Party of the 1850s, which similarly argued that immigrants were taking Americans' jobs and breaking the nation's laws" than with either the People's Party or contemporary progressive populists such as Sanders.[27] Kazin also commented that through most of US history, the progressive form, "a grand form of rhetorical optimism" about what "ordinary Americans" can accomplish, has been dominant.[28]

Although "the great majority of Populist leaders" has been committed to social justice, there is "a long tradition in American politics . . . of appealing for the votes of the 'common man' by combining tough talk against malevolent elites with ugly scapegoating of marginalized groups."[29] Strong emotional reactions are at the core of the nationalist variant as opposed to the progressive variant of populism. Right-wing nationalist populism creates what Mudde and Kaltwasser called a "mental map" "to unite an angry and silent majority . . . [and] mobilize this majority against a defined enemy."[30] Müller noted that nationalist populists are "primarily associated with particular moods and emotions: populists are 'angry'; the voters are 'frustrated' or suffer from 'resentment.'"[31] Müller's discussion of the strong emotion generated by nationalist populists clearly fits Tur's and others' descriptions of Trump's core supporters. Progressive populists express anger in defense of policy reform, whereas nationalist populists incite it and other emotions to tap popular resentment against a "dangerous" Other and elites who refuse to confront that Other.

Progressive Populism

Both the progressive and nationalist variants of populism "include some kind of appeal to 'the people' and a denunciation of 'the elite'" based in a "*moralistic imagination*," but the nature of the attack on elites, the diagnosis of problems facing the nation, and the preferred solutions are quite different.[32] Progressive populists blame primarily the rich, but also other elites who protect them, for the oppression. Contrary to Müller's claim that "populists are always antipluralist," both Kazin and John Judis cite progressive variants that embraced a pluralist vision. Even in the 1890s, some allies of the People's Party in the South "cooperated with the parallel Colored Farmers' Alliance, but others did not."[33] Finally, and in sharp contrast with nationalist populism, the focus of progressive populism is on changing public policy to address social problems in society. Thus, the rhetoric of progressive populism is defined by the following characteristics:

1. Progressive populists claim to represent the people, who are both virtuous and oppressed;
2. progressive populists blame elites, especially the rich, for the oppression of the people and claim that the system is broken;
3. progressive populists use a moralistic tone to call for action;
4. progressive populists focus on changing policies and institutions to produce reform; and
5. because progressive populists focus their ire primarily on rich elites rather than some particular group in society, they use a generally inclusive tone.

This constellation of characteristics defining progressive populism extended from the People's Party of the 1890s to the campaigns of Sanders and Warren in 2016.

The pattern is quite evident, for example, in the Populist Party, also known as the People's Party, platform from 1892.[34] In the preamble, the platform stated, "The fruits of the toil of millions are badly stolen to build up colossal fortunes, for a few, unprecedented in the history of mankind; and the possessors of these, in turn, despise the Republic and endanger liberty." Later, it stated that "grievous wrongs have been inflicted upon the suffering people," that "a vast conspiracy against mankind has been organized on two continents," and that the goal of the party was "to restore the government of the Republic to the hands of the 'plain people.'" In these short passages in the first four paragraphs of the platform, the defense of the people as virtuous and the attack on elites in general and the rich in particular are evident. The

THE ELEMENTS OF TRUMP'S RHETORIC   [9]

moralistic tone is obvious in the first sentence of the preamble, which states, "We meet in the midst of a nation brought to the verge of moral, political, and material ruin."

Although the moralistic narrative that the people must resist the oppression of the elites is present throughout the platform, there is also a strong focus on policy change. The conclusion of the preamble stated that "the existing currency supply is wholly inadequate" and promised to seek a solution "to correct these evils by wise and reasonable legislation." In the remainder of the platform, the People's Party called for nationalization of railroads, creation of "a national currency, safe, sound, and flexible," free silver, establishment of an income tax, and other national actions. Although the platform did include an attack on an immigration policy that "opens our ports to the pauper and criminal classes of the world and crowds out our wage-earners," it also appealed to national unity by referencing "the union of the labor forces of the United States" and stating, "The interests of rural and civil labor are the same; their enemies are identical." Despite the fact that the People's Party developed in the Midwest out of protests by farmers, its platform stated, "We cordially sympathize with the efforts of organized workingmen" and "the Kings of Labor." The People's Party was not an inclusive movement by the standards of progressive movements of the twenty-first century, but it was extremely inclusive for its time.

Studies of the Progressive movement confirm this conclusion. Several chapters in J. Michael Hogan's *Rhetoric and Reform in the Progressive Era* emphasize the reformative focus of progressive populism at the end of the nineteenth and beginning of the twentieth centuries. In the conclusion of the volume, Hogan described the era as "the Age of Reform" and underlined the "pragmatic reform spirit" of progressive populists of the period. This emphasis on pragmatic policy reform was combined with a focus on encouraging "public deliberation." According to Hogan, progressive populists "rewrote the rules of democratic debate and encouraged a broader range of citizens to participate," efforts that reflected the inclusiveness of the movement in the context of the time. In that way, the Progressive movement at the end of the nineteenth and beginning of the twentieth century had a great deal in common with contemporary progressive populists.[35]

A similar pattern was evident 120 years later in the campaign rhetoric of Sanders. A typical example is his speech on the economy and Wall Street in

January 2016, which exhibited all the elements of progressive populist rhetoric.[36] The opening paragraph described how ordinary Americans are being unfairly treated by rich elites:

> The American people are catching on. They understand that something is profoundly wrong when, in our country today, the top one-tenth of 1 percent own almost as much wealth as the bottom 90 percent and when the 20 richest people own more wealth than the bottom 150 million Americans—half our population. They know that the system is rigged when the average person is working longer hours for lower wages, while 58 percent of all new income goes to the top 1 percent.

The first sentence of the second paragraph continued the attack on the rich, stating that ordinary Americans "know that a handful of people on Wall Street have extraordinary power over the economic and political life of our country." This attack on Wall Street and other elites was present throughout the speech. The moralistic tone was evident in the attacks on Wall Street and in many other comments such as his ironic statement, "Greed is not good. In fact, the greed of Wall Street and corporate America is destroying the fabric of our nation."

Although the depiction of ordinary people being oppressed by greedy elites is present throughout the speech, his remarks focused on policy changes that could remedy the situation. He called for much stricter enforcement of antitrust laws, especially on large banks and insurance companies, a policy he summarized with a phrase he attributed to President Theodore "Teddy" Roosevelt: "Break 'em up." Sanders also called for reinstating a "21st Century Glass-Steagall Act to separate commercial banking, investment banking, and insurance services" and advocated prosecuting Wall Street bankers who violate the law, strengthening regulation of large financial firms, establishing "a tax on Wall Street speculators," making "public colleges and universities tuition free," replacing existing credit-rating agencies with "non-profit institutions, independent from Wall Street," capping "interest rates on credit cards and consumer loans at 15 percent," limiting fees banks can charge, and other actions. Notably, Sanders placed more detailed focus on policy in this one speech than Trump did in all of the speeches combined that I discuss in the remainder of this book.

Finally, Sanders presented an inclusive vision of the nation in which the core battle was between ordinary people and greedy elites. Unlike nationalist populists, who often blame some Other for the problems facing the nation, Sanders offered an inclusive definition of the people. He stated, "What this campaign is about is building a political movement which revitalizes American democracy, which brings millions of people together—black and white, Latino, Asian-American, Native American, young and old, men and women, gay and straight, native born and immigrant, people of all religions." This narrative of the people against the greedy rich is especially evident at the end of the speech, in his observation, "They [elites] have an endless supply of money. But we have something they don't have. And that is that when millions of working families stand together, demanding fundamental changes in our financial system, we have the power to bring about that change."

The five defining characteristics of progressive populism are evident in both the platform of the People's Party from 1892 and Sanders's address concerning Wall Street in 2016. Both treated the people as unfairly oppressed by elites and described the conflict between the virtuous people and the elites in moralistic terms. Both provided a detailed list of policy changes to address the elite oppression of the people. And both presented an inclusive vision of the people rather than scapegoating various groups as responsible for the crisis facing the nation. Sanders's message was more explicitly inclusive, but in the context of its time, the platform of the People's Party was also quite inclusive.

The rhetorical appeal of progressive populism is obvious. Progressive populists present a narrative of ordinary people in order to create reasoned anger against their oppression by economic and political elites. The solution is to reduce the power of those elites by enacting progressive policy reforms that aid the people directly. The progressive populist variant is both fundamentally optimistic and entirely consistent with the progress narrative at the heart of the American dream.

Nationalist Populism, Authoritarianism, and the Outsider/Strongman Persona

Nationalist populism is similar to progressive populism in its biting tone and attack on elites, but the remaining content of the message is quite different. Rather than focusing on policy change to address elite domination, nationalist populism is an affective genre that responds to a sense that American identity is threatened by some kind of outside group. The focus is not a policy response to the threat but a message that provides a sense of group solidarity. It is important to understand that the threat need not be real for it to be powerful. The primary functions of the genre are emotional activation and reassurance.

Generic analysis sometimes serves as a heuristic device to illuminate a rhetorical form through comparison to alternative forms. In more restricted cases, genres can be considered ontological categories with an "internal dynamic" that "creates expectations which constrain rhetorical responses" into an identifiable "constellation of forms."[37] Because most ontological genre criticism focuses on categories that are situational in nature, such as eulogies, inaugural addresses, and farewell speeches, it cannot be applied to the vast majority of cases in which the "constellations of element[s]" do not "fuse into unique and indivisible wholes."[38] However, other forms of genre can be useful for explaining discourse patterns organized into a "constellation of forms" that lacks a situational organizational principle. In particular, a focus on a constraining purpose not limited to a single situation can provide useful insight. An affective genre is one such purpose-oriented genre. In "The Symbolic DNA of Terrorism," Robert Rowland and Kirsten Theye argued that an identifiable rhetorical pattern focused on a sense of denied identity, a response negating the identity of the perceived oppressor and an affirmation of a mythically derived identity is found in the rhetorical practice of religious terrorist groups around the world. Rowland and Theye suggested that this "symbolic DNA" can be considered an "epistemic genre" that religious terrorist groups representing all of the world's major religions use to make sense of and justify their actions.[39] Thus, groups such as al Qaeda create a narrative that both explains how they believe the United States and Israel oppress Islam and justifies terrorist action as a response to that perceived threat.

In contrast, nationalist populism does not serve an epistemic but rather an affective function, the need for an emotional response when a nation's economic and political systems no longer seem to function effectively for working-class people. As I demonstrate, nationalist populism is not built around a coherent ideological or policy vision but a rhetorical practice that provides scapegoats to blame for the economic, political, and cultural situation as well as an outsider who can act as the people's savior. The capacity of nationalist populism to fulfill this affective function explains a similar pattern in a number of nations in Europe. In each country, the nationalist populist rhetorical pattern creates a sense of emotional solidarity.

The affective genre of nationalist populism is particularly resonant for people primed by perceptions that economic, political, and social forces threaten their core group identity. These people often possess an authoritarian personality structure. Social psychologists have developed a rich theoretical and empirical literature concerning the impact perceived identity threats have on groups scoring high on measures of authoritarianism. Here, the term authoritarian does not refer to totalitarianism, although people scoring high on an authoritarian personality measure might in fact support totalitarianism in some circumstances. Rather, the term refers to people with a high need for conformity and low tolerance for change they perceive as threatening to their group identity. The authoritarian mind-set can be identified through a series of questions about "childrearing values . . . [that] *reflect one's fundamental orientations* toward authority/uniformity versus autonomy/difference."[40] Stenner described what she calls the "authoritarian dynamic" as follows:

> What remains constant is this familiar triad of racial, political, and moral intolerance: the tendency to glorify some "in-group" and to denigrate "out-groups," . . . to venerate and privilege a set of ideas and practices, and to reward or punish others according to their conformity to this "normative order." Across time and place, we find that those inclined to discriminate against members of other racial and ethnic groups also rush to protect the "common good" by "stamping out" offensive ideas and "cracking down" on misbehavior, and show unusual interest in making public policy about what other people might be up to in private.[41]

Stenner added, "Perceptions of society being filled with groups that pose a threat to the country markedly increase intolerance of specified 'noxious' groups."[42]

A consideration of authoritarian tendencies within the white working class supports the strong evidence that Trump's influence was not tied primarily to ideology but to an emotional response to threatened identity. A Public Religion Research Institute (PRRI) study revealed that "white working-class Americans were much more likely than Americans with a college degree to express a preference for authoritarian traits." PRRI reported in 2016 that "nearly two-thirds (64%) of white working-class Americans have an authoritarian orientation, including 37% who are classified as 'high authoritarian' versus 39% with an authoritarian orientation for 'white college-educated Americans,'" who, of course voted for Trump at a much lower level than did the working-class voters.[43]

Stenner's description of the "normative 'worldview'" of authoritarianism is eerily similar to the themes that dominated Trump's rhetoric and also to the tone of his rallies. She explained that "political demands for authoritative constraints on behavior . . . typically include legal discrimination against minorities and restrictions on immigration" and added that "racial, political, and moral intolerance and punitiveness are 'kindred spirits'" that "are all primarily driven by authoritarianism, fueled by the impulse to enhance unity and conformity, and manifested under conditions of normative threat, that is, conditions that threaten that oneness and sameness."[44]

The idea of normative threat is particularly crucial to understanding the peculiar appeal of Trump's nonprogrammatic affective rhetoric of nationalist populism. Stenner explained how perceived "normative threats" act as "catalysts" that "activate the predisposition [toward authoritarianism] and increase the manifestation of these characteristic attitudes and behaviors."[45] Trump's rhetoric clearly activated that sense of normative threat and, in turn, energized his rallies and social media campaigns. Notably, Trump's appeal cannot be tied to actual threats to society because the emotional activation occurred during a time of consistent job growth, low crime, declining immigration (and in some periods a net outflow of undocumented immigrants), and a quite modest threat from international terrorism.[46] The angry Trump supporters were not responding to actual threats in the same way progressive populists were responding to the real problem of income inequality.

The key to understanding this confusing situation is how a rhetorically created sense of normative threat can activate those with an authoritarian personality structure even in the absence of any significant actual threat. Marc Hetherington and Jonathan Weiler's research concerning threat activation is particularly important to explaining this process. They observed, "Scholars have often demonstrated that threat 'activates' authoritarianism, causing those scoring high in authoritarianism to become less tolerant and more aggressive than usual."[47] Hetherington and Weiler also charted the way the "information environment" has been manipulated to activate authoritarian voters on issues related to race, women's rights, gay rights, immigration, and terrorism.[48] Although these authors' focus was on coverage of issues in the media, the "information environment" might better be understood as the broad rhetorical context in which authoritarian voters operate. That, in turn, suggests that the key to understanding Trump's success in activating authoritarian voters in the white working class is to identify the core characteristics of his rhetoric tied to that activation function. Those core characteristics can be boiled down to nationalist populism and a celebrity outsider persona that evolved over time to that of a strongman with an associated rhetorical style.

Four closely related characteristics define this populist form: expressions of fear and anger at a threatening Other purportedly harming the nation; attacks on political and economic elites for not protecting "real" (white) Americans; a focus not on a detailed policy agenda but on how an outsider with a powerful emotional connection to core supporters can return the nation to a time of prosperity and strength; and a vernacular style consonant with the nationalist, populist, and outsider components of the message.[49]

The nationalist elements in populism are reflected in Taub's description of the "dramatic rise of a new kind of white populism" reflecting "a majoritarian backlash" motivated by "fear of social change; fear of terrorist attacks and other physical threats and the crisis to identity that many whites are experiencing as they struggle to maintain their position." Taub cited shifting gender and racial norms as factors in this backlash and focused on the way "immigration has dramatically reshaped demographics in cities across the United States and set the nation on a path in which whites . . . will no longer be a majority within a few decades."[50] Similarly, Pippa Norris argued that an underlying factor in nationalist populism is "a cultural backlash in Western societies against long-term, ongoing social change" creating a situation in which "[less-]educated and older citizens fear becoming marginalized and left behind within their own countries."[51] Fear of terrorism and rising crime, although terrorism is extremely rare and crime has fallen dramatically since it peaked several decades ago, also strengthened the feeling of threatened identity.[52] The nationalist part of the message produces a sense of threat activation that in turn creates group solidarity and loyalty to the leader by labeling some Other as a danger to the "real" people of the nation.

In response to threatened identity, populism, according to Chip Berlet and Matthew Lyons, "is a way of mobilizing 'the people' into a social or political movement around some form of anti-elitism." Berlet added that populism "is at once an ideology, a strategic organizing frame, and a rhetorical narrative story line that names friends and enemies. While left-wing populism often organizes people around expanding economic fairness, right-wing populism relies on prejudice and bigotry, demonization and scapegoating of an 'Other,' and fears of traitorous, subversive conspiracies."[53] Thus, progressive populism is a coherent ideology indicting economic and political elites, but nationalist populist ideology is incoherent in policy terms and focused on scapegoating to create anger. Müller labels the nationalist form of populism "an exclusionary form of identity politics" in which the "core claim" is that "only some of the people are really the people," a view "that . . . tends to pose a danger for democracy."[54] The nationalist variant focuses on an alien Other that threatens the purity of the people.[55] Mudde noted that nationalist populism "presents a Manichean outlook in which there are only friends and foes. Opponents are not just people with different priorities and values, they are *evil!* Consequently, compromise is impossible, as it 'corrupts' the purity."[56] In the United States, a nationalist populist such as Trump taps into some white Americans' anger about loss of status and political dominance supposedly because of malign actions by people of color and contrasts the present with what Paul Krugman labeled "cultural nostalgia . . . for a vanished past."[57]

Nationalist populism not only focuses on a dangerous Other but also attacks societal elites as weak, corrupt, and "no longer reliably patriotic" as evidenced by their failure to confront the threat posed by the Other.[58] Thomas Greven wrote, "Populism's central and permanent narrative is the juxtaposition of a (corrupt) political class . . . and the people, as whose sole authentic voice the populist party bills itself."[59] Notably, the nationalist populist tends to define "the people" "as culturally homogenous," a crucial definitional move that allows blame to be placed on both elites and the alien Other changing society.[60] Although progressive populists also attack the elites, the nationalist variant draws a "moral distinction between the 'real people' and those who don't belong."[61] One consequence is that nationalist populists can respond to "any criticism or attack" by complaining "of being marginalized vis-à-vis a corrupt political establishment of which the media is simply a part."[62] Trump's constant attacks on the media are an example of how nationalist populists respond to criticism, especially when that criticism is factually correct.

The third element in nationalist populism, the outsider heroic leader, often a celebrity, follows from the other elements. Nationalist populism stems from rage at the dangerous Other and the corrupt elites who allow the Other to threaten society. Mudde noted that nationalist "populism is moralistic rather than programmatic."[63] Müller agreed that nationalist "populism isn't about policy content."[64] Nationalist populism is an affective genre built around feelings of fear and anger about the loss of status. Given the lack of policy agenda, these feelings call for a leader functioning as an authentic hero for the "real" people who through force of will can bring back a fabled "Golden Age." Mudde and Kaltwasser explained, "Populism is generally associated with a strong (male) leader whose charismatic personal appeal, rather than ideological program, is the basis of *his* support." Such leaders rely on charismatic appeal rather than traditional forms of credibility or ethos such as experience or expertise. Mudde and Kaltwasser noted that such leaders "connect directly to the supporters" and act as "the personification of *the* people."[65] On this point, Müller observed that "populists claim that they, and they alone, represent the people" and stated that such leaders "treat their political opponents as 'enemies of the people' and seek to exclude them altogether."[66] The leaders of nationalist populist movements possess these characteristics because the movements are driven by a sense of normative threat to the social order, and thus the leader must both reflect the old social order and not be a political elite within it. In contrast, the leaders of progressive populist movements may be women or members of other marginalized groups who are experts in public policy precisely because the agenda of such groups is programmatic. Trump and Warren are both populists, but they talk in different ways because of their allegiance to nationalist or progressive populism, respectively.

Nationalist populist leaders oppose elites from the perspective of an outsider who speaks as what Kathleen Parker labeled the "voice of the Everyman."[67] Mudde and Kaltwasser observed that a nationalist populist leader often presents himself (the leaders are almost always male) as "a man of action, rather than words, who is not afraid to make difficult and quick decisions, even against 'expert' advice" and who uses "simple and even vulgar language" to present himself as "'one of the boys,'" a description that certainly applies to Trump.[68] Müller explained that nationalist populists "always claim that they, and they alone, properly represent the people" and label their political competitors as "a self-serving, corrupt elite" "who betray the people."[69] The nature of their message requires an outsider persona. Although nationalist populists attack elites, they might themselves come from that class or might have ascended to that class by becoming a celebrity. Mudde and Kaltwasser noted, for instance, "Some of the most famous populists were successful businessmen" who presented themselves as "the voice of the common people."[70]

Given the view of elites as corrupt groups that have undermined the society, traditional norms of leadership such as knowledge and experience or conventional signs of character are suspect; the only alternative is the outsider who can bring fundamental change. As Müller noted, "The populist's promise is not that he is just like any ordinary person; rather, it is that he alone will do what the people want."[71] Notably, the outsider persona is well adapted to "'authoritarian voters': people who have a strong desire to maintain order and hierarchies, along with a powerful fear of outsiders" because this group "finds social change very threatening."[72]

Although the hero in a nationalist populist narrative must be an outsider who takes on elites, several variants of that outsider persona can be used. In some cases, the outsiders might be celebrities who use their status to draw attention. In other cases, the leaders might be rich businesspeople who demonstrate authenticity by taking on members of their class in the business world. Jesse Ventura, the professional wrestler elected governor of Minnesota as a Reform Party candidate, and Ross Perot, the business leader who won millions of votes in the 1992 and 1996 presidential elections, are examples of these two variants of the outsider persona. Once in power, the outsider persona might take on characteristics of the strongman, challenging democratic norms or even established laws or rules, justifying these statements or actions as necessary to cleanse the system of corruption or as a response to political correctness. The key point is that to function effectively in the nationalist populist narrative, the leaders must be from outside the power structure and act in a way that from the perspective of their followers demonstrates authenticity. Acting as an outsider hero, someone who is not part of the system but can bring change, becomes increasingly difficult after election. At that point, maintaining status as an authentic outsider hero can require the leader to assume the role of the strongman.

To this point, I have focused on the narrative defining nationalist populism. It is important to recognize that a particular, quite peculiar stylistic configuration, compared with the norms of American politics, comes out of that narrative. Nationalist populism, unlike progressive populism, is not focused on practical policy advocacy. It, therefore, is not typified by a stylistic pattern based on rational argument and progressive myth, as is the case for progressive populists as well as traditional conservatives such as Ronald Reagan and pragmatic liberals such as Barack Obama. Rather, nationalist populism is typified by a vernacular style adapted to the emotional needs of the in-group that feels threatened.[73] The nationalist component calls for language demonizing the dangerous Other and creating an "us" (the real people of the nation) versus "them" (the dangerous Others) worldview. The populist attack on elites requires an informal style that rejects the pretensions of "experts" and the media, demonized as corrupt elites who do not support the real people. This demonization can be enacted through insults and taunting, what Michael Wolf labeled "insult comedy."[74] The persona of the outsider calls for a style enacting the supposed greatness of the leader, leading to a rhetoric based in bragging and boasting about past and future accomplishments.

It is important to recognize that the vernacular style, as well as the outsider and later strongman leadership role, follows from the overarching nationalist populist message. Contrary to some who have argued that "it is primarily Trump's style" that explains his "rhetorical appeal," the dominant narrative associated with nationalist populism and the outsider/strongman role illuminate Trump's ability to "appeal to angry white voters on a primarily visceral level."[75] Trump's style is important for enacting that message and enabling him to come across as "more authentic than traditional political candidates," but it is not the main source of his appeal.[76] The style is important seasoning for Trump's message, but the message itself, the stew of nationalist rage against the threat posed by dangerous Others, a populist attack on elites as corrupt and disloyal to real (white) Americans, and the claim that the outsider and later strongman hero can bring back a Golden Age of abundant well-paying jobs in a largely white United States is at the core of his political appeal and also what makes him such a danger to US democracy.

New communication technology, especially Twitter, is particularly adapted to enact the vernacular style on which Trump relied.[77] Political leaders such as Obama have used Twitter primarily as a means of reinforcing some aspect of their messages. For Obama or a principled conservative such as Reagan, the core of their message was a coherent ideological and mythic system that justified their view of the proper role of government in moving the nation forward. Twitter could have only played a minor supporting role for presidents like Reagan and Obama because their messages were too complex for the medium to be a primary carrier of their ideological argument and mythic narrative. For the nationalist populist, on the contrary, in addition to boasts about past and promised future accomplishments, the core message is an attack on the Others who threaten hardworking ordinary citizens and the unpatriotic elites who refuse to protect ordinary Americans.

This core message does not call for reasoned argument because the function of the genre is threat activation producing an emotional response rather than policy advocacy, and the message is largely untrue. Transformative political figures such as Reagan and Obama built powerful ideological arguments.

Progressive populists such as Sanders and Warren rely heavily on ideological argument to indict economic and political elites. Nationalist populists, however, are focused on a dangerous Other that exists primarily in their own rhetoric. Notably, in 2016, the nation was not awash with murdering immigrant gangs or foreign terrorists. The defining characteristics of nationalist populism are enacted in a style based on insult, anecdote, and bragging. This pattern perfectly fits the technological limits of Twitter, talk shows focusing on controversy or "breaking news," the carnival atmosphere of political rallies, and the combative structure of primary debates where multiple candidates vie for exposure in a format that provides little time for argument exposition. In contrast, it does not fit contexts such as major speeches on particular topics or general election debates, in which there is vastly more time for policy exposition than in primary debates with multiple candidates.

The stylistic pattern based on insult, anecdote, and bragging is particularly adapted to voters with an authoritarian mind-set. Taub noted, "Authoritarians are thought to express much deeper fears than the rest of the electorate, to seek the imposition of order where they perceive dangerous change, and to desire a strong leader who will defeat those fears with force."[78] She added that the research on authoritarian personality structures suggests a "candidate to match [the predictions of the theory] . . . would look a lot like Donald Trump."[79] A style based on insult, anecdote, and bragging is tailored to fulfilling the needs of authoritarian voters for emotional release. Trump's reduction of "everything to black-and-white extremes of strong versus weak, greatest versus worst, his simple direct promises that he can solve problems that other politicians are too weak to manage," and "his willingness to flout all the conventions of civilized discourse when it comes to the minority groups that authoritarians find so threatening" were perfectly adapted to activating authoritarian voters. He had what political scientist Stanley Feldman called a "classic authoritarian leadership style: simple, powerful and punitive."[80]

Trump's Presidential Announcement Speech Enacts His Core Message

To this point, I have argued that nationalist populism is best understood as an affective genre that produces a strong emotional reaction, serving as a form of rhetorical activation of voters who perceive their economic and social situation and their group identity as threatened by societal change. Unlike progressive populism, nationalist populism is not focused on a policy response to the ills affecting the society but rather is an expression of rage and fear and a call for election of an authentic outsider leader who can bring back a lost time of prosperity and power.[81]

It should be clear that the similarities apparent between Trump's rhetoric and that of nationalist populists in Europe are more than mere coincidence. In confronting fear of rapid social change, along with genuine problems such as income inequality and income stagnation, political figures can respond either at the level of policy or at the level of emotion and narrative. Progressive populists choose the former approach, whereas nationalist populists select the latter. The nationalist variant requires a narrative that provides reassurance for authoritarian voters along with a sense of shared identity and enemies to hate and to blame for societal dysfunction. The pattern is clearly evident in Trump's speech announcing his campaign for president on June 16, 2015.[82]

Trump's announcement speech was strikingly different from typical campaign kickoff speeches. It was not merely that Trump arrived at the site of the announcement by riding down the escalator at Trump Towers but rather what he said. There is no discernable organizational pattern in the speech, and much of it seems to be simply stream of consciousness as he almost randomly presented his nationalist populist message. For example, in the middle of a long passage in which he criticized China for unfair trade practices (67–85), Trump interrupted his attack to say, "Hey, I'm not saying they're stupid. I like China. I sell apartments for—I just sold an apartment for $15 million to somebody from China. Am I supposed to dislike them?" (77). Normally, politicians do not make such interjections.

The speech is also notable for a failure to support claims in any kind of coherent way. For example, early in the speech, Trump stated, "The real number [for the unemployment rate] is anywhere from 18 to 19 and maybe even 21 percent, and nobody talks about it" (22). Of course, this claim was nonsense, a conclusion verified by fact-checking organizations, and as soon as he became president, Trump began claiming credit for the strong economy he had said did not exist.[83]

Although there was no discernible organizational pattern in the speech, and it failed to lay out anything like a coherent argument, the pattern of nationalist populism with an outsider persona was apparent. As was common in his campaign rhetoric, Trump presented a dystopian vision of a nation in crisis. In the beginning of the speech, he said, "Our country is in serious trouble. We don't have victories anymore" (5). He developed that vision throughout the speech, focusing on the economy, especially trade, and various other domestic and international failures. In the middle of the speech, he boiled down his view of the nation, saying simply, "We got nothing but problems" (106). He returned to this conclusion in the third-to-last paragraph: "Sadly, the American dream is dead" (183). Of course, the nation was in the midst of a substantial economic recovery following the Great Recession, and the Obama administration had instituted policies to reduce pollution and otherwise protect the environment, dramatically cut the number of uninsured Americans, put into place a plan to deal with global warming, and so forth. It is revealing that Trump saw the United States during the Obama era as a dystopia.

According to Trump, the nation was threatened by a number of dangerous Others and by the failure of a corrupt political class to confront the threat. Trump began developing the nationalist theme in the introduction, where he referenced the terrorist group Islamic State in Iraq and Syria (ISIS) and failed trade deals with China and Japan. He then focused on undocumented immigrants from Mexico, claiming "They're bringing drugs. They're bringing crime. They're rapists." Late in the speech, he presented his signature policy proposal: "I would build a great wall, and nobody builds walls better than me" (159). In addition, he focused on trade in a number of extended passages to reinforce the nationalist portion of his message, pointed to the threat of terrorism, and at the end of the speech promised, "Nobody would be tougher on ISIS than Donald Trump. Nobody" (161).

The populist theme also was obvious. In his announcement speech, he introduced one of the signature attacks of his campaign, claiming, "Politicians are all talk, no action. Nothing's gonna get done" (29). A few paragraphs later he was prescient in predicting the reaction of ordinary people to other candidates' speeches: "I don't need the rhetoric. I want a job" (33). He also criticized other candidates as incompetent, saying, "If you can't make a good deal with a politician, then there's something wrong with you." He added, "They will never make America great again. They don't even have a chance. They're controlled fully—they're controlled fully by the lobbyists, by the donors, and by the special interests" (38). According to Trump, the underlying problem with the nation's trade policies was that the leaders of other countries "are much smarter than our leaders" (79). In relation to trade, he said, "We have all the cards, but we don't know how to use them" (81). He applied the populist critique to other Republicans running for president, criticizing Jeb Bush and Marco Rubio by name and saying of all his competitors, "They don't have a clue. They can't lead us" (121).

Trump's solution to the problems of the nation was not based in ideology. He mentioned policies he opposed—Obamacare and the Iran deal—and made promises that he would fix infrastructure and other problems, but other than the border wall, he provided few policy specifics, and he never explained a policy position or provided any significant evidence supporting his view. Rather, he enacted the celebrity outsider persona by claiming he would fix problems through the force of his personality and through his capacity as a dealmaker. He said, "Our country needs—our country needs a truly great leader, and we need a truly great leader now. We need a leader that wrote *The Art of the Deal*. We need a leader that can bring back our jobs, can bring back our manufacturing" (40–41). He added, "We need somebody that literally will take this country and make it great again. We can do that" (48). He then shifted from stating what the country needed to what he could accomplish, claiming "I will be the greatest jobs president that God ever created," and "I'll bring back our jobs from China, from Mexico, from Japan, from so many places. I'll bring back our jobs, and I'll bring back our money" (54, 55). He depicted himself as a tough guy who would tell corporate leaders they could not move factories abroad and said those leaders would "have no choice" but to give in to his demands (111). In relation to infrastructure, he provided no details about his policy but promised, "Nobody can do that [rebuild infrastructure] like me. Believe me. It will be done on time, on budget, way below cost, way below what anyone ever thought" (171). In the conclusion of the speech, after stating that the American dream was dead, he promised, "But if I get elected president, I will bring it back bigger and better and stronger than ever before, and we will make America great again" (184).

As part of the celebrity outsider persona, he also bragged about his wealth and accomplishments, thus embracing a vernacular style quite different from that of typical presidential announcements. He claimed he was the only politician who could be trusted because "I'm using my own money. I'm not using the lobbyists. I'm not using donors. I don't care. I'm really rich" (102). He also bragged about his wealth and business accomplishments, ultimately claiming his net worth was "$8,737,549,000" (132–151). Normally, political figures cast their accomplishments as part of the larger story of Americans working together to foster the American dream. They often focus on their humble roots. Trump's approach was quite different. He said the American dream was dead and presented himself as the solution because he was an ultra-rich tough guy beholden to no one.

It certainly was not a typical presidential announcement speech. Joshua Green was on target when he labeled it "mind-bending."[84] Much of the reporting at the time focused on the numerous false claims in the announcement and other early speeches, particularly Trump's claim that undocumented immigrants committed many crimes. The *Washington Post* savaged Trump, concluding that "the facts just are not there" and awarding him the lowest rating for his comments: "Four Pinocchios."[85] Early political reporting viewed Trump's campaign as more of a vanity project than a serious political campaign. For example, Ben Terris noted that "members of team Trump spent the hour before the event out in the streets of midtown Manhattan trying to lure tourists in to fill out the crowd" and added that "few people think Trump has a chance of winning the presidential election."[86] The reporters and analysts did not think a candidate without political experience who violated all the normal rules of politics without laying out a coherent agenda and stated many untruths could possibly be a serious candidate for president. They were wrong.

Conclusion

In this chapter, I laid out the four components that define Trump's message and juxtaposed his nationalist populism with progressive populism. I also demonstrated that the nationalist populist message demanded a celebrity outsider persona and a vernacular style quite different from the norm in American politics. In the next chapter, I begin the process of explaining how and why Trump's message resonated strongly enough for him to win the Republican nomination, and then the presidency, by focusing on one of the key places where he built a strongly affective relationship with supporters—campaign rallies.

2

Trump's Rhetoric of Nationalist Populism in 2016 Campaign Rallies

One of the most distinctive aspects of Trump's 2016 presidential campaign was the way he used a large number of giant rallies that formed the core of his campaign and were widely broadcast on cable television to create a strong following among Republican voters and appeal to working-class white voters, many of whom had voted for Presidents Bill Clinton and Barack Obama.

Rallies were like a concert tour for Trump's core audience. Their function was emotional activation, reassurance, and reinforcement. His rhetoric at these events followed a stream-of-consciousness organizational pattern, very different from typical political rallies but within which the nationalist populist message was dominant. Trump used this message to arouse a sense of threat and then to resolve it by providing an answer in the form of himself. Trump supporters at the rallies and watching them on television or online were transformed into a community of followers.

Trump's nationalist populist strategy of arousal and satiation served three particular emotional functions for his supporters. First, his dystopian narrative activated for those attending or watching the rallies the sense that their role in society was threatened by economic, political, and cultural forces. It, therefore, provided his supporters external enemies to blame for their declining power. Olga Khazan noted, "Trump supporters were also more likely than Clinton voters to feel that . . . high-status groups, like men, Christians, and whites, are discriminated against."[1] By creating a narrative in which hardworking white Trump supporters were threatened by various Others, Trump's rhetoric created an us-versus-them dynamic that reinforced their sense of threatened identity. He attracted "followers by enhancing the perception of dangerous threats to the society and offering simple solutions."[2] Second, the populist portion of Trump's message placed blame for failure to confront the dangerous Others on arrogant liberal elites, Wall Street, and their protectors in the press. In doing so, he not only provided an internal set of enemies to hate but removed all responsibility from Trump supporters for their threatened situation. They were not responsible for declining economic and political power; the arrogant elites and their enablers in the media were to blame. Many clearly felt they had been disrespected by the media and urban elites and used their support for Trump both to reassert their own identity and to lash out at those elites. This aspect of Trump's narrative must have been comforting for the 33 percent of his supporters in the general election who "were white men without a college degree," a group that "put Mr. Trump over the top in disproportionately white working-class battleground states . . . like Pennsylvania, Wisconsin, and Michigan."[3] Third, the celebrity outsider aspect of Trump's persona provided supporters a hero they perceived to be like them and not of the system. Moreover, this hero did not bore them with discussion of policy details or an explanation of the difficulties of passing major legislation but instead promised that through force of will he would "Make America Great Again." In doing so, he would bring back a fabled Golden Age in which their economic and political power had been dominant. The fact that said Golden Age had never existed was irrelevant; it existed in Trump's narrative.

Trump's rally speeches created a strong sense of identity among Trump supporters by fulfilling the three functions I have described. There is persuasive evidence of the emotional resonance of Trump rallies. A number of journalists and social scientists attended rallies and observed the reaction of Trump supporters.[4] Jenna Johnson noted, "Trump rallies often feel like rock concerts. There are groupies who travel to as many rallies as they can and camp out at the front of the line. Many rallygoers show up wearing as much red, white, and blue as possible." She added, "And there are the chants that allow rallygoers to feel even more a part of a movement: 'Lock her up.' 'Drain the swamp.' 'USA!' 'Build that wall.'" The power of creating an us-versus-them identity is obvious in Johnson's description of the rally atmosphere, a point reinforced by her observation that "the rally's loudest moments hit over 100 dB, as loud as a jet takeoff."[5] Gwynn Guilford, who attended several rallies as a form of ethnographic research, also noted that attendees experienced a strong emotional reaction. She explained that the audience at Trump rallies functioned as a "single-voiced creature." She added the thought that even as a researcher, "from within the Trump rally masses, I felt the strange sea-change that turns 20,000 individuals into one being, I felt its power swell, and sometimes it felt good."[6] The strong emotional response Johnson and Guilford described has been labeled by social psychologists "emotional contagion."[7]

Trump's focus on the Others he claimed threaten the nation pertain more to group identity than to rallying the nation to confront a crisis. The opioid crisis, gun violence, and traffic accidents each kill vastly more Americans in a given year than undocumented immigrants, refugees, and terrorists combined. But Trump's focus on these "dangerous" groups and the jobs lost because of unfair trade served a powerful identity-affirmation function. Guilford noted, "The conversation that takes place at Trump rallies is far more fundamental than anything encapsulated in a party platform. The urge that Trump is finally giving voice, authority, and legitimacy to is redefining America's vision of itself—to whom the country belongs, who deserves to live here, who is entitled to its economic bounty, and who must be punished for its perceived decay."[8] Social psychologists Stephen Reicher and Alexander Haslam concluded on the basis of their ethnographic research that "a Trump rally was a dramatic enactment of a specific vision of America," functioning as "an identity festival that embodied a politics of hope" for return to a perceived time of greatness and opportunity. Trump's rhetoric at rallies created "a shared sense of 'us.'"[9] Katy Tur drew a similar conclusion based on her experience covering the campaign for NBC. She noted that "inside a Trump rally, these people are unchained. They can drop their everyday niceties. They can yell and scream and say the things they'd never say out loud on the outside"; she added that in the rally atmosphere, "They aren't deplorables. They are patriots."[10] Tur's comment indicates the great power in Trump's tapping their feeling of being disrespected by elites and the media.

The media served a key function at rallies as "a hate totem for the events, the most reliable targets for ritual humiliation from the stage."[11] According to Johnson, "Whenever the president attacked the media during the rally, his fans would usually start booing and yelling at the reporters in the arena."[12] Tur described one moment when someone in the crowd at a rally yelled, "'Katy sucks!'" and then added, "On Twitter I can see the vitriol rising, the death threats blowing around like loose trash."[13] David Frum noted that "Trump's attacks on the media ventured beyond criticism to outright incitement of violence" and observed that "his campaign rallies triggered furious audience outbursts at members of the media."[14]

Trump's opponents served a similar function. Johnson noted, "Confronting protesters has become a sport of sorts at Trump rallies—one that's especially embraced by young men in the crowd who are excited to yell at liberals." Guilford observed that at the rallies she attended, "just about everyone was on the lookout for protesters," and when they found such interlopers, the crowd chanted "Trump! Trump! Trump!" "to drown out the protesters."[15] Through these forms of emotional release, the rallies produced "a shift—from individual to collective" identity, a shift that "may explain the fistfights, punching, and sporadic tussles between Trump supporters and protesters—many of whom are members of minority groups targeted by Trump's campaign rhetoric."[16] The net result of these strategies was that "crowd members were induced to act as if they were under threat . . . from enemies both without and within."[17]

More broadly, with his attacks on elites, Trump tapped into a sense of being "snubbed," "a feeling shared by many of his supporters, especially those who have never seen the need for a college degree." Johnson added that when Trump reminded supporters Secretary Hillary Clinton had called them "deplorables," "the crowd cheered and then began to chant: 'USA! USA! USA!'"[18] In this way, Trump drew on "a widely held feeling that mainstream culture has turned against" the white working class, a judgment that led Haslam, a researcher on crowd psychology from the University of Queensland, to conclude, "What these unfolding dynamics [at rallies] do is allow people to live out their shared identity in very dramatic ways."[19] One result was that Trump rallies "reinforced" a "self/other dynamic."[20]

There is also strong ethnographic evidence that at the rallies Trump's celebrity outsider persona created both a sense of "shared identity" with him as an everyman and also the sense that he could "Make America Great Again" by force of will. Guilford explained, "Many of the supporters I talked to . . . saw him as a 'regular guy'" and "one of their own." He was "an entrepreneur of identity" who had "construed himself as prototypical of the 'ordinary American' in-group."[21] He also created perceived authenticity by "taking down PC" and, in the words of one supporter, saying "the same things we do around our dinner table." In that way, his most outrageous or offensive comments were proof of his "authenticity."[22] This explains why apparent "gaffes" often helped him. As Reicher and Haslam noted, "His failure to follow the rules of politics and his rejection by the political class validated his in-group status in the eyes of an antipolitical audience" as "'one of us,' not 'one of them.'"[23] Trump's "rough" and "crude" talk was "not the cultured talk of those slick establishment insiders."[24] This strategy made Trump "bulletproof" with core supporters.[25] It allowed him to control the "crowd's moods" with a "rhetorical style" that created an "emotional response" and a "powerful relationship" with the audience that suggested "parallels between Trump and Hitler."[26] As a consequence, "Trump rallies succeeded in large part thanks to an audience that enthusiastically performed its devotion to Trump and . . . acted as a community under threat."[27]

Although the emotional resonance of Trump's message and the rallies themselves as enactment of that message is obvious, commentators and scholars have struggled to explain that response. How did Trump produce the sense of community and the strong emotional reaction described by researchers? In what follows, I show that nationalist populism with a celebrity outsider persona and a vernacular style based on bragging and insults dominated his rally speeches during the 2016 campaign, fulfilling the functions I have described. All four aspects of his message were crucial to producing the emotional resonance. I illustrate that argument by discussing a rally in Pennsylvania on June 28, 2016, focused on trade and a rally in Phoenix on September 1, 2016, in which Trump emphasized immigration.[28] The *New York Times* stated that the speech in Pennsylvania "encapsulated his aspirational strategy for the general election" in its focus on "white working-class men," and the *Guardian* said that "in Arizona we saw the real Donald Trump."[29] After discussing these speeches, I show that the overall pattern of nationalist populism with a celebrity outsider persona and a vernacular style dominated his rallies throughout the campaign.

Trump Rally Speeches

In both the Arizona and Pennsylvania rallies, Trump described a dystopian American landscape. In Phoenix, he said, "Our country is a mess. We don't even know what to look for anymore, folks. Our country has to straighten out. And we have to straighten out fast." At the conclusion of the speech, he claimed his campaign was "our last chance" to confront the danger posed by undocumented immigration and refugees. Trump described both groups as immensely threatening. He said, "Countless innocent American lives have been stolen because our politicians have failed in their duty to secure our borders and enforce our laws." Later, he added that "illegal immigrants and other non-citizens, in our prisons and jails together, had around 25,000 homicide arrests" and concluded that "the media and my opponent discuss one thing and only one thing, the needs of people living here illegally. In many cases, by the way, they're treated better than our vets." In this and similar statements, Trump claimed that the government protected dangerous groups, including immigrants and refugees, whereas it did not care about ordinary, hardworking Americans, a message tailored to appeal to members of the white working class who felt their place in the nation was threatened by racial and demographic change and who also felt disrespected by elites. Of course, the claim that Clinton and the media cared more about undocumented immigrants than they did about ordinary American citizens and veterans was absurd. He also mentioned several ordinary Americans he claimed had been murdered by undocumented immigrants. Later, he attacked Clinton for supporting "amnesty" for immigrants and labeled a plan to "bring in 620,000 new refugees from Syria and that region" a "Trojan horse." With these remarks, he inflamed the audience's fear and anger. He asked, "What the hell are we doing?" He also warned the audience of a significant terrorism threat from "foreign-born individuals." He said, "Right now the largest number of people are under investigation for exactly this [terrorism] than we've ever had in the history of our country." His answer to this threat was to support "extreme vetting. I want extreme. It's going to be so tough." As is evident, the nationalist message dominated the address, which also included a promise to "build a great wall along the southern border" that "Mexico will pay for."

The Arizona rally also featured a populist attack on elites and to a lesser extent the media. Trump said, "The fundamental problem with the immigration system in our country is that it serves the needs of wealthy donors, political activists, and powerful politicians," groups he contrasted with "the concerns that working people, our forgotten working people, have over the record pace of immigration." He also said Clinton had "evaded justice" and claimed of his "special deportation task force" that "maybe they'll be able to deport her."

Trump's outsider persona was apparent when he claimed that his election would essentially produce magical changes across the nation. He claimed about "two million . . . criminal aliens" that in "my first hour in office, those people are gone." He also predicted, "The crime will stop. They're going to be gone. It will be over." He later added that after he was elected, "Our local police will be so happy that they don't have to be abused by these thugs anymore." He also promised "to make great trade deals" and assured the audience that "we're going to bring our jobs back home." Rather than backing up these and other promises with evidence and supporting arguments, he said simply, "It's going to happen, folks. Because I am proudly not a politician, because I am not behold [sic] to any special interest." He concluded, "Nobody owns Trump." Through his outsider leadership, he alleged, "peace and law and justice and prosperity will prevail. Crime will go down. Border crossings will plummet. Gangs will disappear." Of course, these claims were absolute nonsense. In making them, Trump relied on his persona as a celebrity outsider to tap into the view that the real problem was corrupt elites blocking actions to protect the nation from "dangerous" Others. From this perspective, a celebrity outsider beholden to no one could produce immediate and decisive change, leading the nation back to the lost Golden Age.

Trump began the speech in Phoenix stating that it would not "be a rally speech, per se. I'm going to deliver a detailed policy address." Unsurprisingly, he did nothing of the kind but instead gave a typical rally speech. The affective function of Trump's promises is obvious. Even Trump's most ardent supporters had to know that undocumented immigrants would not be deported in the first hour of his presidency and that his election by itself would not yield major reductions in crime or economic gains absent other policy changes. Trump was not building an argument for a coherent conservative agenda. Much of what he claimed would happen was not conservative, and none of it was based in developed ideological argument. Presidents such as Ronald Reagan and Barack Obama used rhetoric to build support for a consistent approach to government: small government conservatism for Reagan and pragmatic liberalism for Obama. Trump's rhetoric served a different function, providing emotional reassurance. Trump treated his core supporters, many of whom had lost ground over decades, as the "real" Americans and promised that dangerous Others would be dealt with and elites would get their comeuppance. It clearly was an emotionally fulfilling message for many in his base of support but was also devoid of policy.

Trump's rally speech in Pennsylvania focused on trade, rather than immigration, but in all other ways presented a nationalist populist message quite similar to what he said in Arizona. The setting for his nationalist populist narrative was a dystopian American landscape. Trump stated, "For years, they [elites] watched on the sidelines as our jobs vanished and our communities were plunged into Depression-level unemployment." He claimed, "Globalization has wiped out our middle class." These major economic losses had occurred, he said, because of unfair competition, especially from China. That unfair competition had created "cities and towns across this country where a third or even half of manufacturing jobs have been wiped out in the last 20 years." Trump's solution was to "declare our economic independence once again." As in Phoenix, the function of the rally was not policy advocacy. Declaring "economic independence" is a slogan, not a coherent policy. The nation was not in a "Depression-level" economic crisis, and the middle class had not been "wiped out." Rather than advocating a clear policy, Trump reassured his base of working-class supporters that the real losses they had experienced were not their fault and that they could return to an imagined Golden Age of economic opportunity without any of the difficulty of actual policy change. His appeal was not ideological but based in emotional reassurance.

Trump not only reassured his audience but gave them villains to hate. In addition to China and other nations cheating American workers with unfair trade practices, the scapegoats were political and business elites "who rigged the system in [sic] their benefit" and "are supporting Hillary Clinton because they know as long as she is in charge nothing will ever change." The nation had "lost our way" because "we stopped believing in our country." The problems the nation confronted were a "politician-made disaster" that was "the consequence of a leadership class that worships globalism over Americanism." Trump focused his attacks on the North American Free Trade Agreement (NAFTA) and allowing China to join the World Trade Organization (WTO), which he blamed on the Clintons. He also strongly attacked the Obama administration trade proposal, the Trans-Pacific Partnership (TPP), which he claimed "will undermine our independence." In this narrative, lost opportunities had nothing to do with new technology or other changes in the economy that lessened reliance on unskilled labor but had occurred because of the nefarious trading practices of China and other countries and because elites, including Secretary Clinton, had "betrayed American workers for Wall Street."

Trump presented himself as a celebrity outsider who could produce instant change. Without explanation or evidence, he promised, "We can turn it all around—and we can turn it around fast." After presenting a laundry list of protectionist proposals, he stated that with his election the "era of economic surrender will finally be over" and "a new era of prosperity will finally begin.

America will be independent once more." Later, he enacted the role of the outsider by promising that as a consequence of his charismatic leadership, companies would "start using American steel for American infrastructure." By putting "American-produced steel back into the backbone of our country," his administration would "create massive numbers of jobs." Trump did not explain how his trade policies would work or provide evidence supporting his claims. He was the celebrity businessman who had made vast sums of money by firing workers on TV. The underlying narrative that Trump would generate massive changes through force of will produced emotional reassurance by denying that technology had fundamentally changed the economy or that many new jobs required more education than in the past and by supporting the reassuring fairytale that his election would produce almost immediate massive job and income gains. The function of Trump's narrative was not just to provide emotional reassurance but also to spur anger against elites and the dangerous Others he claimed threatened the nation.

The pattern of nationalist populism with an outsider persona along with a vernacular style based in attacks, insults, and bragging clearly dominated both rally speeches. The functions of these speeches were to create anger at elites and the dangerous Others, provide emotional reassurance that an imagined Golden Age could be brought back easily, and strengthen a bond between Trump and his supporters. The speeches focused on somewhat different aspects of Trump's dystopian narrative, but both identified Others as villains in this narrative: undocumented immigrants and foreign countries' unfair competition, respectively. They both also placed blame on greedy elites, a political system, and media that protect them. And they both depicted Trump as the outsider, the celebrity businessman who through force of will could bring back the glory days of the 1950s. In both cases, Trump demonstrated his authenticity through use of the vernacular style I have described.

Nationalist Populism: A Consistent Pattern in Trump Rallies in 2016

The pattern of nationalist populism with an outsider persona and an associated vernacular style typified Trump's rallies during the 2016 presidential campaign. In all his rally speeches, he attacked elites, the media, and especially Secretary Clinton as totally corrupt. For example, in a speech in Akron,

Ohio, on August 8, 2016, Trump focused his populist attack on elites on her. He said, "Hillary Clinton has forgotten the first rule of public service. The job of an elected official is to serve the citizens of the United States."[30] Later, he referenced "the vast scope of Hillary Clinton's criminality" and then focused on alleged corruption involving "pay-to-play" in President Clinton's administration, in Arkansas by Governor Clinton, and in the Clinton Foundation. He then tied Secretary Clinton to economic and political elites more broadly, claiming, "Hillary Clinton's campaign is funded by Wall Street and hedge fund managers" who represented the "ruling class."

Trump focused more broadly on attacking elites in a campaign speech in New York on June 22, 2016.[31] After speaking of "crumbling roads and bridges," problems that "can all be fixed" "only by me," Trump said, "We will never be able to fix a rigged system by counting on the same people who rigged it in the first place." He added, "It's not just the political system that's rigged. It's the whole economy." He extended the attack beyond political and business elites, blaming "bureaucrats who are trapping kids in failing schools." He then focused on Secretary Clinton, whom he called "a world-class liar." His "promise to the American voter" was: "I will end the special interest monopoly in Washington."

Trump's populist message was also quite evident in a speech in Charlotte, North Carolina, in mid-August 2016, his first major speech after hiring Steve Bannon as a chief advisor.[32] He claimed to be fighting for "forgotten Americans" and promised that he would "speak the truth for all of you, and for everyone in this country who doesn't have a voice." The fundamental problem, he claimed, was the existence of "a system that gets rich at your expense." It was a system dominated by "arrogant leaders who look down on you instead of serving and protecting you." The emotional function of these comments is quite clear. Trump was fanning his supporters' anger at elites, arguing that elites not only took actions that harmed white working-class people but had no respect for them. He claimed, "Hedge fund managers, the financial lobbyists, the Wall Street investors" were "throwing their money at Hillary Clinton" as a means of the "powerful protecting the powerful." He promised to change all that because "I am fighting for you." Later, he added, "On political corruption, we are going to restore honor to our government."

In these and other rally speeches, Trump expressed the nationalist theme by emphasizing unfair international trade deals, the threat posed by undocumented immigrants, the danger posed by Islamic terrorism in general and refugees in particular, and implicitly Black crime. For example, in Akron, Trump supported an "America First" agenda and again promised that the "era of economic surrender is over." He described major economic losses that he ascribed to "Hillary Clinton trade policies," but he also focused on threats to "law and order" that had resulted in the "more than 2,600 [who] have been shot in Chicago alone since the beginning of the year." Later, he said, "Homicides are up nearly 50 percent in Washington, D.C., and more than 60 percent in Baltimore," referencing the crime rate in cities with a large population of Black Americans. He claimed to be concerned for Black Americans and asked, "What do you have to lose by trying something new?" However, his actual goal was to use the reference to high crime rates as a kind of political "dog whistle" ("subtle code words for race") to scare his largely white audience with the threat of Black crime.[33] Trump did this so effectively that according to E. J. Dionne Jr., Norman Ornstein, and Thomas Mann, he "converted the dog-whistle appeals of the late twentieth century into bull-horn-style racial politics that harkened back to the time of George Wallace."[34]

In other speeches, Trump focused more heavily on the threat posed by immigration or terrorism. In New York, he claimed Secretary Clinton "refuses to acknowledge the threat posed by Radical Islam" and then said she "would admit hundreds of thousands of refugees from the most dangerous countries on Earth—with no way to screen who they are or what they believe." He went as far as to claim, "Hillary Clinton wants to bring in people who believe women should be enslaved." In that speech, he also spoke of the danger posed by undocumented immigrants who would take jobs from "poor African American and Hispanic workers." After quoting a letter from the mother of a police officer killed by illegal immigrants, he said Secretary Clinton "has the blood of so many on her hands" and accused her of supporting "an open-door policy to criminals and terrorists to enter our country."

Although he often focused on one aspect of what he later called "American carnage" by identifying a dangerous Other he claimed threatened the nation, on occasion he presented the complete cast of villains. In the speech following his hiring Bannon, he spoke of the dangers of "Radical Islamic Terrorism" as well as the risks posed by unfair trade deals such as NAFTA and the perils posed by "our open border," which "has allowed drugs and crime and gangs to pour into our communities." In the same speech, he also said he was "going to restore law and order to this country" and cited "chaos and violence on our streets and the assaults on law enforcement," referring to protests after police violence against Black Americans. Trump's nationalist message was designed to arouse his core audience's fear of Islamic terrorism, job losses as a result of bad trade deals, and crime committed by undocumented immigrants and Black Americans.

His dystopian narrative of a nation threatened by dangerous enemies had great emotional power despite the fact that it was a fundamentally false story. The nation did not face "Depression-level" economic problems. Crime was quite close to a forty-year low. Islamic terrorism was a modest problem in the United States and no larger than the problem of radical right-wing terrorism. No Americans had been killed in terrorist attacks by refugees. Trump was not building a case for policy change. He was successfully creating fear and anger in audience members who saw themselves as losing dominance in society.[35]

In all of these rallies, Trump depicted himself as a hero who would represent the people and through force of will quickly produce massive change. In the speech after hiring Bannon, he promised, "If I am elected President, this chaos and violence will end—and it will end very quickly." As president, by "fighting for these forgotten Americans" and serving as "a champion for the people," he would "restore honor to our government." He was the outsider who "will fix it." In New York, he claimed that "I'm with you: the American people" and promised that "it's going to be America First."

Trump's statement that problems could be fixed "only by me" in the speech in New York is representative of the many times he made grandiose claims about the instant and magical results his election would produce. It also indicates that the populist message and his celebrity outsider persona were closely linked. Typical political figures, including progressive populists, never claim that only they could fix a problem both for fear of coming across as arrogant and because their message is about what they can accomplish working with and for the people as an enactment of the American dream. In contrast, the hero of a nationalist populist narrative must be an outsider who is not part of the corrupt system. In Trump's case, he was the celebrity businessman variant of the outsider who had triumphed on television and would do so just as easily in real life. Of course, this was nonsense, but the campaign more than the show made for good TV.

Conclusion

In the rally speeches, Trump adapted his message to events of the moment in the campaign and also to local concerns. Thus, he focused more on immigration in Arizona and more on lost manufacturing jobs in Pennsylvania. But there was much less variation than is the norm in presidential campaigns. Trump did not give major addresses focusing on a particular issue as is common in campaigns. In Arizona he claimed he was going to present such a speech and then did nothing of the kind. In fact, the rally speeches contained almost no developed policy argument. Although his policy on undocumented immigration was quite simplistic (build a wall and create a deportation force), it was also in comparison with other issues one of Trump's most detailed positions. On other topics, he primarily made grandiose claims that provided emotional reassurance to his supporters by appealing to popular nostalgia for a time when the United States had been the preeminent industrial power in the world. For example, in Akron he claimed, "My tax reforms will add millions of new jobs and thousands of new small businesses. My energy reforms will create millions of new jobs and lower the price of your energy bill. My trade reforms will raise wages, grow jobs, and add trillions in new wealth into our country." These statements were less about public policy than they were a declaration of the power of his charismatic leadership. The keys to that power were that he was an outsider who claimed to be consubstantial with and fighting for his core supporters. At the beginning of the conclusion of the rally speech in Akron, he said, "I am fighting for everyone who doesn't have a voice. The forgotten men and women of America. I am your voice." He added later, "I am fighting for you" and noted that he wore the "opposition [of elites] as a badge of honor. Because it means I am fighting for REAL change," or what he called "peaceful regime change in our own country." He added, "The media-donor political complex that's bled this country dry has to be replaced with a new government of, by, and for the people." Trump described himself as the enactment of that government and promised, "We Will Make America Great Again."

The rhetorical pattern of nationalist populism with an outsider persona dominated Trump's campaign rallies. The primary difference among the rally speeches was which villainous Other he attacked. In some speeches, he focused on undocumented immigrants, refugees, Islamic terrorists, or unfair trade deals; in others, he painted a picture of a broader dystopian landscape that included all of these villains. Sometimes by implication, he also warned his largely white audience of inner-city (Black) crime. Regardless, elites were to blame for the Others who threatened the nation. Trump was always the outsider hero who was consubstantial with his supporters and would bring instantaneous magical change that would "Make America Great Again."

One of the puzzles of the 2016 campaign was Trump's popularity despite the fact that he made so little effort to show that his policy proposals would actually work. Other than on immigration and refugee policy, he made very few specific proposals, and the few specifics he did provide were widely labeled as unrealistic by fact checkers on the left and right. Many of his promises were, frankly, unbelievable. It is difficult to believe that even his firmest supporters thought Mexico would pay for a wall on the border or that undocumented immigrants would be deported during the first hour of a Trump presidency. There is no evidence that many of his supporters actually believed his promise that the industrial economy of past decades would quickly be reborn upon his election.

In contrast with Trump's speeches, it is common for presidential candidates to lay out a relatively detailed policy position. For example, Reagan presented major speeches in October 1980 that described in considerable detail his variant of small-government conservatism and provided a rationale for his domestic and foreign/defense policy agendas.[36] Other nominees have spoken in even more detail about their policy agenda. For example, Obama presented major speeches on a host of topics during the 2008 campaign.[37] I have focused on Reagan and Obama as particularly skillful presidential persuaders, but a similar point could be made about virtually every major party nominee since the World War II. All of them felt the need to lay out and defend their agenda in some detail.

In contrast, Trump's appeal was not tied to public policy. Except for general policy statements about the various Others he depicted as threatening the nation, his policy positions were often quite ambiguous. For example, although he constantly labeled "Obamacare" a disaster, on occasion he seemed to endorse a single-payer health system similar to that advocated by Senator Bernie Sanders in the Democratic primaries in 2016.[38] Trump's appeal was not tied to policy advocacy but was based in the emotional connection he made with core supporters. He provided these supporters villains to hate (the media and elites) and to fear (the various Others he claimed were creating an American dystopia) and a hero who stood with them and would vanquish their foes. For the tens of millions of Americans who felt threatened by demographic and other cultural change and who perceived that the press and other elites often talked down to them, Trump was the hero who would fight for them. The chants at Trump rallies were not primarily support for a policy agenda. Trump's strongest supporters tended to be low-information voters who lacked a strong ideological worldview; in the past many had strongly supported small-government conservative Republicans who favored free trade or pragmatic liberals such as Presidents Clinton and Obama. In 2016, Trump was their guy. The chants and cheers at Trump rallies were akin to those at a rally for a beloved sports team. Supporters wore Trump hats for the same reason Green Bay Packer fans wear cheeseheads. He was their guy, and they were going to cheer for him.

There is grave danger in political allegiance becoming a tribal matter, as it is in sports. One danger is that tribal loyalty usually transcends reason. Good arguments will not turn a Denver Broncos fan into a supporter of the Kansas City Chiefs. Tribal allegiance also often leads to demonization of the other side, and such demonization can produce violence. Fights between fans of rival teams are a common occurrence. Those fights are much more dangerous if they involve political leaders with the power to enforce or change the law. Charles Homans's observation that "it is hard to get through a Trump rally now without thinking of the Philippines' Rodrigo Duterte, Turkey's Recept Tayyip Erdogan, or the other authoritarians for whom Trump has openly expressed his admiration" points to the potential dangers of the political conflict evident at Trump rallies.[39] More fundamentally, hatred of some group described as a threatening Other can undermine the ties that bind together a pluralistic democracy such as the United States. In his rally speeches, Trump urged his audience not to judge the country based on ideals defining the American dream but on the basis of race or religion or political loyalty. His core supporters cheered for him and screamed at opponents for the same reason that Auburn football fans boo the Crimson Tide. Basing politics and governance in tribal identity can be a dangerous approach indeed. Those dangers would become still more evident in the rallies that occurred after Trump's inauguration.

3

Nationalist Populism in Debates, the Republican National Convention, and the Inaugural

Trump's message of nationalist populism was well adapted to campaign rallies, where he tapped resentment against elites and fed fear of various Others. The rallies allowed him to speak for an extended period and create a persona as a celebrity businessman outsider, producing for many an atmosphere like a concert tour or NASCAR race. The rallies also were widely carried on cable television and were available for streaming or viewing after the fact, allowing Trump to extend the rally experience into virtual space, creating a strong bond with core supporters. Although Trump's message perfectly fit the rally atmosphere, the connection he made was more emotional than ideological. One consequence was that Trump avoided major policy speeches in which candidates typically lay out their agenda and critique that of their opponents.

Trump's message was adapted to the rally context, but there were two other campaign contexts he could not avoid in which it was not as good a fit: debates and his acceptance address at the Republican National Convention (RNC). The message was still less a fit for his Inaugural Address, which began his presidency. In this chapter, I show that in debates and the convention address, where rhetorical norms called for a very different kind of message than in his rally speeches, Trump ignored those norms and presented the same nationalist populist message with an outsider persona and the vernacular rhetorical style I have described. I then show that despite rhetorical norms calling for an inclusive and optimistic message, Trump used his Inaugural Address to present a dystopian vision of the nation that contained the same key rhetorical components as in his campaign.

Primary and General Election Debates

Campaign debates presented a potential challenge for Trump. Either moderators or other candidates could challenge him to back up his claims with evidence; explain how his proposals would work; or respond to attacks on his proposals, rhetoric, or actions. In other words, debates might force Trump to actually build an argument in support of his views or respond to the arguments of his opponents. In rallies, Trump never developed detailed proposals, cited strong evidence for his views, or responded with argument as opposed to insults to his opponents. Given the demands of the situation and the nature of his message, one might have expected primary debates to pose a serious problem for his campaign. In fact, they did not. Trump dominated Republican primary debates using the same approach as in his announcement speech and primary rallies. In fact, over time, he transformed primary debates into something more like competing rally speeches rather than actual debates. His use of a vernacular style, associated with the underlying pattern of nationalist populism with an outsider persona, was particularly important. He enacted that vernacular style by insulting his opponents and bragging about his accomplishments. Over the course of the primary debates, some of his opponents attempted to counter his approach with a vernacular style of their own. In particular, Senators Marco Rubio and Ted Cruz hit back at Trump with his own weapons, a tactic that did little to undercut Trump's appeal. By the end of the primary debate process, only Governor John Kasich was treating the events as something resembling a real debate.

To show that nationalist populism dominated Trump's debate performances, I focus on the first primary debate on *Fox News* on August 6, 2015, and another *Fox News* debate on March 3, 2016, when the primary field had dwindled to Trump, Rubio, Cruz, and Kasich.[1] The first debate was important for setting the tone for the Republican primary campaign and cementing Trump's role as the front-runner. The second *Fox News* debate came "at a crucial point" in the primary season when Trump was on the verge of winning the nomination, but Rubio, Cruz, and Kasich were doing everything possible to stop him from securing enough delegates to win an outright majority before the convention.[2] The two debates played a central role in the campaign and were broadly reflective of the other primary debates.

In the debate in August 2015, ten candidates shared the stage, and there had been another debate with additional candidates. With so many candidates, the event was more a joint press interview, with occasional interaction between the candidates, than a debate. Trump dominated the event by sticking to his basic message. In the opening, the anchors from Fox pressed all the candidates to raise their hands to agree that they would support the eventual Republican nominee. All but Trump did so; Trump promised only, "If I'm the nominee, I will pledge." Although the transcript reports that Trump was booed when he failed to raise his hand, his refusal was entirely consistent with the populist and outsider aspects of his message and also with the vernacular style he used throughout the primaries and the general election campaign.

It became quite clear that Trump would not stray from this pattern when Megyn Kelly used the first question to Trump to challenge him on insulting things he had said about women. Trump's initial response was to joke that his comments had been about "only Rosie O'Donnell," a longtime critic of Trump. After Kelly pushed Trump by mentioning a number of extremely offensive comments, he pivoted to the populist portion of his basic message, stating, "I think the big problem this country has is being politically correct." He then linked the populist and nationalist themes, adding, "I don't frankly have time for total political correctness. And to be honest with you, this country doesn't have time either. This country is in big trouble. We don't win anymore. We lose to China. We lose to Mexico both in trade and at the border. We lose to everybody." Trump concluded the answer by saying, "We need strength, we need energy, we need quickness, and we need brains in this country to turn it around," implying that only he could overcome political correctness to address the crisis he described.

In these statements, Trump made no attempt to address Kelly's question seriously or deny that he had said awful things about women. After the debate, he even went after Kelly directly, attacking her for asking "all sorts of ridiculous questions" and then saying, "You could see there was blood coming out of her eyes, blood coming out of her wherever."[3] This comment was both odious, drawing on offensive stereotypes about women, and typical of Trump's populist message and vernacular style. During the debate and afterward, Trump made no attempt to demonstrate that he respected women.

The same pattern of nationalist populism with an outsider persona and a vernacular style would continue throughout the debate. When Chris Wallace raised the immigration issue, the first thing Trump did was take credit for the focus on the topic: "So, if it weren't for me, you wouldn't even be talking about illegal immigration." Trump cast himself as the celebrity outsider who had forced the party to confront the problem despite the fact that "very dishonest" reporters were not "cover[ing] my statement the way I said it." He claimed to have forced the party to face "the fact . . . [of] many killings, murders, crime, drugs pouring across the border" and the "need to build a wall, and it has to be built quickly." Later, Trump again emphasized the nationalist portion of his message, stating, "The Mexican government is much smarter, much sharper, much more cunning. And they send the bad ones over because they don't want to pay for them." After Wallace pushed Trump to provide "specific evidence" that the Mexican government was, in fact, sending criminals to the United States, Trump responded, "I was at the border last week. Border patrol, people that I deal with, that I talk to, say this is what's happening. Because our leaders are stupid." Of course, Trump made the original comment months before his visit to the border, there was no documentation that border patrol officials had made any such statements, and the underlying claim had been widely debunked. The key point is that Trump treated the "debate" as a nationally televised opportunity to present his core message and ignored the norm for debates that candidates should present arguments and evidence in support of their positions. Although he had been booed in the opening moments of the event when he refused to pledge support for the eventual Republican nominee, after the exchange on immigration, the *Washington Post* transcript reported "cheering and applause."

Trump used the same approach throughout the debate. For example, when he was challenged about having made political donations to Democrats, he justified his actions by emphasizing the populist portion of his message, saying, "Our system is broken. I gave to many people, before this, before two months ago, I was a businessman. I give to everybody. When they call, I give." He then added, "When I need something from them two years later, three years later, I call them, they are there." Here, he depicted himself as the skilled businessman who knew how the corrupt system worked and had "built a net worth of more than $10 billion." In this way, he enacted the business variant of the outsider persona. He did the same thing when after talking about his record in business, he said, "And by the way, this country right now owes $19 trillion. And they need somebody like me to straighten out that mess."

In the first Republican primary debate, all aspects of Trump's nationalist populist message were present, although his focus was on the populist rather than the nationalist theme. He again and again emphasized the corruption of the system. On the nationalist aspect of his message, in addition to focusing on trade and immigration, he also spoke of Islamic terrorism, emphasizing the threat by stating, "When you have people that are cutting Christians' heads off, when you have a world that the border and at so many places, that is medieval times . . . it almost has to be as bad as it ever was in terms of the violence and the horror." He then concluded, "We have to go out and get the job done." The outsider persona was less evident than it would be in later debates or in other contexts, although Trump bragged about his business credentials and used his final statement to promise, "We have to make our country great again, and I will do that." Similarly, the vernacular style associated with nationalist populism was present, although Trump did not insult his opponents to the same degree he did in later debates and campaign rallies. At one point, he even praised Governor Jeb Bush as "a real gentleman." Even so, his bragging, refusal to apologize for demeaning comments about women, cruel joke about O'Donnell, and other comments were strikingly different from the norm in political primary debates.

Clearly, Trump did not treat the event as a debate. Unlike the other candidates, especially Bush and Kasich, he made no genuine effort to lay out or support a position. This was apparent when Wallace demanded that he cite support for his claim about the Mexican government sending criminals to the United States, and Trump responded with an entirely unverifiable reference to something he had heard at the border the week before. Rather than a debate, Trump treated the event as a competitive joint interview with the other candidates and an opportunity to use his nationalist populist message to set himself apart from them. There is considerable evidence that he succeeded. He went into the debate with support "double that of his closest competitors," a level based "on his unfettered style" as "the first post-policy candidate."[4] The debate drew 24 million viewers, more than three times the audience than in any Republican primary debate in 2012, largely because "the public can't get enough of Donald Trump's presidential bid."[5] Karen Tumulty and Phillip Rucker observed, "Donald Trump landed on the Republican debate stage like a hand grenade," tapping "into a genuine current of public outrage and exasperation" and "overshadowing the bids" of the other candidates.[6] Ezra Klein said of Trump's performance in the debate, "You cannot embarrass Donald Trump" and added, "The crowd loves him for it."[7] Although Trump's appeal was evident in polling before the debate and the enormous audience that he drew to the debate, many commentators still doubted his campaign had any real chance of winning the nomination. *Politico* printed the "snap reactions" of "23 political experts," most of whom thought Trump had lost the debate and had little chance of winning the nomination.[8] What the experts did not recognize was how potent Trump's appeal was in tapping into public anger and fear and how his campaign was changing the norms for how a presidential candidate should talk.

By the *Fox News* debate on March 3, 2016, the power of that appeal was obvious. Trump had just won multiple primaries on Super Tuesday and was in such a strong position to win the Republican nomination that his remaining opponents were focused not on winning the nomination itself in the remaining primaries but in preventing Trump from gaining a majority of delegates and therefore forcing a brokered convention. Trump's approach in the debate was strikingly similar to that of the earlier debate, with one exception. His style was much harsher than in the earlier debate, and on several occasions, he taunted Cruz and Rubio by referring to them with the insulting names "Lyin' Ted" and "Little Marco." As with the earlier debate, Trump did not develop a coherent policy platform, cite clear evidence for his position, or respond to objections to his views. Cruz and Rubio in some ways mirrored Trump's approach; only Kasich treated the event as a debate and laid out a coherent position. It did him little good.

Trump's approach was evident in his answer to the first question of the debate from Wallace, who challenged him "to answer with substance, not insults" a sustained attack on Trump's candidacy by 2012 Republican nominee Mitt Romney. Trump chose insults rather than substance and immediately labeled Romney "a failed candidate" who "should have beaten President Obama very badly." Trump then attacked Romney for supporting "free trade," which he said was "killing our country." He added, "Both at the border, and with trade—and every other country we do business with we are getting absolutely crushed on trade." He then shifted to the businessman outsider portion of his message, claiming, "I have the greatest businesspeople in the world lined up to do it. We will make great trade deals." As was typical of

Trump, he did not explain either what the "great trade deals" would look like or how he could achieve them. In this answer, the populist, nationalist, and outsider aspects of his message were apparent.

The same pattern was present throughout the debate. Trump attacked China, Mexico, and Japan for devaluing "their currencies"; labeled the Trans-Pacific Partnership (TPP), a trade agreement negotiated by the Obama administration, "a total disaster"; said that "we have a tremendous problem with crime"; added that "the border is a disaster, it's like a piece of Swiss cheese"; and claimed that "Mexico is going to pay for the wall." He also defended waterboarding as an appropriate response to Middle East terrorism, saying, "We should go for waterboarding, and we should go tougher than waterboarding." Trump stated the populist portion of his message when he responded to Cruz's claim that it "would be a disaster" to nominate Trump by stating, "I don't believe these politicians. All talk, no action."

Trump also enacted the celebrity businessman outsider persona by boasting several times about his poll results. At one point, he repeated five times, "I beat Hillary Clinton in many polls." He also bragged about his business empire: "I started off with $1 million. I built a company that's worth more than $10 billion. And I say it not in a bragging way, but that's the kind of thinking we need." Trump was a master of bragging while claiming simultaneously not to do so. Late in the debate, he said, "I will prove to be a great leader" and then supported this statement not with discussion of policy or citation of past examples of leadership but by saying, "Every single poll when it comes to ISIS and the military and the border say, by far, Trump is the best." Similarly, in his concluding statement, he bragged, "I am going to bring jobs back to the United States like nobody else can" and added, "And you're going to be very, very proud of this country in just a few years if I'm elected president." It was precisely the same message he used in his rallies.

Trump's use of a more extreme vernacular style than in the first debate became obvious early in the debate, when he labeled Rubio a "lightweight" and then made a vulgar response to Rubio's comment that Trump had small hands. Shockingly, Trump stated, "And he referred to my hands, if they are small, something else must be small. I guarantee you there is no problem." It is impossible to imagine any other serious presidential candidate boasting about the size of his genitalia. Another aspect of this style was obvious when Trump interrupted the answers of his opponents, something he would do constantly in the debates with Clinton and then again in 2020 with

Democratic nominee Joe Biden. For example, when Rubio disputed Trump's claim to be a great businessman, noting that "he inherited over $100 million," Trump interjected, "Wrong. Wrong." Trump also often resorted to name-calling or otherwise insulting his opponents. For example, he responded to attacks from Cruz by saying several times, "You're the liar." When Rubio attacked Trump University as a "scam" training program, Trump responded that "the real con artist is Senator Marco Rubio," who "scammed the people of Florida." And, of course, he used the nicknames "Lyin' Ted" and "Little Marco" to demean his opponents.

Trump's failure to make a coherent policy argument was especially evident when Wallace pushed him to reply to the charge that his proposed tax cut would "add $10 trillion to the nation's debt over 10 years." Trump responded to Wallace by saying that he would make cuts in the Common Core program in the Department of Education and major cuts in the Environmental Protection Agency (EPA). Wallace then noted that the total budget of the Department of Education and the EPA combined was $86 billion, which included any number of programs, such as Pell Grants, Trump did not propose to cut. Trump then shifted to claiming that he could save "hundreds of billions of dollars in waste" by setting up "proper bidding procedures" for buying drugs via Medicare. When Wallace pointed out that Medicare "only spends $78 billion a year on drugs," Trump claimed that based on his business prowess, "through negotiation throughout the economy, you will save $300 billion a year." The key point is that Trump did not present a coherent policy proposal for cutting the deficit but simply made wild and untruthful claims based on his record as a celebrity businessman. This was bluster, not policy analysis. The contrast with Kasich, who laid out a case for a small-government Reaganesque domestic policy, was particularly striking.

The debate was widely perceived as, in the words of Republican pollster Frank Luntz, "embarrassing," a conclusion echoed by Frank Bruni, who labeled it "a fetid farce." David Graham noted in the *Atlantic* that based on the debate, "the Republican Party appears on the edge of collapse."[9] Patrick Healy and Jonathan Martin said the debate "deteriorated into the kind of junior high school taunts that have startled many Republican elders but have done little to dent Mr. Trump's broad appeal."[10] Writing in the *Washington Post*, Tumulty called it a "substance-free shout-fest" and added that it raised "the question . . . [of] how close the Grand Old Party [GOP] will come to annihilating itself and what it stands for."[11] In fact, the debate reflected the

GOP becoming the party of Trump. There was no question, as Chris Cillizza noted, that "Trump totally dominated the debate."[12] In fact, one of the three moderators, Bret Baier, said that based on the "conversation on Facebook surrounding the remaining candidates," "Donald Trump clearly dominates the field." The debate revealed both the underlying power of Trump's message of nationalist populism and the outsider persona as well as how this rhetoric was changing politics, moving it toward more focus on identity and less on ideology, and all but eliminating the standards of decorum and eloquence that had ruled political debate for decades. Trump did nothing in the debate to demonstrate that he had a grasp of the issues, a coherent agenda, or the knowledge and temperament to be an effective president. He said many things that undercut all of those conclusions, but they did not hurt him. Trump's successful use of a vernacular style in support of a nationalist populist message reflected a substantial change in debate practice and, more broadly, American politics.

Trump followed a similar pattern in the general election debates. I noted earlier the consensus that Trump badly lost those debates and violated standards of political decorum and that the literature on debates suggests that in previous elections his debate performance probably would have been viewed as disqualifying by enough voters to doom his candidacy. That did not happen in 2016 because of the potency of his message of nationalist populism with an outsider persona. His rhetoric in the general election debates was so similar to that in the primary debates, and for that matter his rally speeches, that only a brief analysis of the first debate is needed to demonstrate this similarity.[13]

Trump began his answer to the first question of the debate by emphasizing the nationalist theme. He said, "Our jobs are fleeing the country. They're going to Mexico. They're going to many other countries." Later, he called NAFTA "the single worst trade deal ever approved in this country." He made similar charges many times in the debate and also focused on undocumented immigration, terrorism, and crime rates in major cities.

Trump expressed the populist theme by blaming Clinton for not solving problems despite being at the center of power since her husband was elected president. Early in the debate, he blamed her for thirty years of decline in manufacturing jobs, stating, "You haven't done it in 30 years" and later adding, "Typical politician. All talk, no action. Sounds good, doesn't work. Never going to happen." Here, Trump used almost precisely the same words he did in campaign rallies and primary debates. Late in the debate, when pressed about his untruthful claim to have opposed the war in Iraq from the beginning, Trump baldly stated, "I did not support the war in Iraq" and then attacked the media: "That is a [sic] mainstream media nonsense put out by her, because she—frankly, I think the best person in her campaign is mainstream media."

The businessman variant of the outsider persona was evident when Trump promised without evidence, "I'm really calling for major jobs because the wealthy are going to create tremendous jobs. They're going to expand their companies. They're going to do a tremendous job." On several occasions, he cited his success as a businessman as proof of his leadership. In response to a question about his false claim that Obama had not been born in the United States, Trump actually took credit for resolving the issue. He said, "But I was the one that got him to produce the birth certificate. And I think I did a good job." The chutzpah of this answer was astonishing. At the end of the debate, to some laughter, Trump even claimed, "I have much better judgment than she does. There's no question about that. I also have much better temperament than she has." Trump, the outsider, was unwilling to concede any errors or weakness. As the debate progressed, and Trump apparently became angry, he relied on the vernacular style I have described, for example, interrupting Clinton by saying "wrong" on several occasions.

Trump's message in the general election debates in 2016 and then again in 2020 was the same as in the primary debates and in his rallies. Some candidates shift their message over the course of a campaign to account for the development of the campaign or domestic or international events. In 2008, Obama adapted his message to the growing economic crisis over the course of the fall. Candidates also often shift to a more formal tone in general election debates compared with that of rally speeches or early primary debates. Trump made no such adaptation. Nationalist populism with an outsider persona and an associated vernacular style was not only at the core of his appeal but also it was the only message he had. Moreover, a shift to a more optimistic message and a more formal tone risked undercutting his perceived authenticity with core supporters. Trump had created a bond with these supporters in part by rejecting what he called political correctness both in the content of what he said and by using a vernacular style based on bragging and insults. A shift away from that content and style could have made him look like just another politician. In 2012, Romney used the debates to shift toward the center and away from the extremely conservative positions he had taken in the primaries. If Trump had used a similar tactic, it would have risked weakening his bond with his supporters as an authentic outsider and a regular guy who was on their side.

Nationalist Populism at the RNC

The convention speech can be treated as a summation of Trump's campaign message, a sampling of greatest hits from the campaign. Healy and Martin called the speech "an unusually vehement appeal to Americans who feel that their country is spiraling out of control and yearn for a leader who will take aggressive, even extreme, actions to protect them" and added that it was filled with "dark imagery and an almost angry tone" and "made a sharp departure from the optimistic talk about American possibility that has characterized Republican presidential candidates since Ronald Reagan redefined the party."[14] Similarly, Alex Altman observed that the convention speech closely mirrored Trump's "dominant narrative thread" of describing "an American dystopia" to create a "a fiesta of fear."[15] In this way, the convention address enacted the same themes Trump first used in his announcement speech and emphasized throughout the campaign. As a number of commentators and academics noted, one of the dominant tactics in the convention address was to create fear by using "tried-and-true code words to gin up racial animosity and fear among America's white voters."[16]

It is also important to recognize how different Trump's remarks at the RNC were from other convention acceptance addresses, which generally retell party history as a means of unifying and energizing the party. Additionally, convention addresses also present the policy agenda of the candidate, often linking it to the heroic history of the party and claiming it is essential to enacting or protecting the American dream. Through these strategies, the convention acceptance address is designed to motivate the faithful and appeal to potential swing voters.[17] Trump took a different approach by essentially ignoring party history and policy advocacy. It is particularly notable that he did not even mention Reagan, the most important Republican hero of the previous forty years. He did not lay out a clear agenda except for calling for strong action to enact the nationalist portion of his message.

The one aspect of Trump's convention speech similar to other convention acceptance addresses was his attack on the nominee of the other party. In most cases, these attacks are made primarily by the vice-presidential nominee and other speakers at the convention, but they are also common in acceptance speeches. At the RNC, Trump restated the quite brutal attacks on Clinton he made throughout the campaign. At one point, he boiled down the "legacy of Hillary Clinton" to "death, destruction, terrorism, and weakness."[18]

Although many presidential nominees have painted an optimistic picture of a nation facing problems but with limitless opportunity for further progress toward achieving the American dream, Trump painted a picture of a nation under siege, a kind of dystopian variant of the American dream. In the introduction, he claimed, "Our convention occurs at a moment of crisis for our nation. The attacks on our police and the terrorism in our cities threaten our way of life" (5). He particularly emphasized crime in major cities, noting, "Homicides last year increased by 17 percent in America's 50 largest cities. That's the largest increase in 25 years" (17). He tied this increase to "illegal immigrants with criminal records" who "are being released by the tens of thousands into our communities with no regard for the impact on public safety or resources" (22). Later, he fleshed out the dystopian vision, claiming vast increases "in poverty," loss of jobs with "14 million people" having "left the workforce entirely," massive loss of income, and huge trade and budget deficits had occurred (27–33). He said these economic problems were occurring in a nation where "our roads and bridges are falling apart, our airports are in Third World condition, and 43 million Americans are on food stamps" (34). The situation was, if anything, worse in foreign policy, in which the nation had "lived through one international humiliation after another" (36). Of course, Trump's description of a nation in crisis bore little resemblance to the actual state of the nation, which had experienced strong job creation, low crime rates, a declining rate of undocumented immigration, a modest internal terrorism risk, and a substantial reduction in military losses as the nation reduced its forces in Afghanistan and Iraq.[19] In contrast with that reality, Trump claimed that his description of a nation in crisis was "the plain facts that have been edited out of your nightly news" (26).

Trump emphasized all of the main themes of nationalist populism with a celebrity businessman outsider persona in the speech. The nationalist theme received particular emphasis in passages in which Trump described immigrants as violent and dangerous. For example, he cited the case of a young woman murdered by a "border-crosser" and labeled her "one more child to sacrifice on the altar of open borders" (23, 24). He also spoke of "the mothers and fathers who have lost their children to violence spilling across our borders" and promised that he would "build a great border wall to stop illegal immigration, to stop the gangs and the violence, and to stop the drugs from pouring into our communities" (121, 131). The nationalist message was also obvious in relation to trade. He spoke of "communities crushed by our horrible and unfair trade deals" (74). He also emphasized the threat of Islamic terrorism, describing "the damage and devastation that can be inflicted by Islamic radicals," and made what can only be described as the bizarre promise, given strong support for his candidacy from the religious right, that he would "do everything in my power to protect our L.G.B.T.Q. citizens from the violence and oppression of a hateful foreign ideology" (105, 107). Trump also presented a thoroughly nativist message by promising to "suspend immigration from any nation that has been compromised by terrorism" and attacking Clinton for supporting "massive refugee flows coming into our country" (114, 115).

Trump also appealed to racial division by strongly attacking Obama for "using the pulpit of the presidency to divide us by race and color," a particularly odious claim given Trump's history of challenging Obama's identity as an American (99). He also used multiple references to crime in "inner cities" to appeal to racial stereotyping by tapping into fear of Black crime among members of his almost totally white audience (100). This strategy was evident in his claim "I am the law and order candidate" (98). Throughout the address, Trump appealed to his audience by creating fear of the Other in the form of immigrants, Islamic Americans, refugees, and Black Americans who commit crime.

He also tapped into the nationalist theme by wildly mischaracterizing the gun policies of Clinton, who, he claimed, "wants to essentially abolish the Second Amendment." In response to this imaginary threat, Trump promised to "protect the right of all Americans to keep their families safe" (184). By claiming that Clinton wanted to "abolish the Second Amendment," Trump tapped into fears the government could seize privately owned guns, which have become a key aspect of populist nationalist culture. It is telling commentary on American political discourse that Clinton's support for modest gun safety regulation could be characterized as favoring abolition of the second amendment without producing public backlash.

Trump promoted the populist theme by strongly attacking political elites and the media. He critiqued the media, claiming that he would "present the facts plainly and honestly," and juxtaposed his plain facts with "corporate spin, the carefully crafted lies, and the media myths" of the elites (11, 13). He asserted that progress depended on rejection of elite domination: "The problems we face now—poverty and violence at home, war and destruction abroad—will last only as long as we continue relying on the same politicians who created them" (55). According to Trump, Clinton was the "puppet" of elites who "pull the strings" (69). He claimed that on a variety of issues, elites were blocking solutions to real problems. For example, he maintained in relation to education policy, "My opponent would rather protect bureaucrats than serve American children" (175). Trump said that unlike Clinton, he spoke for "the forgotten men and women of our country. People who work hard but no longer have a voice" (74). He added, "I am your voice" (75).

The irony is that Clinton actually supported a broadly progressive agenda that not only would have increased social programs to aid the working class (as well as other Americans) but also strengthened financial, environmental, and other regulatory efforts many business elites opposed. But Trump's campaign was not about policy. In his narrative, he was the friend of the ordinary Joe or Jane, whereas Clinton was held hostage by elites.

It is notable not only that Trump's dystopian narrative of a nation in crisis was not remotely accurate but also that he failed to present a coherent policy agenda with any level of specificity. The most specific parts of his agenda were related to the nationalist theme, with which he called for strict limits on immigration and refugees and "a great border wall." On other issues, he was quite vague. For example, he summarized his "plan of action for America" by saying, "The most important difference between our plan and that of our opponents is that our plan will put America first. Americanism, not globalism, will be our credo" (57–59). Because no candidate of a major party has ever embraced anything but "Americanism," this statement was not revealing in ideological terms, but it was important as a narrative theme. Trump drew support from many who felt left out and disrespected.

Rather than having a clear ideological agenda, Trump presented himself as a truth-teller who would "present the facts plainly and honestly" (11). He claimed he would bring major change through force of will, saying, "I have no patience for injustice, no tolerance for government incompetence, no sympathy for leaders who fail their citizens" (77). In a statement typical of the businessman variant of the outsider persona, he claimed that precisely because he understood the corrupt system, he could fix the system: "Nobody knows the system better than me, which is why I alone can fix it" (84). He amplified this claim, noting, "I have made billions of dollars in business making deals—now I'm going to make our country rich again." He then added, "I am going to bring back our jobs to Ohio, and Pennsylvania, and New York. . . . and I am not going to let companies move to other countries" (145, 150). A few paragraphs later, he said, "Our country is going to start building and making things again." He added, "Middle-income Americans and businesses will experience profound relief, and taxes will be greatly simplified for everyone" (161, 164). In these passages, Trump provided no explanation for how he could accomplish any of the economic miracles he promised, except for a reference to his business experience. The breadth of his bravado is shocking. He apparently was arguing that his knowledge of a corrupt system was a sign not of his political corruption but that only he could change that system despite the fact that he opposed campaign finance and other political reform proposals Clinton and other Democrats supported. It is a sign of the level of alienation in American politics that such an argument did not produce universal derision.

Leaders with an outsider persona often claim their strength comes from their role as an enactment of the will of the people. Trump embraced this aspect of the outsider persona in the conclusion of the address, in which he stated his "pledge" to the nation: "I'm With You—the American People," and "I am your voice" (207, 208). This statement was both quite simplistic and implied that neither Clinton nor Obama had been on the side of the American people, a message that tapped into the fear of cultural change on the part of many of his core supporters. Although the speech did not present a coherent agenda and cited almost no supporting evidence, Trump claimed again and again that his election would essentially produce magical changes in the nation. He was the outsider who would force the elites to act in order to transform the nation. On crime, he said, "The crime and violence that today afflicts our nation will soon come to an end. Beginning on January 20, 2017, safety will be restored" (8). He promised, "The day I take the oath of office, Americans will finally wake up in a country where the laws of the United States are enforced" (137). In the conclusion of the convention address, Trump claimed his outsider leadership would transform the nation:

> We will make America strong again.
> We will make America proud again.
> We will make America safe again.
> And we will make America great again. (211–215)

Although nomination speeches rarely provide a detailed policy agenda with supporting data, they generally sketch an ideological vision for approaching the problems of the day. For example, both Reagan and Obama sketched a coherent policy agenda for the country—small-government conservatism and a tough Soviet policy for Reagan and pragmatic liberalism for Obama—in their convention acceptance addresses.[20] Trump took another course and claimed that because of his outsider celebrity role, he could magically transform the nation.

Trump's nationalist populist narrative and outsider persona were designed to appeal to those who felt threatened by cultural change, those who felt left behind by economic developments during and after the Great Recession, and those committed Republican partisans who loathed both Obama and Democratic nominee Clinton. The dominance of nationalist populism in the convention address is particularly notable because the situation demanded a different kind of message. Trump's failure to adapt to generic norms for convention addresses is strong evidence of the exceptional nature of his campaign in US history. The optimistic small-government narrative popularized by Reagan, which had dominated the Republican Party for more than a generation, had been vanquished in favor of a dark dystopian narrative appealing most strongly to those with authoritarian leanings.

Nationalist Populism and the Outsider in the Inaugural Address

Although sharply in conflict with postwar norms for the Inaugural Address, Trump used his address to present the same themes that defined his campaign rhetoric and that later typified his presidential rhetoric. Jeff Shesol was precisely right when he observed that the Inaugural Address "was mostly a buttoned-up version of his campaign stump speech, aimed at the same audience of 'forgotten men and women' who share his disgust toward" elites, and added that it failed "to honor the stark differences in opinion that exist in the country, differences that he has widened and exploited."[21] Pulitzer Prize–winning columnist Thomas Friedman aptly labeled Trump's Inaugural Address as "dystopian," a conclusion supported by Peter Baker and Michael Shear, who described "Trump's view of the United States . . . [as] strikingly grim for an Inaugural Address." Similarly, Mark Ladler stated that Trump's "uncompromising . . . tone [was] . . . entirely in keeping with his insurgent campaign," and David Sanger cited the "dark, hard-line alternative" set of policies in the address, whereas Maggie Haberman and Glenn Thrush labeled the Inaugural Address an "America-in-decline speech, aimed at his base" that "echoed the dark antiglobalist pitch he delivered at the Republican Convention."[22]

Despite generic norms that inaugural addresses should heal the wounds of the campaign, reaffirm widely shared basic American values, and present an optimistic vision of the ideological vision of the administration, Trump's Inaugural Address closely mirrored the convention speech and clearly possessed the characteristics of nationalist populism.[23] It is striking that he paid so little attention to fulfilling the functions and forms of an inaugural. In the first five paragraphs of the address, Trump adhered to those norms, speaking of the "challenges" that "we" the people "will confront" and praising the Obamas for "their gracious aid throughout this transition."[24] In the conclusion, he also briefly referenced national unity, citing the "old wisdom" of "our soldiers" that "whether we are black or brown or white, we all bleed the same red blood of patriots" (66). He added, "Whether a child is born in the urban sprawl of Detroit or the windswept plains of Nebraska, they look up at the same night sky, they fill their heart with the same dreams, and they are infused with the breath of life by the same almighty Creator" (67). These brief passages were, however, the exception, and the remainder of the address expressed the key components of his rhetoric of nationalist populism.

Trump began to express the populist portion of his message in the sixth paragraph, when he promised that this "ceremony . . . has very special meaning. Because today we are not merely transferring power from one Administration to another, or from one party to another—but we are transferring power from Washington, D.C., and giving it back to you, the American people." Trump followed by attacking corrupt elites: "For too long, a small group in our nation's Capital has reaped the rewards of government while the people have borne the cost." He added, "Politicians prospered—but the jobs left and factories closed" (7, 8). After foregrounding the populist message that elites had failed to serve the American people as a whole, Trump shifted to present a dystopian vision of what he called "American carnage" (25).

In the remainder of the address, Trump presented a picture of a nation in crisis, blamed that crisis on threatening Others and greedy elites, and presented himself as the savior—the voice of the people, who would bring

dramatic change through force of will—change that would produce immediate results. In other words, despite vast generic differences across varied
rhetorical situations, Trump presented the same narrative that dominated
his announcement speech, primary debates, campaign rallies, general election debates, and convention speech. He described an American nightmare:
"Mothers and children trapped in poverty in our inner cities; rusted-out
factories scattered like tombstones across the landscape of our nation; an
education system, flush with cash, but which leaves our young and beautiful
students deprived of knowledge; and the crime and gangs and drugs that
have stolen too many lives and robbed our country of so much unrealized
potential" (24). Trump promised that "American carnage" "stops right here
and stops right now" (25).

As in the announcement, rallies, debates, and convention speech, two
primary villains were responsible for the carnage: a number of dangerous
Others who threatened American lives and American identity itself and
villainous elites—along with their allies in the press—who filled their own
pockets but failed to protect the people. In the middle of the speech, Trump
focused on the nationalist theme and the Others who threatened the nation
when he claimed, "For many decades, we've enriched foreign industry at the
expense of American industry," "defended other nations' borders while refus-
ing to defend our own," "spent trillions of dollars overseas while America's
infrastructure has fallen into disrepair and decay," and "made other countries
rich while the wealth, strength, and confidence of our country has disappeared over the horizon" (28–32). As a consequence, "the factories shuttered
and left our shores," rendering "millions of American workers left behind,"
and "the wealth of our middle class has been ripped from their homes and
then redistributed across the entire world" (33, 34). In this passage. Trump
sounded an "America First" theme, placing blame for economic losses on
unfair competition, ruinous immigration, and elite complicity in these problems (38). He assured the audience that he would put "America First" and
added, "Every decision on trade, on taxes, on immigration, on foreign affairs,
will be made to benefit American workers and American families" (39). In
response to the threat posed by refugees and terrorists infiltrating the nation,
he promised to "unite the civilized world against Radical Islamic Terrorism,
which we will eradicate completely from the face of the earth" (49). All of
these threats could be stopped by adhering to a policy of "total allegiance to
the United States of America" (50). Trump's "America First" agenda was both

exceedingly simplistic and implied that his predecessors had not shared that commitment to the nation.

Trump attacked elites throughout the address, blaming both parties for "American carnage." He said, "The establishment protected itself, but not the citizens of our country. Their victories have not been your victories; their triumphs have not been your triumphs," producing a situation in which "there was little to celebrate for struggling families all across our land" (10, 11). At the end of the address, Trump claimed, "We will no longer accept politicians who are all talk and no action—constantly complaining but never doing anything about it. The time for empty talk is over. Now arrives the hour of action" (59–61). Given that Trump did not present a coherent policy agenda and that calls for cracking down on immigration and foreign trade were among the very few specific polices that he endorsed, there was considerable irony in his attack on politicians "who are all talk and no action."

As during the campaign, Trump promised to be the voice of the people and that his leadership would produce immediate and transformative change. Early in the address, he guaranteed "that all changes—starting right here, and right now, because this moment is your moment; it belongs to you." He added, "This is your day. This is your celebration" (12, 14). In this passage, he portrayed himself as the enactment of the people's will, a view he reemphasized by saying, "January 20th, 2017, will be remembered as the day the people became the rulers of this nation again. The forgotten men and women of our country will be forgotten no longer" (17, 18). Stating a theme quite common in nationalist populism, Trump presented himself as a business outsider who, because he represented the people's will, could produce immediate action. Trump's claim to be the voice of the people was an odd one for a new president who lost the popular vote by almost 3 million votes. In contrast to the reality of the popular vote, Trump claimed to have won an overwhelming victory by leading "a historic movement the likes of which the world has never seen before" (20). Later in the speech, he again depicted himself as the voice of the people: "I will fight for you with every breath in my body—and I will never, ever let you down" (41).

As in the campaign speeches, Trump enacted the role of the transformative outsider who through sheer force of will would produce immediate and amazing results. He promised, "America will start winning again, winning like never before" (42). As was the norm in his speeches, there was no explanation of either the policies he supported or how they would work. He promised amazing results based on the power of his leadership alone: "We will bring back our jobs. We will bring back our borders. We will bring back our wealth. And we will bring back our dreams" (43). All of this would occur because his administration would follow "two simple rules: Buy American and Hire American" (46). Again, Trump's "America First" worldview was built on the implication that past leaders of both parties had not been committed to protecting the people and that major accomplishments could be produced easily through the wave of his outsider's hand. In the conclusion, he promised, "We will not fail. Our country will thrive and prosper again" and then emphasized his personal role as the voice of the people, proclaiming, "You will never be ignored again" (69). The final words of the speech echoed the grandiose promises of so many of his speeches. He guaranteed that he would "Make America Strong Again," "Make America Wealthy Again," "Make America Proud Again," "Make America Safe Again," and "Make America Great Again" (71–75).

Trump's message in his Inaugural Address was quite similar to that of his campaign addresses. In the campaign and his Inaugural Address, he described a nation facing crisis, blamed the crisis on elites in both parties who had destroyed American greatness through bad trade deals and a failure to enforce immigration laws or confront the threat of terrorism, and promised that he would produce transformative and immediate change by enacting the will of the people. As in the campaign, he did not present any coherent explanation of the policies he supported or indicate how they would produce the magical results he promised. Rather, he relied on tired clichés, such as "America First," that also reinforced both the nativist and populist themes, implying that previous administrations had placed "America Last."

There were differences between his campaign speeches and his Inaugural Address. In his Inaugural Address, Trump expressed the nationalist theme primarily in economic terms, focusing less on threats posed by undocumented immigrants, refugees, or terrorists. Those threats were mentioned but not emphasized to the same degree as in the convention and other campaign speeches. In other ways, notably the depiction of a dystopian American landscape wildly at odds with the actual state of the nation, and in his enactment of the outsider persona who as the voice of the people would bring immediate change, the speeches were quite similar.

Trump's Inaugural Address was a striking contrast with most inaugurals, which lay out a positive agenda, reinforce shared values, and attempt to heal the wounds of the campaign. Trump's address included passages at the beginning and the end that fulfilled the generic functions of an inaugural, but the bulk of the speech worked primarily to create a visceral emotional reaction.[25] Many commentators noted that the address was far outside the norm for inaugurals. Carl Hulse spoke with considerable understatement when he said that the address "was a remarkable departure from past inaugurals."[26] Marc Fisher called the speech a "blunt, searing talk about a crippled nation in dire need of bold, immediate action" that "spurned the poetry and grandeur of most inaugural speeches" in favor of "a rallying cry, reminiscent of his stream-of-consciousness campaign talks." He added, "Never before had an American president used words such as 'carnage,' 'depletion,' 'disrepair,' and 'sad' to describe his own country in an inaugural address."[27] Michael Gerson, a *Washington Post* columnist and former speechwriter for President George W. Bush, scathingly labeled the address a "funeral oration at the death of Reaganism, and of conservatism more broadly" and added that Trump demonstrated "no respect for norms of presidential magnanimity and self-restraint."[28] His former boss presented a similar sentiment in earthier language, labeling the speech "some weird shit."[29] Other principled conservatives echoed Gerson's comments. George Will said simply that the speech was "the most dreadful inaugural address in history."[30]

Television commentators interpreted the address as an attack on the political system; in the words of Bob Schieffer of CBS, "He basically took the hide off everybody." *New York Times* critic James Poniewozik drew a similar conclusion, labeling the speech "pugilistic" and an "us-vs.-them polemic . . . aimed to delight his base."[31] The *New York Times* called the speech "a graceless and disturbingly ahistoric vision of America" and a "sweeping exaggeration" of the national condition and said it was focused "on inspiring only his base of aggrieved or anxious white Americans."[32]

In fact, the aim of the speech was not to "inspire" but to reinforce feelings of anger and fear about cultural change. Leonard Pitts observed that in his Inaugural Address, Trump "promised a magic solution through the sheer force of his will." Pitts then added, "The magical thinking embodied in Trump's speech is not a recipe for fixing problems, nor even for addressing them. It is rather, a primal scream, viscerally satisfying in the short term, but masturbatory and useless in the long term." He finally observed, "Bluster is not governance."[33] Although "bluster is not governance," it was central to Trump's nationalist populism. Whereas other presidents sought to unify and inspire, Trump sought to create fear and hate of Others and blind love for himself. It is clear that with his core audience, he succeeded.

Conclusion

Trump's consistent presentation of nationalist populism and an outsider persona throughout the 2016 presidential campaign and in his Inaugural Address is striking. He kept to that message in his announcement, rallies, debates, convention address, and Inaugural Address despite generic norms that called for adapting his message to these different situations. Trump's success with this message is also revealing. In almost all cases, successful political figures present an optimistic and uplifting message, even when facing an immediate crisis. Obama honestly confronted the economic crisis in 2009, but he also presented a coherent economic program he claimed would lead to a better future. Reagan used a similar approach in 1981. There is simply no precedent for a president using his Inaugural Address to describe the state of the nation as "American carnage."

Trump's successful use of a rhetoric of nationalist populism with an outsider persona and a vernacular style indicates the strong desire in a large section of the public for immediate action, even if his supporters did not know exactly what that action should be. It also indicates that a large portion of the voting public felt threatened by the changing demography. I have noted several times that Trump's message that undocumented immigrants and Islamic terrorists were major threats to the nation was simply untrue. A similar point can be made about Trump's claim that unfair trade was the primary cause of a decline in manufacturing or that the nation was experiencing near-Depression-level unemployment. It is enormously revealing about the American electorate that the nationalist portion of Trump's message resonated so strongly despite being false.

The Transition from Outsider
to Strongman in Trump's
Formal Presidential Rhetoric

Rhetoric plays a key role in presidents' efforts to shape public opinion, build support in Congress for their agenda, and more broadly create or reinforce an ideological and value-based view of the nation.[1] In that way, the "genres" of presidential rhetoric act "as the structural supports for the edifice of the presidency," and, as a consequence, for any president, "the identity and character of the presidency arise out of such discourse."[2] The "centrality of rhetoric to presidential power" is obvious in the speeches of Lyndon B. Johnson in support of the War on Poverty; of Ronald Reagan in support of tax cuts, deregulation, and a strong defense; of Barack Obama in support of health-care reform and regulation of Wall Street; and in the rhetoric of every other president who tried to move forward an ideological agenda.[3]

Rhetoric is also the means presidents use to talk about the nature of American identity itself. Karlyn Kohrs Campbell and Kathleen Hall Jamieson noted, "Public communication is the medium through which the national fabric is woven." They added that especially on ceremonial occasions such as inaugural addresses; eulogies for important citizens, which they call *national eulogies*; and farewell addresses, the president acts as a "national priest" and is the "custodian of national values."[4] Similarly, Vanessa Beasley has focused on "how U.S. presidents have constructed American identity," concluding "that presidents have used a civil religious rhetoric of American nationalism to promote national unity."[5] Eloquent presidents such as Theodore and Franklin Delano Roosevelt, John F. Kennedy,

Reagan, and Obama not only advocated for particular policies but spoke of what it means to be an American and reinforced and redefined fundamental values. They also helped the nation cope with national tragedy or the death of an important political or cultural figure, as Reagan did after the *Challenger* accident, Bill Clinton did after the Oklahoma City bombing, and Obama did after far too many gun murders.

Formal Policy Speeches

Trump's formal presidential rhetoric was strikingly different from the norms of presidential discourse. With the exception of his Inaugural Address, his policy-oriented addresses as president were largely formulaic and, frankly, of little import. Presidents such as Reagan and Obama invested enormous effort into crafting powerful defenses of major policy proposals.[6] For example, a search for health-care town halls on the archived Obama Whitehouse.gov site revealed more than fifteen town hall meetings in 2009 and 2010 and dozens more dealing with the economy and other administration issues. Of course, Obama also made any number of other important speeches on his administration's agenda, including an address to Congress on health-care reform. One of the most memorable moments in the debate concerning the Affordable Care Act (ACA) occurred when Obama answered questions and made a case for the bill at a meeting with House Republicans on January 29, 2010. The televised meeting lasted almost ninety minutes, and the transcript contains more than 12,000 words. In the long exchange, Obama both responded to objections and suggested that the proper way forward was to focus on the real issues.[7] At the end of the exchange, he said of the way both parties had approached messaging on health care, "It's all tactics, and it's not solving problems." He then promised he was willing to have a serious conversation about entitlement programs, including Social Security and Medicare, with Republicans. Clearly, Obama used speeches, town hall addresses, and other meetings to sell his agenda. In these sessions, he also made a real effort to persuade the people and even Republicans, who almost always opposed him in Congress, of the merit in his proposals.

Obama was hardly alone in taking this approach. Reagan made a similar effort in selling his economic proposals in 1981. The Reagan Presidential

Library includes five major economic addresses by the president defending his economic agenda from the inauguration through September 1981.[8] Amos Kiewe and Davis Houck noted that the Reagan administration created "a 'rhetorical agenda' for the first 100 days" in which it "designed a thematic approach to speeches incorporated as a 'rhetorical package'" focusing "solely on economic issues."[9] The product of that effort included "unprecedented tax cuts, major cuts in social welfare programs, and the increase in defense spending," accomplishments that made "Reagan's first year as president truly extraordinary."[10] The key point is that effective presidents have made a concerted effort to persuade the public to support their agenda. In many cases, as was true with Reagan and especially Obama, they worked hard to account for the objections of critics as part of that effort.

In contrast, Trump made little effort to lay out policy proposals or defend them against attack. In fact, he rarely made major speeches about his agenda.[11] A review of Trump's remarks on health care is quite revealing. Both in the campaign and as president, Trump often labeled Obamacare as a disaster, but he made almost no effort to persuade the American people that his proposals would in fact improve the health-care system. A search of Whitehouse .gov reveals no significant speech in which the president either laid out his opposition to the ACA or made a case for any of the Republican alternatives.[12] Moreover, there are surprisingly few instances in which he even made brief remarks about the proposed alternatives to the ACA. In a brief weekly address on March 10, 2017, he said the ACA "is collapsing around us" and praised a Republican plan "that gets rid of this terrible law and replaces it with reforms that empower states and consumers." His entire discussion and defense of this proposal consisted of the following assertions:

> You will have the choice and the freedom to make the decisions that are right for your family. The House plan follows the guidelines I laid out in my recent address to Congress—expanding choice, lowering costs, and providing health-care access for all.
>
> This plan is part of a three-pronged reform process. In concert with the plan in front of Congress, I have directed Dr. Tom Price, our Secretary of Health and Human Services, to use his authority to reduce regulations that are driving up costs of care.
>
> We are also working on reforms that lower the costs of care, like allowing Americans to purchase health insurance across state lines. You've heard me say that many, many times during the debates.

It is notable that what he labeled the "principles" in the speech that served as a substitute for the State of the Union Address were, in fact, quite general goals rather than a description of actual policy proposals, a point I will develop later when I discuss that speech. In another statement the same day as the weekly address, "Remarks by President Trump in a Health-care Discussion with Key House Committee Chairmen," his comments were even more general. On May 4, 2017; June 13, 2017; and in a weekly address on June 23, 2017, he made similarly brief and quite general defenses of the proposed alternative to the ACA. Although he mentioned the ACA in interviews and tweets, he discussed it in the most detail in the speeches I have described.

Presidents normally use multiple major speeches and often town hall presentations to defend their agenda. Trump made no such effort on repealing the ACA, which along with a tax cut and enacting a restrictive immigration policy were his most important domestic initiatives. Whitehouse.gov includes fewer than a thousand words from Trump defending his position on health care. Obama provided vastly more support for the ACA in any number of single events than Trump did opposing it in all of his speeches or question-and-answer sessions discussing it.

The underlying point is that Trump did not use rhetoric to support his agenda in anything like the same way other contemporary presidents did. Although Trump did not use presidential speeches to support his agenda in the same way as other presidents, it is nevertheless important to consider major policy speeches because they reveal the centrality of nationalist populism to his rhetorical practice. One way to make this point is to consider Trump's rhetoric on occasions that essentially required major speeches, when he could not avoid providing at least some support for his agenda. The most obvious of these occasions is the State of the Union Address, but the president also made other important speeches on an annual basis at such venues as the meeting of the UN General Assembly. In such cases, the formal demands of the situation led to a suppression to some extent of his normal vernacular style. Consequently, major policy speeches contained language that sounded much like that of mainstream conservatives, including George H. W. Bush, George W. Bush, and especially Reagan. Although Trump's style was much flatter and more formal than at rallies, in interviews, or on Twitter, these speeches still embraced the nationalist populist worldview. That position had to be there, or Trump risked sounding inauthentic to his base as just another conservative Republican, the kind of politician he had savaged in the Republican primary contest in 2016.

Although Trump's formal speeches reflected the nationalist populist worldview, there was a significant shift in the role he played within the speeches. As a candidate, he was the celebrity business outsider who promised he would bring instant change. After he became president, two things changed. First, over time, pressure built for him not to merely promise change but to actually fulfill the promises he had made. As a candidate, he could claim that winning a trade war was easy. As president, he faced pressure to actually win that trade war. Second, after he became president, he had vastly more power to directly influence events by taking action of some kind. Moreover, as president, a claim that he was an outsider lost credibility. The changed situation led to an evolution in the persona he played. Whereas previously he had been the celebrity outsider, over time he assumed the role of a strongman who claimed to have already produced vast progress. Unlike most presidents, who focus on what the nation has accomplished, often speaking of what "we" have done together, Trump as strongman often personalized the claim, stating what he had personally achieved. In addition, Trump also made grandiose claims about his own power and on occasion threatened to use that power to confront or attack a real or perceived enemy, either foreign or domestic. This change in role was most apparent in campaign rallies, interviews, and on Twitter, but the evolution also was present to a lesser degree in formal presidential addresses. Moreover, whereas previously he often insulted his political opponents and the press, after becoming president he had an additional weapon, the explicit or implicit threat. He was not a strongman in the same sense as an autocratic leader in South or Central America (or Europe) during the nineteenth or twentieth century, but he often threatened to take action to punish or block his opponents, even when that action undercut basic democratic norms. His attacks on democratic norms became more prevalent as various investigations of his business and presidency proceeded.

To illustrate the evolution of Trump's formal presidential speeches, I focus in detail on the State of the Union Address on January 30, 2018, and then show that the same pattern was present in the speech he made as a substitute for an official state of the union address in 2017, a speech he presented to the UN General Assembly in September 2017, and a short address during the government shutdown in January 2019.[13]

Nationalist Populism and the Outsider/Strongman
in the 2018 State of the Union Address

Trump's 2018 State of the Union Address, clearly the most important formal speech of his first two years in office, illustrates the point that his formal presidential rhetoric did not fulfill the same function as for other postwar presidents. It was both the third longest such address in the last half-century and one of the least important.[14] A state of the union address is normally a vehicle for laying out and building support for the president's agenda. As Campbell and Jamieson explain, "Viewed generically, the State of the Union address is characterized by three processes: (1) public meditations on values, (2) assessments of information and issues, and (3) policy recommendations."[15] Trump included these formal elements in an address that for the most part sounded more like those of other conservative presidents than did his campaign or rally speeches, but underneath the surface the nationalist populist message with an outsider/strongman persona was evident.

In the speech, Trump focused on the first element defining the genre, the discussion of shared values. He did this primarily by discussing "American heroes" who "show us what we can be" (5). He honored a Coast Guard officer, Ashlee Leppert, who helped "save more than 40 lives" in Houston during Hurricane Harvey (8); a firefighter in California, David Dahlberg, who rescued "almost 60 children trapped at a California summer camp threatened by wildfires" (9); and ordinary people in the "Cajun Navy" and in Las Vegas who saved lives during Hurricane Harvey and a mass shooting event. He said these heroes reflected the American spirit, and "no people on Earth are so fearless, or daring, or determined as Americans." Later in the speech, he praised police officer Ryan Holet of Albuquerque, who along with his wife adopted the baby of a heroin addict (97–99). He also honored the family of American college student Otto Warmbier, who died after he was jailed in North Korea (124–126). In recognizing American heroes and having several of them present in the chamber during the speech, Trump continued a tradition Reagan started of extolling "basic values" and redefining "the people as heroes."[16]

Trump sounded still more like Reagan in the conclusion of the speech, in which he used the Capitol and the monuments "to Washington and Jefferson—to Lincoln and King" as well as other memorials on the National Mall to praise the American people as heroes (135–139). In language reminiscent of Reagan's First Inaugural Address, he said American heroes "live not only in the past, but all around us—defending hope, pride, and the American way" (139). He added, "They work in every trade. They sacrifice to raise a family. They care for our children at home. They defend our flag abroad. They are strong moms and brave kids. They are firefighters, police officers, border agents, medics, and Marines."[17]

Many presidents have used a "heroes in the room" strategy to reinforce American values, but Trump explicitly claimed to be discussing American heroism to send a message of unity. He emphasized that his goal was "to seek out common ground, and to summon the unity we need to deliver for the people we were elected to serve" (13). Later, he said that he wanted "to talk about what kind of future we are going to have and what kind of Nation we are going to be. All of us, together, as one team, one people, and one American family. We all share the same home, the same heart, the same destiny, and the same great American flag" (33–34).

In these passages, Trump sounded much like Reagan and other presidents, but his underlying message was quite different. His reference to "the same great American flag" in his call for unity was one strong signal that his real purpose was to reinforce his divisive nationalist populist message. He presented his State of the Union Address at the end of a professional football season in which the president had attacked National Football League (NFL) players who refused to stand during the national anthem.[18] For example, on November 28, 2017, he tweeted, "At least 24 players kneeling this weekend at NFL stadiums that are now having a very hard time filling up. The American public is fed up with the disrespect the NFL is paying to our Country, our Flag, and our National Anthem. Weak and out of control!"[19] In referencing the flag in the speech to Congress, Trump was using a narrow definition of patriotism to appeal to core supporters, "many of whom also nurse racist resentment against highly paid African American athletes."[20] On the surface, his comments seemed inclusive, but under the surface they functioned as a dog whistle to activate those within his base of support. The nationalist populist message was embedded within the boiler-plate discussion of policy and the Reaganesque appeal to an entirely faux sense of unity.

Trump focused the policy-oriented portion of the speech on praising his administration and describing policy proposals in the most general terms possible. In the fourth paragraph he claimed, "Over the last year, we have made incredible progress and achieved extraordinary success. We have faced challenges we expected and others we could never have imagined. We have shared in the heights of victory and the pains of hardship. We endured floods and fires and storms. But through it all, we have seen the beauty of America's soul, and the steel in America's spine." The emptiness of the address is already evident at this point. He detailed the progress in relation to jobs created, declining unemployment, and "massive tax cuts" that "provide tremendous relief for the middle class and small businesses" (17–21). In fact, the economic trends he described were largely a continuation of what had occurred during the Obama administration, although at a slightly slower rate of job creation.[21] Despite his claim that because of the tax cut "millions of Americans will have more take-home pay starting next month," ordinary Americans saw only a small bump in income, and the overwhelming proportion of the cuts went to corporations and the rich, a result that led Republican candidates in the 2018 elections to avoid mentioning it (22).[22] Trump described the state of the nation during the Obama years as "American carnage," but in his 2018 State of the Union Address, he described essentially the same nation as one where "a new tide of optimism" is "sweeping across our land" (2). The point is that Trump's description of the nation was shaped not only by whether he could take credit for it but also by the fact that the function of the address was not to lay out evidence of problems and then advocate for policies to address those problems but instead to minimally fulfill the generic form of a state of the union address and embed within it his nationalist populist message.

In the remainder of the address, Trump took credit for a number of other trends that preexisted his administration.[23] For example, he claimed, "We are defending our Second Amendment and have taken historic actions to protect religious liberty" (43). Because there were no efforts to undermine either the Second Amendment or religious liberty in the previous administration, unless one defined support for quite modest gun safety regulation or regulation that allowed employees of organizations with ties to the Catholic Church or other groups opposed to birth control to access a standard prescription drug program without directly involving the church or religious organization as such a threat, his comment was entirely empty as a policy prescription.[24] It actually functioned as part of Trump's nationalist message for the portion of his base that perceived major threats to either gun rights or religious liberty. Similarly, he claimed to have "ended the war on American Energy," a statement that both ignored the enormous boom in oil and natural gas production during the Obama years and mischaracterized air pollution and global warming regulation as a "war" on energy companies (48).

A relatively small proportion of the speech focused on laying out new policy proposals. Trump used one paragraph to call for giving the terminally ill access to experimental drugs (54), stated the need to address high drug prices (55), mentioned the importance of prison reform (71), and supported keeping open the Guantanamo Bay prison (110). He spent only slightly more time calling for increased defense spending and tough enforcement to confront the opioid epidemic (93–95, 102–103).

The policy positions cited to this point were consistent with the views of the traditional conservatives Trump defeated in the 2016 Republican primaries. Most notable was the way he presented those objectives, such as his misleading comments about a "war" on energy companies. The point is that even when defending orthodox conservative policy, he did so in a way designed to create an emotional reaction among supporters and opponents alike. Another example of this strategy was his support for the longtime conservative goal of undermining the protections in the Civil Service system. He cited the need to care for veterans as rationale "to empower every Cabinet Secretary with the authority to reward good workers—and to remove Federal employees who undermine the public trust or fail the American people" (46). Here, Trump cloaked a proposal to undermine Civil Service protections as a means to care for veterans.[25]

The most developed policy discussions reflected the nationalist and to a lesser degree the populist aspects of his message. On immigration, Trump claimed, "For decades, open borders have allowed drugs and gangs to pour into our most vulnerable communities. They have allowed millions of low-wage workers to compete for jobs and wages against the poorest Americans. More tragically, they have caused the loss of many innocent lives" (73). He then cited the case of two teenage girls killed by the MS-13 gang and recognized the girls' parents, his guests at the speech. He also cloaked his anti-immigration message in a veneer of compassion, claiming, "My greatest compassion, and my constant concern is for America's children" (77). He made this clear when he said, "Americans are dreamers too," a reference to the Obama policy of protecting "dreamers" (immigrants who came as young children to the United States and had lived here for many years) from deportation. Of course, American citizens who dream of a better life are not subject to deportation.

Trump followed the passage concerning American "dreamers" by describing what he labeled a "bipartisan approach to immigration reform" that included a path to citizenship for "dreamers" but also a border wall, along with expanding border enforcement, ending "the dangerous practice of 'catch and release,'" ending the "visa lottery system," and "ending chain migration." He called this plan "a down-the-middle compromise" (82–90). In fact, it was a repackaging of the same anti-immigration message he presented in the 2016 campaign.

He took a similar hard line on what he called "unfair trade deals that sacrificed our prosperity and shipped away our companies, our jobs, and our Nation's wealth," promising his supporters that "the era of economic surrender is over" (56, 57). As is the norm in his speeches, there was little detail and no explanation of how to "fix bad trade deals and negotiate new ones" (59). Trump's discussion of trade and immigration was less about making a case for a policy proposal than it was about sending a message of strength to his supporters. He was telling them that he would remain committed to the nationalist message he expressed more directly and colorfully in rallies and tweets.

Trump also reinforced the nationalist message when he told the story of Preston Sharp, a twelve-year-old boy who "started a movement that has now placed 40,000 flags at the graves of our great heroes" in military cemeteries (38). He added, "Preston's reverence for those who have served our Nation reminds us why we salute our flag, why we put our hands on our hearts for the pledge of allegiance, and why we proudly stand for the national anthem" (39). Here, Trump implicitly juxtaposed Sharp, the white patriot he had invited to the speech, with the Black NFL players who protested police violence during the national anthem. In this passage, Trump used praise for a small boy as a dog-whistle to activate the emotional reaction of core supporters who felt threatened by demographic change.

Trump also warned of the danger posed by terrorists, focusing both on terrorism abroad and "two terrorist attacks in New York [that] were made possible by the visa lottery and chain migration" (88). Abroad, he said, "when possible, we annihilate them" and added that "when captured overseas they should be treated like the terrorists they are" (108). Here, he drew on fear of terrorism in general and Islamic terrorism in particular. He also reinforced the nationalist portion of his message when calling for punishing nations that had protested when the Trump administration "recognized Jerusalem as the capital of Israel" (113). He threatened to cut funding to "dozens of countries" that had voted "against America's sovereign right to make this recognition," adding that "American taxpayers generously send those same countries billions of dollars in aid every year" (114). He said foreign aid should "always serve American interests, and only go to America's friends" (115). In this passage, Trump drew on the common misconception that the United States spends roughly 25 percent of its budget on foreign aid (the real figure is 1 percent) to ungrateful countries that then oppose it.[26]

The populist message was less evident than in other contexts, perhaps because a speech to Congress and the nation as president is an odd place to attack the political system itself. Still, there were moments in the address when Trump made it clear that he remained committed to the populist themes he expressed during his campaign. This message was implicit in a general discussion of infrastructure policy. He called on Congress "to produce a bill that generates at least $1.5 trillion for the new infrastructure investment we need" and said that "every Federal dollar should be leveraged by partnering with State and local governments and, where appropriate, tapping private sector investment—to permanently fix the infrastructure deficit" (64, 65). He neglected to provide any explanation of how this plan would work or how it would be funded. However, he did imply that his plan would succeed because he would cut through bureaucratic barriers to action. He referenced his business as a developer, telling the audience, "America is a nation of builders. We built the Empire State Building in just 1 year—is it not a disgrace that it can now take 10 years just to get a permit approved for a simple road?" (62). He said, "Any bill must also streamline the permitting and approval process" and again alluded to his work as a developer, promising that "together, we can reclaim our building heritage" (67).

Trump's outsider/strongman persona and the vernacular style that enacted it were subdued in the speech, largely because they did not fit the generic demands of a state of the union address. At the same time, the grand claims about "incredible progress" and "extraordinary success," as well as his statement that "we have faced challenges we expected" and achieved the "heights of victory" were consistent with this persona (4). There was less explicit bragging about what he alone could accomplish than in campaign speeches, rally addresses as president, or on Twitter, but the outsider/strongman persona was still present.

One aspect of the outsider/strongman persona was Trump's expression of enormous vanity about accomplishments. I have already quoted several examples illustrating his vanity in the speech. At the end of the address, almost immediately before the Reaganesque conclusion, he spoke about "the depraved character of the North Korean regime" and a policy of "maximum pressure" to confront the regime (122, 124). He noted, "No regime has oppressed its own citizens more totally or brutally than the cruel dictatorship in North Korea" and spoke of the case of Otto Warmbier, the American student imprisoned in North Korea who later died of injuries sustained there.

Trump paired his discussion of North Korea in the speech with an attack on the Iran agreement negotiated by the Obama administration. Yet, Trump's harsh attacks on North Korea in his 2018 State of the Union Address are revealing because of the change in his tone that would occur after a meeting with the North Korean leader in summer 2018. After that meeting, Trump's language changed dramatically despite the failure of the North Korean regime to take tangible steps to cut production of either nuclear weapons or missile delivery systems. Of course, the regime also made no changes in the way it treats its own citizens.[27] In his 2018 State of the Union Address, Trump described North Korea as a barbaric regime that oppressed its own citizens and threatened the world. After a meeting in which the North Koreans agreed to nothing but a symbolic long-term commitment to denuclearization, his tone changed dramatically. Trump stated, "He's the head of a country, and I mean he's the strong head." He added, "Don't let anyone think anything different. He speaks and his people sit up at attention. I want my people to do the same."[28] At the same time, Trump continued to attack Iran and the Iranian deal Obama had negotiated despite the fact that it placed real constraints on Iran's capacity to produce nuclear weapons.[29] The shift in tone made little sense if Trump truly supported a policy of "maximum pressure." But it made perfect sense as a reflection of the strongman persona. After he completed the summit with Kim Jong Un, Trump's strongman persona essentially required him to take credit for it. Because he had consistently identified himself as the consummate dealmaker, the summit must have been historic in its accomplishments. The fact that the summit produced no tangible results beyond the meeting itself was irrelevant.

In his 2018 State of the Union Address, Trump seemed to embrace a bipartisan and inclusive perspective and to defend an orthodox conservative agenda. Some reporting focused on the "conciliatory tone" of the address, which, as Karen Tumulty and Phillip Rucker noted, "was sharply at odds with the combative manner in which he has conducted his presidency." Conservative commentator Marc Thiessen said the "speech was moving. It was reasonable. It was bipartisan."[30] Some saw Trump's tone in the speech as "traditionally presidential." Marc Fisher referenced this use of "a more nuanced rhetoric for official occasions" as "Special Occasion Trump."[31] The speech was also praised as theater. James Hohmann noted, "Trump is a consummate showman, and his stagecraft was top notch." Hohmann added, "Trump's approval rating could easily be 10 points higher right now if he just behaved the way he did last night, even while pursuing an identical agenda."[32]

Even though Trump called for bipartisanship and unity, the nationalist populist message was present in the address. In fact, "Special Occasion Trump" did nothing to fundamentally shift his message. He only moderated his tone for a special occasion. He made the nationalist populist message quite clear in his discussion of trade, immigration, the flag, and other issues. Labeling his immigration proposals "bipartisan" did not change the reality that his proposals were stridently nationalist and his tone even more so. Moreover, in a number of passages, he fanned racial division with comments about patriotism in general and honoring the flag and the national anthem in particular. Always an astute commentator, E. J. Dionne recognized that Trump "kept coming back to the most divisive themes of his presidency" and added that "without the heroes, there would hardly have been any speech at all."[33] Similarly, the *Washington Post* editorialized that Trump included "divisive references to hot-button issues," and Dana Milbank cited the use of "several cultural wedges" in what was more a "campaign event" than a traditional discussion of the issues facing the nation.[34] "Special Occasion Trump" could not fundamentally change his message because that message was "a feature, not a bug" and "part of his enduring appeal to the GOP base."[35] Absent the nationalist populist message and the outsider/strongman persona, Trump would sound like just another conservative Republican, a result that would undermine his perceived authenticity and potentially undercut his ties to his base of support.

"Special Occasion Trump" in Other Formal Policy Speeches

Although "Special Occasion Trump" minimally met the demands of the occasion for major policy addresses and tamped down both the tone and the strongman persona he increasingly used on Twitter, in interviews, and in rally speeches to enact his nationalist populist message, that message was still very much in evidence. His remarks to Congress on February 28, 2017, which took the place of a state of the union address for the first year of his presidency, and his speech at the United Nations on September 19, 2017, illustrate these points.[36] In the speech to Congress, Trump began by referencing "our celebration of Black History Month" and said that "each American generation passes the torch of truth, liberty, and justice in an unbroken chain all the way down to the present." Trump's language echoed Kennedy's Inaugural Address, although lacking the eloquence of Kennedy's remarks. In the conclusion, he spoke of "the wonders our country could know in America's 250th year" in 2026 and appealed to unity in words quite similar to those of his Inaugural Address, stating, "We all bleed the same blood. We all salute the same great American flag." He added, "The time for trivial fights is behind us."

In the speech to Congress, Trump also discussed policy proposals but, as in the address the following year, only in highly general and sometimes misleading terms. For example, he used two short paragraphs to support what he called "a big, big [tax] cut." He also laid out what he called his five "principles" for repealing the ACA. In fact, his statement of "principles" indicated that his health-care program was more a slogan than an actual policy. The first "principle" illustrates this point. He said, "First, we should ensure that Americans with preexisting conditions have access to coverage and that we have a stable transition for Americans currently enrolled in the health-care exchanges." As would become apparent in the debate about repealing the ACA, preexisting conditions could not be covered in a stable program without both a mandate banning insurance companies from denying coverage or setting premiums based on them and a program of government subsidies to support coverage. Trump's first principle was the kind of statement that works well in a campaign context but falls apart under any significant scrutiny. The other segments of the speech discussing public policy followed a similar pattern.

As in Trump's State of the Union Address the following year, the nationalist and populist themes that dominated his rhetoric were present in the 2017 speech, in which he described an American dystopia quite similar to his portrayal in his Inaugural Address. He said that "our own borders" are "wide open for anyone to cross and for drugs to pour in at a now unprecedented rate" and later called for building "a great, great wall along our southern border." He warned of the danger of "radical Islamic terrorism," said it was "reckless to allow uncontrolled entry from places where proper vetting cannot occur," and added that "we cannot allow a beachhead of terrorism to form inside America." His tone was slightly less inflammatory than in his rally speeches but substantively the same.

On trade, Trump said, "We've lost more than one-fourth of our manufacturing jobs since NAFTA was approved, and we've lost 60,000 factories since China joined the World Trade Organization." He also implicitly attacked those associated with Black Lives Matter and others who protested unfair policing tactics that disproportionately affect Black Americans and other minorities, stating, "We must work with, not against—not against—the men and women of law enforcement." If anything, the nationalist message was stronger in 2017 than it was a year later.

The populist message was also present. Trump claimed his administration had already "begun to drain the swamp of government corruption" and would "massively reduce job-crushing regulations, creating a deregulation task force inside every government agency."

Trump's celebrity business outsider persona, which sometimes included statements and actions consistent with that of a strongman, was more evident in 2017 than the following year. He predicted stupendous results from his leadership:

> Dying industries will come roaring back to life. Heroic veterans will get the care they so desperately need, and our military will be given the resources its brave warriors so richly deserve. Crumbling infrastructure will be replaced with new roads, bridges, tunnels, airports, and railways gleaming across our very, very beautiful land. Our terrible drug epidemic will slow down and ultimately stop. And our neglected inner cities will see a rebirth of hope, safety, and opportunity.

Apparently, his strong leadership would magically produce these changes because he failed to lay out any coherent agenda.

A similar point can be made about his UN address. The form for a speech to the United Nations is less fixed than that of a state of the union address; however, normally a president speaks of the basic values that undergird US foreign policy and lays out the foreign policy agenda of the administration. This message is expressed in broadly ceremonial language, and the commitment of the United States to the United Nations and international norms is reaffirmed. There were portions of the speech in which Trump enacted these norms. He spoke of American values in stating, "We do not seek to impose our way of life on anyone, but rather to let it shine as an example for everyone to watch." He also praised the Marshall Plan as "built on the noble idea that the whole world is safer when nations are strong, independent, and free."

Most of the remainder of the speech, in contrast, enacted Trump's nationalist populist message, and in some cases, he attacked international norms and institutions. The populist message was most obvious when he attacked the United Nations itself. He said that in paying for the United Nations, "The United States bears an unfair cost burden" and added at the end of the address that "we cannot wait for someone else, for faraway countries or far-off bureaucrats—we can't do it. We must solve our problems, to build prosperity, to secure our futures, or we will be vulnerable to decay, domination, and defeat." In domestic speeches, he called for the people to take power from the politicians, bureaucrats, and lobbyists. In this speech, he said the "basic question" for the people of the world is: "Are we still patriots? Do we love our nations enough to protect their sovereignty and to take ownership of their futures?" Implicitly, Trump was attacking international institutions and calling for the people of the world to take back control of their own countries.

The nationalist message dominated the address. Trump emphasized a litany of threats that dangerous Others posed to the United States and the world. He said, "Terrorists and extremists have gathered strength and spread to every region of the world," warned of the danger of "uncontrolled migration," and claimed "mammoth multinational trade deals, unaccountable international tribunals, and powerful global bureaucracies" had created a situation in which "millions of jobs vanished and thousands of factories disappeared." The result was that "our great middle class . . . was forgotten and left behind, but they are forgotten no more."

Trump also again called the Iran deal "one of the worst and most one-sided transactions the United States has ever entered into." It was "an embarrassment." He attacked Iran as "a corrupt dictatorship" and "a rogue state." He used still harsher language to discuss North Korea, stating that the government was "responsible for the starvation deaths of millions of North Koreans and for the imprisonment, torture, killing, and oppression of countless more." He then warned North Korea, "The United States has great strength and patience, but if it is forced to defend itself or its allies, we will have no choice but to totally destroy North Korea." He added in astonishingly harsh language, "Rocket Man [Kim Jong Un] is on a suicide mission for himself and for his regime."

In response to these dangers, Trump promised to "always put America first." He explained, "But we can no longer be taken advantage of, or enter into a one-sided deal where the United States gets nothing in return." Trump essentially told the United Nations that the United States would support international norms, treaty commitments, and the like if we thought those commitments helped us. Otherwise, all bets were off.

Trump's speech at the United Nations in some ways followed those of other presidents by stating support for at least some international institutions. This led David Ignatius to comment, "When you discount the rhetorical overkill, the most surprising thing about President Trump's address to the United Nations on Tuesday was how conventional it was. He supported human rights and democracy; he opposed rogue regimes; he espoused a global community of strong, sovereign nations."[37] Ignatius attempted to reassure readers that in the speech Trump "operated within the four walls of rationality." Yet, if there is anything Trump's campaign and presidency teach, it is that it is never wise to "discount the rhetorical overkill." Fundamentally, the speech enacted the nationalist populist message that dominates Trump's rhetoric. David Rothkopf explained:

> President Trump delivered a speech to his alt-right, anti-globalist base from the podium of the United Nations General Assembly on Tuesday. He offered a vision of America's role in the world starkly different from any of his predecessors who stood in the same spot before the leaders of the world. In the end, Trump offered up remarks that were antithetical to the ideas and ideals that led the United States to play a central role in the U.N.'s founding in the wake of World War II.[38]

In the UN address, Trump gave lip service to the values that had defined US foreign policy for presidents of both parties for decades, but he also strongly embraced the populist and especially nationalist components of his message, thereby undercutting international norms. And especially in the sentence labeling Kim Jong Un as "Rocket Man," he used a vernacular style entirely consistent with the strongman persona.

In major policy addresses, "Special Occasion Trump" tamped down his normal tone and minimally enacted the norms for policy rhetoric. But he made little effort to describe in detail or support his policy proposals and even less effort to account for possible objections. Underlying his message, moreover, were the same nationalist and populist themes that dominated all his rhetoric. It was the essence of his message. Moreover, after becoming president, the role he enacted shifted somewhat. No longer could he place all blame on elites in Washington because he was president and Republicans controlled both the House and the Senate for the first two years of his presidency. Moreover, as president he had vastly more power than he did as a candidate. Thus, his role evolved from a business outsider toward that of a strongman. His bragging shifted from prediction to claims of present accomplishments, and his attacks on the media and dangerous Others were veiled in the power of the presidency, sometimes with the implication that direct action could be taken against them. This shift was much more evident in rallies, interviews, and on social media, especially Twitter, but it also occurred in formal policy speeches.

On the rare occasions Trump focused on public policy outside a special occasion, such as his State of the Union Address, his remarks were quite similar to a typical rally speech. The most notable example was the Oval Office address on January 8, 2019, in the midst of a government shutdown precipitated by his demand that Congress fund a border wall. The speech reflected the nationalist portion of his message and was aimed at "stoking visceral fear of people crossing the border."[39] It depicted undocumented immigration as a "growing humanitarian and security crisis" that "strains public resources and drives down jobs and wages," produces a huge number of crimes, and causes thousands of deaths from illegal drugs every year. In contrast, a border wall "would very quickly pay for itself" and was the solution that could end "this crisis."[40] His remarks were essentially the same as in a rally speech and were "littered with falsehoods," apparently designed to appeal only to his base of support. As Jennifer Rubin noted, "It's difficult to imagine Trump would change the mind of any voter not already devoted to his cause and immunized against reality," a conclusion later supported when public anger over the shutdown forced Trump to end it without funding for a border wall, which he later provided by shifting funds from other programs.[41]

Rather than making a case for a policy or ideological perspective as other contemporary presidents had done, Trump used policy speeches to energize his base and as a form of bargaining, what he called "truthful hyperbole."[42] The same pattern was present in his 2019 State of the Union Address, which began and ended with appeals to unity.[43] In between the call for national unity was what the *Washington Post* called "the same old polarizing demagoguery" as well as "a thinly veiled attempt to fend off investigation," with no coherent policy advocacy and many outright falsehoods.[44] Michael Gerson labeled "the call for healing and unity . . . a very typical Trumpian ploy." He said of the remainder of the speech, "When you strip away all the hatred and fearmongering, there is always another layer of hatred and fearmongering beneath."[45] The underlying pattern of nationalist populism was still present even on special occasions, such as his State of the Union Address. Trump's policy rhetoric was not focused on informing the public and building a case for action. Rather, Trump's rhetoric of nationalist populism served an affective, as opposed to a deliberative, function. It activated fear and anger and undercut the ground for the compromises required in reasonable policy change.

Ceremonial Rhetoric:
Trump's Rejection of the Role of National Priest

As I noted earlier, presidents often speak on ceremonial occasions, including national holidays; eulogies of major public figures or after national tragedies, such as the *Challenger* disaster or mass shootings; and, of course, in their Inaugural Addresses, which contain both ceremonial and deliberative elements.[46] Ceremonial addresses are designed to celebrate or mourn. Presidents celebrate on the Fourth of July, Veteran's Day, or when they "pardon" the national turkey prior to Thanksgiving. And they mourn the loss of significant political figures, foreign leaders, or citizens. But still more fundamentally, ceremonial addresses support a sense of American identity by reinforcing or redefining basic values. Abraham Lincoln, both Roosevelts, Kennedy, Reagan, Clinton, and Obama were particularly skillful at that kind of value affirmation. For example, Reagan's eulogy for the *Challenger* astronauts and Obama's multiple mass shooting eulogies helped Americans cope with the loss of life in those tragedies but also pointed the way forward by reaffirming values about who we are. In the midst of the Civil War, Lincoln did the same thing at Gettysburg in what is probably the most praised speech by an American or perhaps the most praised speech in the English language.

Some of the most memorable presidential speeches of the past half century have been ceremonial in nature, including Reagan's speech in Normandy, which I will discuss in a moment, and Clinton's remarks after the Oklahoma City bombing. The notable point about Trump's ceremonial rhetoric is that with the single exception of his speech in Normandy on the seventy-fifth anniversary of the D-Day invasion, he presented no important ceremonial speeches. Of course, there were national tragedies during his presidency and holidays and other events to be celebrated, but he made no important speeches save for his remarks in Normandy.[47] A close look at that speech and a comparison with Reagan's speech thirty-five years before is revealing.

In his D-Day speech, Trump spoke movingly about the bravery and sacrifice of those who "enlisted their lives in a Great Crusade."[48] He described the preparations for the invasion and the landing itself and focused on the stories of several American soldiers who had shown great bravery that day and seventy-five years later were present at the ceremony. He also praised American allies, including "the British, whose nobility and fortitude saw them through the worst of Dunkirk and the London Blitz," "the Canadians, whose robust sense of honor and loyalty compelled them to take up arms alongside Britain," "the fighting Poles, the tough Norwegians, and the intrepid Aussies," and "the gallant French commandos." The stories about medic Ray Lambert, Captain Joe Dawson, and others were genuinely powerful.

The response of commentators and political figures was near unanimous praise. Ian Bremmer called it the "best speech of Trump's presidency," Alex Ward labeled it "great," and even Speaker of the House Nancy Pelosi, a Democrat, said, "The president made a very fine speech."[49] Conservative commentators were unrestrained in their praise, with Steven Presser saying the speech possessed "subtle eloquence" and demonstrated "what it means to Make America Great Again."[50] Perhaps the *Wall Street Journal* best captured the response to the speech when it editorialized, "Hell froze over . . . as Donald Trump delivered a speech in Europe that even his critics applauded."[51]

Yet, there was also a widely shared sense that the speech was moving but also not important. Commentators noted that Trump's avoidance of service during the Vietnam War and his many attacks on the North Atlantic Treaty Organization (NATO) undercut his message; he "was only mouthing words," as Bret Stephens argued.[52] Others said that his behavior on the trip was wildly inappropriate, including immediately prior to the speech giving an interview to *Fox News* in which he attacked Robert Mueller and Nancy Pelosi with the American military cemetery visible directly behind him, a moment conservative commentator Max Boot called a "sacrilege" that exposed the emptiness of his speech.[53]

The critics are right that Trump's words and behavior both earlier in his administration and on the trip, as well as his personal behavior, weakened his message. But the more fundamental problem was that he spoke movingly about the courage and sacrifice of the soldiers but not about larger values that animated their effort. At Normandy, nearly all those Trump honored had already passed away. His remarks about the few remaining servicemen and -women were powerful, but such ceremonies are about the present and the future even more than the past. Ceremonial rhetoric honors and mourns in the service of the living. In such moments, our greatest leaders have helped the nation recommit to basic values or, when necessary, shift those values, both of which Lincoln achieved at Gettysburg.[54]

In Normandy, Trump honored the heroes who fought there but said little of the values that energized their action or of what those values meant for the present or the future. And the few words about the meaning of D-Day were consistent with his nationalist populist message. Although he praised the soldiers from the various nations who participated in the landings and noted that the Americans "came from the arms of a vast heartland, the streets of glowing cities, and the forges of mighty industrial towns," he did not add that they also represented the diversity of the American experience in race, ethnicity, and religion. Moreover, his reference in particular to "forges of mighty industrial towns" was consistent with his underlying nationalist message and call to return to the nation of the 1940s, 1950s, and early 1960s, when the manufacturing economy was much stronger and the nation much less diverse. Although he noted of NATO that "our cherished alliance was forged in the heat of battle," added that "our bond is unbreakable," and said that the soldiers fought "for liberty, democracy, and self-rule," he made it clear that underlying this effort was a sense of American nationalism. He said the armed forces "pressed on for love of home and country—the Main Streets, the schoolyard, the churches and neighbors" and then spoke of the "national culture that inspired the entire world." Trump's vision was not of sacrifice for fundamental values but in the service of "national culture," a theme conservative commentators praised. The *Wall Street Journal* noted that at the core of the speech was "a concept of nationalism" and that Trump's words functioned as part of a battle of "nationalists versus 'globalists.'"[55]

Reagan understood that the most important purpose of ceremonial rhetoric is value affirmation. When he spoke at Normandy, only about half of the speech was focused on "the boys of Pointe du Hoc."[56] The remainder was focused on what their sacrifice meant then and moving forward for the nation. In the beginning of the speech, he made it clear that the United States was fighting not only for national interest but for something larger: "to reclaim this continent to liberty," a fight against "tyranny," and to free the "Jews [who] cried out in the camps, millions cried out for liberation." "The men of Normandy . . . fought for all humanity" because they knew that "democracy is worth dying for, because it's the most deeply honorable form of government." He spoke of how after "the war was over," "there was a new peace to be assured," so the United States and our allies "rebuilt a new Europe together." In 1984 that effort was not complete because "liberated countries were lost" to Soviet armies. In contrast with the Soviet invasion of Eastern Europe, "uninvited, unwanted, unyielding," American forces remained in Europe "for only one purpose—to protect and defend democracy. The only territories we hold are memorials like this one and graveyards where our heroes rest." Reagan continued to look forward and draw meaning from the courage and sacrifice at Normandy, saying, "We've learned that isolationism never was and never will be an acceptable response to tyrannical governments with an expansionist intent." The lesson of Normandy was that the West must be "prepared to deter aggression" but also be "prepared to negotiate the reduction of arms . . . in the spirit of reconciliation." After praising the Russian people for the "terrible price" they paid during World War II, he called for efforts "to wipe from the face of the earth the terrible weapons that man now has in his hands" and "to renew our commitment to each other, to our freedom, and to the alliance that protects it" in the hope that someday the Soviets might "give up the ways of conquest." From the sacrifice that day, Reagan concluded, "strengthened by their courage, heartened by their value [valor], and borne by their memory, let us continue to stand for the ideals for which they lived and died."

Reagan's words were moving not only because they honored the courage and sacrifice of the "men of Normandy" but because they spoke to the present and the future. He reaffirmed a commitment not only to NATO and to American allies in Europe but also to freedom, democracy, the humanity of all people, and the hope for reconciliation and real arms reductions, efforts that eventually bore fruit. Reagan was committed to the United States, but he believed in values that transcended the nation's borders and simple self-interest. The speech was moving because it reaffirmed the most basic values at the heart of the American experiment with democracy, the idea that the nation was defined by ideals worth fighting and dying for. Trump's speech was empty despite the description of courage and sacrifice because it stood for nothing beyond his nationalist worldview that there are no larger values but only national self-interest.

In the memorable ceremonial speeches I mentioned, presidents spoke not only of tragedy or honored achievement but also about values shared by all Americans. They used the speeches to reflect on American identity itself and to call for a recommitment to what Lincoln in his First Inaugural Address called the "better angels of our nature." Trump's rhetoric of nationalist populism with an outsider/strongman persona was a message fundamentally defined by division, not unity—by an appeal to the basest values, not those of our "better angels." Such a message does not lead to important ceremonial addresses. The fundamental emptiness of his message was quite evident when Trump spoke from the Lincoln Memorial on July 4, 2019.[57] This speech was widely panned for its near total focus on the US military and its presentation of the story of the nation likened to "an angry grandpa reading a fifth grader's book report on American military history." Trump was critiqued because of inaccuracies "peppered throughout the speech." He also was widely mocked when he said of George Washington's army that it "took over the airports, it did everything it had to do."[58] Writing in the *Guardian*, Edward Helmore noted that Trump's claim about Washington's prowess in conquering airports "spurred a slew of memes," one of which referenced "the Battle of the Baggage Claim."[59] Trump attributed his error to a problem with the teleprompter, but the real problem was that he had nothing to say about the meaning of the Revolution.

By summer 2020, in the midst of the COVID-19 pandemic, Trump's ceremonial addresses had essentially become rally speeches. He presented an angry and divisive speech at Mount Rushmore on July 3, ostensibly celebrating Independence Day but in fact mounting "a full-on culture war against a straw-man version of the left that he portrayed as inciting mayhem and moving the country toward totalitarianism." In response to largely peaceful protests calling for social justice and taking down Confederate statues, he warned of the danger of "a new far-left fascism that demands absolute allegiance." The following day, from the lawn of the White House, he "repeated the themes" he had expressed at Mount Rushmore, using "exaggerated, apocalyptic language" in a speech that "sounded like a campaign rally." At a time of national crisis, he doubled down on his nationalist populist message, hoping "to drive home his alternate version of reality."[60]

Given his message of division, it is understandable that Trump was asked not to attend the funerals of Barbara Bush and John McCain in 2018. Rather, he occupied "the role of pariah—both unwelcome and unwilling to perform the basic rituals and ceremonies of the presidency, from public displays of mourning to cultural ceremonies."[61] Trump's role as "pariah" was reemphasized at the funeral for George H. W. Bush in December 2018. Knowing his death was coming, the senior Bush had insisted that Trump be invited to his funeral as a sign of his personal graciousness. At the funeral, Trump "was an outsider," barely greeted by the living ex-presidents and their spouses.[62] The eulogies for Bush focused on the forty-first president's patriotism, commitment to service, and bipartisanship, a message that functioned as "an implicit rebuke of everything Trump is" and emphasized the "smallness (and meanness)" of his presidency.[63] The death of a former president provides the nation an important opportunity not only to mourn but also to reflect on what it means to be Americans and the values that unify and energize the nation. It is telling that at the funeral for a much-admired ex-president, Trump had nothing to say, and those eulogizing Bush had a great deal to say about what they feared Trump was doing to the nation. Trump's message of division was totally unfit for such an occasion or for any other moment requiring reflection on the meaning of the nation.

Conclusion

The most important presidential speeches normally fall into two categories: policy focused and ceremonial. Presidents use the policy speeches to present and sell their agendas. With the exception of his Inaugural Address, important more for violating generic norms than enacting them, Trump's major policy addresses were not central to his presidency. The tone of these speeches was much more subdued than his rally speeches or Twitter comments, and he often minimally fulfilled some of the generic expectations of the occasions by describing in extremely general terms the policy he supported. But he never took the time to lay out that policy in detail, present substantial evidence to support it, or respond to potential objections to it. His core message of nationalist populism was still present, even in contexts in which it was grossly inappropriate. Obama spent almost a third of his address to Congress on health care responding to potential objections to the proposal.[64] That single case of extended refutation from Obama dwarfed all instances in which Trump publicly responded to objections to his agenda in the first three years of his presidency.

Obama, Reagan, and other modern presidents used rhetoric to inform Americans about their policy proposals, reflecting the ideal that citizens of a democracy need to understand the reasoning behind any proposed action. In contrast, Trump made little effort to explain the rationale behind his administration's proposals. Trump's policy speeches focused so little on policy because his presidency was not driven by ideology but by emotions, especially anger and fear. Moreover, his narrative of a nation under siege from dangerous Others who threatened ordinary (white) Americans was fundamentally false. Informing the public could not advance his agenda; only activating fear and hatred could do so.

In contrast with policy speeches, Trump spoke frequently on ceremonial occasions, but his remarks were essentially empty. Presidents use ceremonial rhetoric to honor achievement and mourn loss and more fundamentally tell us what it means to be American. Trump's message of division as opposed to unity made his ceremonial rhetoric quite dissonant with the reaffirmation of values and the American dream in the remarks of our most eloquent presidents. Most presidents use ceremonial rhetoric to focus on the ties that bind the nation together, comfort those who suffer loss, and point the way to a brighter future to be shared by all. Trump's entire approach was to activate a sense of grievance, of fear, and of hatred of some perceived dangerous Others. One cannot console or unify the nation or call the people together to serve a higher purpose by activating fear, hatred, or grievances. That message was much better suited to the presidential rallies Trump continued from the beginning of his administration.

5

Trump Rallies the Base with a Never-Ending Campaign of Nationalist Populism

After inauguration, most presidents focus their attention on developing a program, managing the administration of government, responding to crises, and using speeches and other acts of presidential persuasion to present and sell their agenda. Until the midterm campaign begins in earnest after Labor Day, roughly twenty months after the inauguration, and then again following the midterm elections until the general election campaign begins in earnest in the summer before the election, presidents do not generally conduct campaign-style rallies. Once again, Trump took a sharply different course and held more than fifty campaign-style rallies during the first thirty months of his presidency.

Why did Trump continue to hold campaign rallies rather than present major speeches or host town hall events in support of his agenda? One part of the answer, as I explained, is that Trump had little patience for or facility with making an extended argument in favor of a given policy. Another part of the answer is that he seemed to draw energy from the adulation he received at rallies. In that way, his "speaking to a crowd" at rallies created "a symbiotic feedback loop."[1] The final piece in the puzzle is that the underlying pattern of all Trump's rhetoric, nationalist populism with first an outsider and later a strongman persona, was not a good fit for a major policy address but fit perfectly the rally atmosphere, especially when he was threatened by investigations and growing frustration of his core supporters that their wages and other aspects of their lives were not improving rapidly. Trump himself seemed to understand that dynamic and in a rally in West Virginia on April 5, 2018, first commented that his prepared speech "would have been a little boring" and then threw away the remaining text of the speech.[2] Trump understood that his core message was not adaptable to a speech laying out the rationale for policy change on a complex issue such as health care or tax reform. But his rhetoric of nationalist populism perfectly fit the goal of creating a strong emotional bond with his core audience. It was a message of constant campaign rather than of governance.

In rally speeches as president, Trump continued to present a message of nationalist populism, but his role evolved from the celebrity businessman outsider to that of a strongman. As with his rallies during the campaign, the primary function of his ongoing message was emotional activation. Trump used the rally speeches to activate fear of the Other by claiming that undocumented immigrants, refugees, Islamic terrorists, Black protesters, and unfair foreign trade agreements posed a threat to the nation. His attacks on these groups and activities provided the audience an external enemy to blame for their own misfortune and to hate. However, there was some shift in emphasis on the domestic enemies he attacked. During his campaign, he attacked elites he said maintained rather than drained the swamp, along with the journalists who supported them. Because for the first two years of Trump's presidency Republicans were in charge of both houses of Congress and the presidency, and conservatives were a majority on the Supreme Court, blaming elites for the nation's problems became much more difficult. As a consequence, he increased his attacks on the media, calling any critical story "fake news" and sometimes labeling journalists the "enemy of the people." He also attacked his opponents, especially those investigating him, as representatives of the "deep state." Although the results of the 2018 election appeared devastating for Trump, the Democratic takeover of the House provided Trump a foil to blame for the failures of his own administration.

Finally, Trump again offered himself as the hero who could return the nation to greatness. During his campaign, he had promised that through force of will, he would bring almost magical change immediately upon becoming president. As his term progressed, he increasingly presented himself as the strongman who had achieved that magical progress. No longer did he decry economic statistics as fake news as he did during the 2016 campaign, when he alleged that the actual unemployment rate was an astronomical 42 percent, or even higher. Instead, Trump took credit for the continuation of the economic recovery that began early in Barack Obama's administration.[3] In many cases, he took credit for accomplishments that had not in fact occurred or that he exaggerated, leading fact checkers to identify more and more false statements. As president, Trump also increasingly made statements that undercut the norms of the democratic process itself, reflecting the shift in his persona toward that of a strongman. This development became much more common as the investigations led by Special Counsel Robert Mueller, congressional committees, the press, and later the House impeachment inquiry progressed.

Nationalist Populism in Presidential Rally Speeches

To demonstrate the evolution of Trump's nationalist populist message as president, I first outline its components in major rallies in Youngstown, Ohio, on July 26, 2017; Phoenix, Arizona, on August 23, 2017; and Wilkes-Barre, Pennsylvania, on March 10, 2018. I then explain how his message evolved in rallies during the 2018 midterm campaign. Next, I examine how his message developed after the midterm election with a discussion of his more than two-hour speech at the Conservative Political Action Conference (CPAC) on March 2, 2019.[4] Finally, I show how he transformed briefings about the COVID-19 pandemic into something like rally speeches while the country was largely shut down and he could not hold rallies in spring 2020.

In the rallies in Youngstown, Phoenix, and Wilkes-Barre, Trump continued to focus upon essentially the same external enemies he did during his campaign. By describing undocumented immigrants, refugees, Islamic terrorists, and his other frequent targets as major threats, he activated fear of Others, continuing to identify an enemy for his core supporters to go on fearing and hating. In Youngstown, he claimed the nation remained under threat, but major progress already had been made. Regarding immigration, he said, "We are actually liberating towns and cities. We are liberating—people are screaming from their windows, thank you to the border patrol." He added, "We are destroying the bloodthirsty criminal gangs." In this speech, he defended the crackdown on immigration and refugees by stating, "We don't want radical Islamic terrorists in our country. We've seen the total devastation in Europe." On trade, he claimed that whereas under previous administrations "those jobs have left Ohio. They're all coming back." Finally, he used a reference to the flag and praise for law enforcement as a dog-whistle to create anger at groups, such as Black Lives Matter, focused on high rates of police violence against people of color. Trump said, "We believe that schools should teach our children to have pride in our history and respect for that great American flag. We all believe in the rule of law, and we support the incredible men and women of law enforcement." Of course, many of these claims were simple nonsense. There were, for example, no towns or cities "liberated" from gangs of undocumented immigrants.[5]

The speech in Phoenix occurred shortly after a violent white supremacist rally in Charlottesville, Virginia, resulted in multiple injuries and one death. In the aftermath of Charlottesville, Trump was widely criticized for stating there were "very fine people on both sides" rather than blaming the white supremacists and neo-Nazis for the violence.[6] His primary method of dealing with the controversy was to attack the "fake media" and claim they "make up stories," but it is important to recognize that even in a situation in which there were strong pressures on him to moderate his rhetoric, he continued to focus on the same dangerous Others he did in his campaign rallies. In Phoenix, he spoke of the "deadly and heartbreaking consequences of illegal immigration, the lost lives, the drugs, the gangs, the cartels, the crisis of smuggling and trafficking" and again claimed his administration was "liberating towns" from criminal gangs of undocumented immigrants who "don't shoot people because it's too fast and not painful. They cut them up into little pieces. These are animals." Later, he led the crowd in chanting, "Build that wall!" He again claimed major progress on trade, stating that "struggling American workers" are "starting to see the light because plants are coming pouring back into our country." Late in the speech, he promised, "No longer will we allow other countries to close our factories, steal our jobs, and drain our wealth." He also again activated negative attitudes toward attempts by such groups as Black Lives Matter to reduce police violence. He attacked "the unaccountable hostility against our incredible police, who work so hard at such a dangerous job" and also referenced efforts to remove Confederate monuments from cities across the South, claiming "they are trying to take away our history and our heritage," a comment that led the audience to boo. In the aftermath of Charlottesville, he continued to sharply criticize those who wanted to take down monuments to a society that enslaved Black people.

Trump made similar comments in Wilkes-Barre in March 2018. At that rally, he activated fear of crime and anger at undocumented immigrants by claiming Democrats "like to protect criminals, they like to protect MS-13" (a gang originally organized by undocumented immigrants from Central

America) and again promised to "build the wall for people, for gangs, for drugs."[7] On trade, he claimed credit for "companies coming back into the United States." He also attacked US Representative Maxine Waters (D-CA), as "a very low-IQ individual." This long-serving and outspoken Black member of Congress had been one of his strongest critics in the capital. His attack appealed to supporters, including not only the alt right but also the significant number of Americans with an authoritarian mind-set, uncomfortable with changes in the racial makeup of the nation. In rallies, on Twitter, and in other comments, Trump demonstrated a strong tendency to attack women and people of color with labels such as "low IQ."[8] In the three rallies I discuss here, the "dangerous" Others he named were largely the same as in his campaign, but Trump was already claiming credit for major progress reducing the threat to the nation posed by the "alien" (nonwhite Others) despite the fact that no significant legislation addressing immigration reform issues had been passed and little actual change had occurred.

In presidential rallies, Trump often expressed the populist theme as an even stronger attack on the media than he did during his campaign. Early in his speech in Youngstown, he said his goal was "to cut through the fake news filter and to speak straight to the American people," which produced chants of "fake news" and "drain the swamp." A little later he outlined a populist theme, exclaiming, "We believe that family and faith, not government and bureaucracy, are the foundation of our society." He then added, "We don't worship government" and "we are restoring our government's allegiance to its people, to its citizens." This comment, similar to what he had said during the campaign, posed a problem. He would need to show that what he called the restoration of government was making a real difference in the lives of his supporters. Because the actual administrative and legislative agenda of his administration focused on cutting taxes primarily for corporations and the wealthy and instituting deregulation for businesses, he would have difficulty pointing to tangible advances for his core audience in the white working class.

In Phoenix, Trump stridently attacked "the very dishonest media, those people right up there with all the cameras." He added, "Truly dishonest people in the media and the fake media, they make up stories." He then devoted several minutes to attacking the media for accurately reporting his comment that there were "some very fine people on both sides" in Charlottesville. He said his purpose was "to show you how damned dishonest these people are." He later attacked the "failing *New York Times*, which is like so bad," claimed the *Washington Post* was "a lobbying tool for Amazon," and said CNN "is so bad and so pathetic, and their ratings are going down," which led the crowd to chant "CNN sucks!" Trump continued his attack on the media for several more minutes in what *Time* labeled a rant.[9] Later in the speech, he linked the nationalist and populist themes, claiming, "The media turns a blind eye to the gang violence on our streets . . . [and] the destruction of our wealth at the hands of the terrible, terrible trade deals." He also criticized the media for "the unaccountable hostility against our incredible police." The same populist theme surfaced in Wilkes-Barre, where he attacked the "fake" media seven times in the first eleven minutes of his speech. Although at other rallies he continued to present "greatest hits" from his 2016 campaign, including calling for Hillary Clinton to be locked up, this populist theme was much less prevalent because he was now president. He needed a new foil to attack, and that led to a much greater focus on the media. This trend escalated as the media reported on various investigations of his administration.

The strongman persona was present in all three speeches. During his campaign, Trump often claimed he would accomplish amazing things because he was the voice of the people. As president, he claimed those amazing accomplishments already were occurring. For example, in Youngstown, he responded to criticism that he did not act presidential by claiming, "With the exception of the late great Abraham Lincoln, I can be more presidential than any president that's ever held this office." He then added, "With few exceptions no president has done anywhere near what we've done in his first six months. Not even close." Of course, this was nonsense. Many presidents had far more actual accomplishments early in their presidencies than did Trump. Trump also took credit for the continuation of economic trends that began in Obama's first term and compared himself to presidents depicted on Mount Rushmore, concluding, "We are going to bring back our dreams, and we are going to bring back, once again, our sovereignty as a nation." It is difficult to imagine another president comparing himself to the presidents depicted on Mount Rushmore, but Trump's strongman persona dictated that kind of self-praise.

The pattern was similar in Phoenix. Trump began the speech by personally claiming credit for job creation. Astonishingly, he did so in the context of discussing race relations, which he said "were pretty bad under Barack Obama." Trump then observed, "If we continue to create jobs at levels that I'm creating jobs, I think that's going to have a tremendously positive impact on race relations." This comment is revealing in two ways. First, after only a few months in office and with no significant legislative or other accomplishments, Trump alleged he was personally creating jobs. Second, the statement that race relations were bad under Obama is another indication of his focus on supporters uncomfortable with the changing racial balance in American society. His comments about job creation were less an appeal to Black voters than an attempt to activate core supporters, including in the alt right, uncomfortable with racial change in American society, by demeaning the accomplishments of Obama.

At other points in the speech, Trump embraced a theme often used by strongmen, that he was fully consubstantial with core supporters. Late in the speech, he stated, "I came to Washington for you. Your dreams are my dreams. Your hopes are my hopes. And your future is what I'm fighting for each and every day." In the conclusion, he linked his strongman persona with the nationalist theme by saying he was "in the proud tradition of America's great leaders, from George Washington . . . to Lincoln, to Teddy Roosevelt." He added of Washington, "Please, don't take his statue down." He concluded the passage, stating, "They're trying to take away our culture. They are trying to take away our history." Here, he appealed to a sense of grievance felt by many supporters through depicting himself as the savior protecting (white) American history values from Black activists.

In the speech in Wilkes-Barre, the strongman persona was enacted primarily through a series of egocentric statements. Trump claimed, "Without Donald Trump the Olympics would have been a total failure." He went on to praise himself for producing "a big hit" with *The Apprentice* and then made the bizarre assertion that he personally had achieved major progress in controlling the nuclear program in North Korea despite the fact that a meeting with Kim Jong Un that produced nothing tangible was still several months off. Trump said, "So here they [the media] are. They're outside, these wonderful representatives, very high-level from South Korea are saying all of these things—de-nuke and all of the things that they can't believe, because it's like five years ahead of schedule." Later he claimed, "We have done more than any first-term administration in the history of our country." He added the false statement, "We passed the biggest tax cut in the history of our country." Later in the speech, he claimed other politicians "go out, they get 50 people, they're satisfied," whereas, "if I go to a small place and they have 2,000 people." He added "So, is there any more fun than at a Trump rally?" Later, he claimed, "Those people are coming out of the hills. They're coming out of the valleys" to vote for candidates Trump supported. In this quite disjointed and strikingly self-referential passage, Trump depicted himself as the strongman savior of his supporters.

The rhetoric of nationalist populism with a strongman persona dominated Trump's rally speeches in Youngstown, Phoenix, and Wilkes-Barre. In some ways, Trump's rally rhetoric had shifted from that of his campaign, notably in his more stridently attacking the media. Moreover, in his presidential rally speeches, his persona shifted from outsider to strongman, a message he enacted by making claims of incredible accomplishments, often about trends that preexisted his presidency or about events that had not happened.

Midterm Rallies

The trends that developed over time in Trump's rally speeches were quite evident in Houston at the end of the midterm campaign in 2018. The nationalist, populist, and strongman elements of his message, along with the vernacular style, all were present in an exaggerated form. As at other rallies, Trump enacted the populist message by attacking the "fake news media" and instigating a chant of "CNN sucks!" Rather than attacking the political system, he specifically attacked Democrats, often combined with a nationalist appeal. For example, he said a victory by Democrats in the midterm would cause a "radical Democrat mob [to] take a giant wrecking ball and destroy our country and our economy." Unlike the Democrats, "we're putting America first," whereas "radical Democrats want to turn back the clock for the rule of corrupt power-hungry globalists." He said, "Democrats want to replace freedom with socialism," were "against your military," favored "open borders," would "replace the rule of law with the rule of the mob," and "have launched an assault on the sovereignty of our country." He also claimed, "Democrats don't care what their extremist immigration agenda will do to your neighborhoods, to your hospitals, or to your schools. They don't care that the mass illegal immigration will totally bankrupt our country." The speech also included standard attacks on unfair trade deals and other nationalist themes, and Trump proudly embraced the label of "nationalist." Striking, however, was the combination of the populist and nationalist themes in attacks not just on the media but on the Democratic Party.

There is a long tradition in American politics of sharply contesting political campaigns but always recognizing that members of the opposing party were the loyal opposition and loved their country and their families. Trump flouted that tradition with attacks that were extreme, untrue, and ridiculous in policy terms. Trump labeled Democrats, the press, and other critics un-American. His strategy at the rally in Houston and others at the end of the midterm campaign was based on "brazen racial and xenophobic fear-mongering" in order to make "supporters . . . feel besieged by dark-skinned people, immigrants, women, religious minorities, and, of course, the media."[10] Trump's escalation in tone also reflected the movement from the outsider to the strongman persona; he was willing to sharply undercut democratic norms in order to protect his own power.

Trump also expressed the strongman persona with utterly shameless bragging, often about accomplishments that simply had not occurred. For example, he claimed that "the plants and factories are coming back like never before," that he had passed the "biggest tax cut," that he had "started the wall," and that he had achieved other astonishing results, accomplishments he summarized with the statement, "I produced." The vernacular style was evident in stream-of-consciousness, often difficult to follow sections of the speech, such as four paragraphs early on in comparing his record in appointing judges with that of Washington himself.

In addition to the bragging, the speech also contained name-calling and other personal attacks. As was common, he focused on women and people of color, calling Senator Elizabeth Warren "a total fraud" and adding, "I can't use the name Pocahontas anymore" because "she has no Indian blood" despite the fact that Warren had released a DNA test proving she had Native American ancestry.[11] Trump also again labeled Representative Waters a "low-IQ individual" and attacked Senator Cory Booker (D-NJ) as "a horrible mayor." It was no accident that the personal insults were aimed at women and Black Americans.

Trump's rally speech in Houston enacted the defining elements of his rhetorical approach in a way that reflected the trends I have described. It was a mean-spirited speech that misstated the policy positions of Democrats in the campaign, leading Glenn Kessler, the chief fact checker of the *Washington Post,* to note that "at least 70 percent of the factual claims he makes at his rallies are false or misleading." Kessler added that Trump's portrayal of himself "as a super-action hero, slashing regulations, creating jobs, even saving money on embassy construction" was fundamentally inaccurate.[12]

Trump at the Conservative Political Action Conference

Trump's stream-of-consciousness speech at CPAC represented the evolution of his rhetoric after the Democrats captured the House in the 2018 midterms. It also reflected his total domination of the Republican Party, now fully the party of Trump. It was, by any standard for eloquence or even simple coherence, an undisciplined and mean-spirited speech. There was no discernable organization to the speech, which as Michael Gerson, former speechwriter for George W. Bush, noted, "skipped from enemy to enemy—a taunt here, a mock there." Gerson, a traditional conservative and before Trump a loyal Republican, assessed the quality of the speech by saying, "To a former speechwriter, it was like watching a wound drain; it was like eating toothpaste canapés." Gerson said that the speech comprised a "flood of lies" that came across as "the rhetorical spawn of Fidel Castro and George Wallace, combining demagoguery with bigotry in equal measure" and that it "confirmed Trump's place as the worst speaker in presidential history."[13]

Gerson's commentary was harsh but entirely understandable, given the many strange moments during the speech, which included Trump hugging the flag; swearing multiple times; bragging about going off-script; mocking his former attorney general, Jeff Sessions, from Alabama, by using a fake southern accent; and attacking opponents or restating grievances repeatedly. Vox identified the "7 Most Bizarre Moments," the *Hill* focused on the "Top 9 Moments from Trump's Two-Hour CPAC Speech," and CNN identified the "67 Most Stunning Lines."[14] The speech, which included "more than 100 false or misleading claims," was not designed to lay out a case for Trump's agenda.[15] There was almost no actual policy argument. Rather, the speech expressed the grievance, anger, fear, and vanity at the heart of Trump's rhetoric of nationalist populism with a strongman persona. It also reflected the strong emotional connection Trump had created with his core supporters. Press reporting described attendees as "a rapt audience" and "an exuberant crowd chanting 'Trump!'" and labeled the event a "lovefest."[16]

Trump's CPAC speech contained all the defining elements of his rhetoric of nationalist populism. He emphasized the nationalist theme on trade and the "lawless chaos on our southern border," which he claimed "provides a lucrative cash flow to some of the most dangerous criminal organizations on the planet" that they use to "flood our cities with drugs that kill thousands and thousands" (173). He claimed vast numbers of crimes were committed by undocumented immigrants (176–182) as well as focusing on the threat posed by "caravans" of these immigrants, including many "stone-cold killers" (187). He summarized, "We're being invaded by drugs, by people, by criminals" and returned to his "greatest hits" from the 2016 campaign, warning about "sanctuary cities" and saying he was going to "end 'catch-and-release'" policies and the "visa lottery" (198, 199, 201). Neither his claims about an immigration crisis nor his incredible accomplishments in resolving it were true. But the falseness of his narrative did not undercut the power of his message.

At other points, Trump focused on international trade, claiming his administration was "reversing decades of blunders and betrayals" committed by "the failed ruling class that enriched foreign countries at our expense. It wasn't 'America first.' In many cases, it was 'America last'" (10). He hit this theme again and again throughout the speech. In the conclusion he claimed, "Now you have a president who is standing up for America" and added that "after decades of building up foreign nations, we are finally building up our nation" (246, 247). Trump's dominance of the Republican Party was evident in his nationalist message on trade. For decades prior to Trump, Republicans had been proudly supportive of free trade. At CPAC, the formerly free-trade conservatives screamed their support for Trump.

Trump also made clear his core nationalist theme when he said, "Every day we're restoring common sense and the timeless values that unite us all. We believe in the Constitution and the rule of law. We believe in the First Amendment right. And we believe in religious liberty. And [we] believe strong[ly] in the Second Amendment and the right to keep and bear arms, which is under siege" (169). He then added what was essentially a campaign slogan for 2020, "We believe in the American Dream, not the socialist nightmare. And we believe in the words of our national motto: In God We Trust," a comment that appealed strongly to his base of support among evangelicals (170). Of course, not one of the freedoms Trump claimed to protect was under attack except freedom of the press, by Trump himself.

Trump supported his populist message with multiple attacks on the "fake news" (23, 25, 216). He excoriated the Mueller investigation, "this witch hunt, this phony deal that they put together; this phony thing that now looks like it's dying" (32, 226). He also claimed that the people investigating him "are sick" and labeled Adam Schiff, chair of the House Intelligence Committee, "little Shifty Schiff" and mocked his "collusion delusion" (32, 33). Trump claimed that Mueller's investigation was led by "13 of the angriest Democrats in the history of our country," that he "had a nasty business transaction with Robert Mueller," and that Mueller "wanted the job as FBI director" before he shifted to attacking the former director of the FBI as "Lyin' James Comey," who he said "did a horrible job at the FBI" (37, 38, 42). Trump also sampled from the "greatest hits" of his populist message in the 2016 campaign by referencing "Crooked Hillary" (93).

Trump also reflected the populist portion of his message by depicting political opponents as people who "hate our country" (78, 79) and attacking Democrats for supporting socialism, which he said was based on "power for the ruling class" (147). He claimed Democrats and the "hard left" supported "oppressive speech codes, censorship, [and] political correctness" (153) and were willing to "execute the baby after birth" (207). In Trump's narrative, he loved the United States, and his opponents did not. The extremist nature of Trump's attack on those investigating him and on his political opponents along with a torrent of lies undercut the democratic norms that had guided both parties in the postwar era.

By spring 2019, Trump's strongman persona was quite evident, reflected in multiple instances of bragging about his campaign and presidential accomplishments. It is notable that he focused on political as opposed to policy success. Early in the speech, he claimed, "What we did in 2016 . . . it's never been done before," a false claim false because a number of recent presidents had amassed more electoral votes than Trump *and* had won the national popular vote (3). Later, he claimed, "We had the greatest election," greater than "Andrew Jackson" or "Ronald Reagan," "the greatest of all time" (34–36). He also bragged about how during the campaign "we never had an empty seat" (52) before complaining bitterly that he had not been given credit for the enormous crowd at his inauguration (57–61), his claims of which had been widely debunked.[17] Trump also boasted about how "incredible" he had been in his 2019 State of the Union Address (63, 64) and claimed that his opponents in the Republican Party, "the Never Trumpers," "are on mouth-to-mouth resuscitation" (101). Astonishingly, he even claimed that the 2018 midterm elections, in which Republicans lost control of the House, had been "a tremendous victory," for which "we get no credit at all" (217, 229). He also boasted about what he had achieved in meetings with Kim Jong Un, when no substantive agreements had been reached at the meetings (236–244). At the end of the speech, he bragged that "not one person has left" during his more than two-hour speech, surely more a sign of the ego needs the speech filled for him than an accurate statement about the audience (251).

Enacting a theme common among strongmen around the world, Trump claimed he personally had implemented policies that produced massive benefits. For example, he maintained he personally "found some very old laws from when our country was rich—really rich" that he was using in the various tariff battles (14–18). It is notable that he mentioned 1888 as a time when the nation "didn't know what to do with all of the money we were making" (18). Of course, the nation was much poorer in 1888 than at any point in recent history, but in 1888 white male dominance was unquestioned. Later, he bragged about how in the tariff battle with China "billions of dollars, right now, are pouring into our Treasury" and praised himself for various other accomplishments that either had not happened or that continued economic trends going back to the second year of the Obama presidency (29). Representative examples include: "I'm building the wall," "companies are roaring back into our country," the "world respects our country again," and "America is now booming like never before" (76, 77, 89, 90). Although no significant new wall was being built, the nation was much less respected in the world than during Obama's presidency, and economic trends were quite similar to those of the second Obama administration, Trump's persona required that he brag about major accomplishments even if they were largely imaginary.[18]

Throughout the speech, Trump relied on the vernacular style I have described. At several points, he violated normal presidential decorum by swearing (194), at one point bragged about how in the midterm election "we kicked their ass" (222), and at another claimed his critics were "trying to take you out with bullshit" (36). Clearly, his norm violation was designed to send the message that he was an authentic leader who understood the needs of his supporters. He repeatedly emphasized this message by telling the audience "I'm totally off-script" and even claiming that "I got elected, by being off-script" (19, 72).

The vernacular style was most obvious when Trump mocked his critics. For example, in the middle of his discussion of tariffs, for no apparent reason he mocked supporters of a proposal to dramatically increase use of renewable energy known as the Green New Deal by claiming there would be "no planes. No energy" (21). He imitated a supporter of the proposal, asking, "Darling, is the wind blowing today? I'd like to watch television, darling"

(21). Later in the speech, he made fun of the Green New Deal itself, claiming it would require taking "trains to Hawaii" and would ban air travel to Europe (96). He also ridiculed an unidentified female senator from Hawaii (apparently Mazie Hirono), claiming she said of the Green New Deal, "Well, I don't know how people are going to get to Hawaii, but I'm in favor of the plan" (141). He also mocked those who opposed his immigration policies, claiming they said about someone who "killed four people": "'Oh, here's a wonderful person. Wonderful'" (204). The point of these examples was not argument but derision. They are a sign of how little facts matter at Trump rallies or, more broadly, in many contexts in American politics.

Watching or reading the CPAC speech makes it easy to understand why Gerson critiqued it so strongly. Yet the video, the transcript, and the press reporting all make clear that the audience responded positively to the speech. They expressed the emotional bond Trump had created with core supporters who, it seems, had become forever Trumpers. Trump's consistent polling also indicates the strength of this emotional bond. His CPAC speech defied all conventional standards, but the nationalist and populist themes, along with the outsider/strongman persona and vernacular style present in the speech, clearly cemented the emotional bond he had developed with his supporters.

Trump's speech at CPAC reflected the evolution of his rhetoric after the midterm election. His speeches were aimed at creating fear, anger, and a sense of grievance through variations on the central message of his campaign/presidency, nationalist populism, an outsider image that took on characteristics of the strongman over time, and a vernacular style. A rally speech on July 17, 2019, in North Carolina illustrates how his escalation of tactics at CPAC dominated his rallies after the midterm election and how he adapted his speeches not to the issues of the moment but to the grievance of the moment.[19] The speech in North Carolina drew a lot of press attention because it included an attack on Representative Ilhan Omar (D-MN), who Trump claimed "looks down with contempt on the hardworking" in an obvious attempt to produce the same kind of anger over disrespect for white working-class supporters he had activated in the 2016 campaign. In response to his attacks and a tweet in which he suggested Omar and three other women-of-color US representatives should leave the country, the crowd chanted "Send her back!" twelve times, according to the transcript.[20]

The North Carolina speech, the chant it produced, and the tweet were widely criticized "for stoking racial divisions," and the House of Representatives later passed a resolution condemning Trump's words.[21] In fact, both the tweet and the speech were part of a strategy of activating fear and a sense of grievance to create emotional solidarity with Trump. The pattern that dominated all his rhetoric was clearly present in this speech. He enacted the nationalist theme by bragging about progress against free trade and warning of terrible crimes committed by undocumented immigrants. The populist theme was reflected in three attacks on the Mueller and congressional investigations of the "Russian hoax" or just "the hoax"; two attacks on the "fake news"; multiple attacks on Democrats as "left-wing extremists" or the "radical left" or similar labels; attacks on particular Democratic candidates, including a reference to former vice president Joe Biden as "Sleepy Joe"; and five references to Warren as "Pocahontas" in addition to the attack on Omar. He demonized Democrats as anti-American, saying, for example, "They want to demolish our Constitution, weaken our military, eliminate the values that built this magnificent country." He also said, "The Democrat agenda is anti-worker, anti-jobs, anti-citizen, anti-family, and anti–common sense" and added that the party was "being violent, so vicious, moving so far left, it's out of control." He claimed Democrats want "to take away your guns" and support policies that would allow "ripping babies straight from the mother's womb right up until the moment of birth." The claims were outrageous and obviously false, but along with attacks on the media, they were the only available means of stating his populist message given Republican control of the Senate and presidency but Democratic control of the House.

The other aspects of Trump's core message also were present. The business outsider persona was evident in constant bragging about the economy, his victory in the 2016 election, and how respected he was in the world. The vernacular style was obvious in the stream-of-consciousness organization, the personal attacks, and the use of the word "bullshit." And the evolution toward a strongman persona was present in not only the attack on investigations of his presidency and the media but also in a discussion of the idea that he might serve more than two terms, about which he said, "Maybe that is a good idea."

For brief moments, Trump actually did discuss public policy, including a false claim that "patients with preexisting conditions are protected by Republicans much more so than protected by Democrats," but the policy section of the speech was mostly bragging about the continuation of economic trends from the Obama years. And of course, the speech was widely attacked for expressing racist and un-American views and, like all his rally speeches, was filled with lies.[22] In other words, it was quite similar to what he said at CPAC and reflected the evolution of his message after the Democrats took control of the House of Representatives. He said dangerous Others were threatening the nation; blamed Democrats, the media, and those investigating him for protecting those Others or other sins; presented himself as a heroic friend to ordinary citizens; and used a vernacular style to reinforce a sense of authenticity. It was a pattern designed to create anger and fear, activate a sense of grievance, and construct a strong emotional bond with Trump. Despite the falsity of many of his claims, his message clearly resonated with his supporters.

Trump continued to hold multiple rallies throughout 2019 and in January and February 2020 in which he presented a message similar to what he had said at CPAC and in North Carolina, expressing particular anger toward Democrats and the media and decrying his impeachment by the House of Representatives. The rallies, including ten in early 2020, continued until the spread of the COVID-19 virus created a pandemic and the Centers for Disease Control (CDC) recommended that people not gather in large crowds. This led Trump to seek a substitute for the rally atmosphere. He found that substitute with increased use of Twitter, interviews with friendly news organizations, and confrontational news briefings about the pandemic.

Transforming Pandemic Briefings into Rallies

Although Trump received "warnings about the novel coronavirus in more than a dozen classified briefings . . . in January and February" 2020, and numerous studies had "seen a coronavirus-like pandemic as a threat," "he continued to play down the threat," claiming on January 22, 2020, to have the virus "totally under control." In this period, he consistently rejected expert scientific opinion and minimized the threat posed by the virus.[23] As late as February 26, 2020, he said of the virus, "Within a couple of days [it] is going to be down to close to zero" cases in the country.[24] Peter Baker observed of this statement, "In the annals of the American presidency, it would be hard to recall a more catastrophically wrong prediction."[25] When it became clear that the COVID-19 virus was spreading rapidly and threatening to kill hundreds of thousands of Americans or, according to one estimate, as many as

2 million, states banned mass events and the Trump campaign was forced to stop holding rallies, although he did invite himself to Tulsa, Oklahoma, and Phoenix, Arizona, against local authorities' wishes, to hold ill-advised rallies with attendees unmasked and not distancing from each other.[26]

Experts agreed that the crisis called for a shutdown of many businesses, widespread wearing of face masks, strict social distancing rules limiting how people interacted, a massive program of testing to identify both the infected and the rate of spread of the virus, and contact tracing of all those potentially exposed by infected people.[27] These steps would limit the spread of the virus to a manageable level, not overwhelming the health-care system until a treatment or vaccine could be developed. Several developed nations, including Australia, Germany, New Zealand, and Norway, used such a strategy to limit the toll of the disease. Although experts in the United States recognized the scope of the problem and the actions that must be taken to control the crisis, the Trump administration failed to rapidly implement the required strategy.[28] The result was a much higher death total than in much of the developed world, with the United States eventually having one-quarter of the worldwide cases.[29] Commentators and experts agreed that considerable blame for the nation's failures rested with the Trump administration.[30] Dana Milbank's comment that "Trump has abandoned attempts to control the pandemic" reflects the consensus view.[31]

The COVID-19 pandemic was a public health catastrophe and also an economic crisis because the shutdown caused tens of millions of workers to be fired, laid off, or furloughed from their jobs.[32] The pandemic also created a political crisis for the administration. With the pandemic and associated economic collapse, Trump could no longer point to the strong economy as a rationale for his reelection and, therefore, had to implement or support legislation responding to the twin crises and use rhetoric to both inform members of the American public about how to lessen their risk of exposure and reassure them that the country would weather the storm. Rather than following this course, Trump largely outsourced policy to the states and Congress, transformed briefings about the crisis into quasi–campaign rallies, and refused to set an example for his supporters by wearing a mask in public.[33]

In past public health emergencies, briefings were usually handled by the Centers for Disease Control (CDC), with the head of the agency often taking the lead to educate and reassure the public about the crisis. For example, when Ebola threatened the nation, Obama largely left public briefings to his head of the CDC, Thomas Frieden. In taking this course, the Obama administration was following the plan developed by public health professionals for how to communicate publicly in a crisis.[34]

Trump took a different approach by first assigning Vice President Mike Pence to lead the pandemic response and then taking over the press briefings himself, putting the nation's top public health experts in a secondary position by essentially forcing them to operate under a "gag order."[35] Trump's approach broke "almost every rule" in the CDC's "450-page manual outlining how U.S. leaders should talk to the public during crises."[36] The press briefings quickly became a substitute for campaign rallies, drawing 8.5 million viewers on cable networks and many more on the internet and broadcast TV.[37] As in Trump's rally speeches, the nationalist, populist, and strongman themes were evident, along with a vernacular style quite different from the careful and calm precision found in CDC briefings about earlier public health threats.

The briefings typically began with a formal statement from the president, usually restrained in tone and focused on new developments supporting the underlying claim that his administration was doing a great job. Such political statements are not normally found in public health briefings, but the briefings were also dissimilar from Trump's rally speeches, somewhat resembling the "special occasion" stylistic pattern found in scripted aspects of Trump's formal policy speeches. After the formal statements, in the question-and-answer portion of the briefings, Trump presented the same message that dominated his presidential rallies. A study found that in thirty-five briefings between March 16 and April 25, 2020, Trump spoke for a total of more than twenty-eight hours, or more than 60 percent of the time, in all the briefings. In a three-week period, Trump spent "two hours . . . on attacks" in his answers to "113 out of 346 questions," "45 minutes praising himself," and "just 4.5 minutes expressing condolences for coronavirus victims." He also made "false or misleading [statements] in nearly a quarter" of his prepared statements or answers to questions, amounting to forty-seven minutes of briefing time. Rather than providing information and reassurance, Trump used the sessions "to vent and rage; to dispense dubious and even dangerous medical advice; and to lavish praise upon himself and his government" in what was called "a daily talk show, hosted by a self-centered blowhard worried only about his poll numbers."[38] Similarly, a *New York Times* analysis of 260,000 words in briefings from March 9 through mid-April found that "the most recurring utterances from Mr. Trump in the briefings are self-congratulations, roughly 600 of them, which are often predicated on exaggerations and false-hoods." Trump also often blamed China or others for the virus and often bragged about his decision to shut down travel from China.[39] Empathy for those sickened or killed by the virus or those who lost jobs in the crashing economy was not a focus of the briefings, leading one commentator to conclude, "Trump is simply incapable of offering the kind of emotional support the country needs at a time like this."[40]

In briefings early in the crisis, Trump was much more restrained in his language and overall message than he would be later when the briefings became more and more similar to rallies. For example, most of his first briefing on March 13, 2020, consisted of reporting on the status of the outbreak as well as discussion of new regulations to control the virus and actions by various federal agencies and corporations. Only at the end of this briefing, in the question-and-answer segment, did nationalist populism emerge. When asked whether he took responsibility for a lag in testing, he denied responsibility, blamed the Obama administration for "regulations, and specifications from a different time," and then called Obama's response to a swine flu epidemic in which 14,000 died a "disaster." He later labeled a question about his administration having dissolved the White House office focused on planning for a pandemic as "nasty." In the conclusion to the briefing, the populist, outsider/strongman, and vernacular style of his rhetoric were evident. At this point, the nationalist message was largely absent because he was still praising a trade deal he had made with China.[41]

This pattern of partial restraint was also evident on March 16, when Trump answered a question about social distancing by saying, "Let me just have the professionals answer that." By the end of the briefing that day, however, he was taking the lead again, rating his administration's performance a "10" and implicitly blaming the Obama administration for the CDC's botched testing plan, claiming, "We really took over an obsolete system. . . . And we're doing something that's never been done in this country. And I think that we are doing very well."[42] In this briefing, the nationalist theme was also beginning to emerge when he implicitly blamed China for the virus by taking credit for shutting down travel between the two nations, bragging, "We did make a good decision; we closed our borders to China very quickly, very rapidly" and adding that "otherwise, . . . we'd be in a very bad position, much worse than we would be right now." Just two days later, he was more explicit in first putting responsibility for the pandemic on China, stating, "It could have been stopped right where it came from—China," then taking credit for limiting travel from China to the United States, saying, "I called for a ban from people coming in from China long before anybody thought it was—in fact, it was your network—I believe they called me a racist because I did that."[43] He bragged about the travel ban or explicitly shifted blame to China in several other early briefings as well.[44] The nationalist theme was also evident in Secretary of State Mike Pompeo's consistent labeling of COVID-19 the "Wuhan virus," thereby vilifying the country where it originated.[45] Trump also enacted the nationalist theme by blaming the World Health Organization (WHO) for failing to act rapidly to confront the virus.[46] Unsurprisingly, Trump's attacks on China for failing to control the virus became a common topic in right-wing media.[47]

Trump enacted the populist theme by undercutting the idea of expertise itself. This occurred most prominently when Trump praised the drug hydroxychloroquine, saying there are "very strong, powerful signs" that it worked against COVID-19. He later denied expertise was essential for making judgments about treatment, saying, "I'm not a doctor. But I have common sense," appealing to the antielitist sentiment in his base and reinforcing his persona as the outsider/strongman who knew better than the experts.[48] Trump also touted the drug to conservative media, pressed the Food and Drug Administration (FDA) to allow emergency use of the drug to fight COVID-19, which it did, and reportedly took the drug himself to guard against infection. When studies demonstrated that risks of using the drug were quite serious, the FDA was forced to issue warnings about its use and revoke the emergency-use authorization.[49] But even as Trump's "common sense" was undercut, it is important to recognize that his advocacy for hydroxychloroquine reinforced his image as the outsider who knew better than the experts. Unfortunately, his failure to follow experts both increased the overall death rate because of treatment failure and led to cases of poisoning and death.[50]

The role of an outsider/strongman and an associated vernacular style was also beginning to be evident in the press briefings. In the briefing on March 16, when the virus was spreading rapidly, Trump bragged, "We've done a fantastic job from just about every standpoint." In addition, he "repeatedly accused the news media, governors, Democratic members of Congress, and former President Barack Obama of being responsible for the number of cases overwhelming the nation's hospitals."[51] In this narrative, Trump's enemies, foreign and domestic, were to blame for the crisis, and he could deny any culpability. Trump also demanded "more gratitude" from Democratic governors of hard-hit states such as Washington and Michigan for the help his administration had provided, in so doing enacting the populist and strongman themes in his rhetoric.[52] On occasion, he used the briefings to send a political message similar to that of his rallies. For example, in one briefing, he "lapsed back into complaints about the impeachment 'hoax' and renewed his attack on critics like James B. Comey, the former F.B.I. director."[53] He also lashed out at reporters who questioned any aspect of his blame shifting and credit taking.[54] The attacks on the media came "in torrents" aimed at "solidifying a population of supporters who believe Trump over the media even when presented with evidence upending their inclinations."[55]

In the briefings, Trump claimed to be totally in charge while simultaneously displacing both blame and responsibility onto governors and other officials, in this way enacting the strongman persona and attempting to deflect responsibility for the growing death total. For example, in a briefing on April 13, 2020, he expressed the strongman persona, stating, "When somebody is the president of the United States, the authority is total," a claim not, in fact, true.[56] At the same time, he made no attempt to dictate policy to governors, preferring to urge them to reopen business, a position that allowed him to take credit for the economic benefits of reopening but also deny responsibility for any surge in cases and deaths.[57] In the briefing on March 13, 2020, he said simply, "I don't take responsibility at all."[58] At the same time he denied responsibility for government failures, he took credit for all successes, often claiming to have "done a great job." He linked that "great job" to the nationalist and populist themes, claiming, "It started with the fact that we kept a very highly infected country—despite all of the—even the professionals saying, 'No, it's too early to do that.' We were very, very early with respect to China."[59]

The "picked fights [and] childish slights," along with the bragging and falsehoods, were "an attempt to divert attention away from a historic fiasco," with a strategy of producing "chaos and mystification" so that people did not realize "what a catastrophic failure Trump has been."[60] Trump's strategy was "to try to frame the political narrative on his own terms, even when at variance with the facts, through relentless repetition and the power of his bully pulpit" to support the view that, in Trump's words, "we did all the right moves."[61] The ultimate impact was not to change views, because polling indicated a sharp "partisan split on trusting the information" he provided, but to confirm "preconceived notions about him."[62]

The transformation of public health briefings into quasi–campaign rallies was perhaps most apparent in the April 23, 2020, press briefing.[63] The briefing looked nothing like those normally conducted by CDC officials during a public health emergency. Although Trump had emphasized the nationalist theme in earlier briefings by blaming China, the WHO, or Democrats for the growing pandemic, he moved away from that theme in this case because it did not fit with his message about surmounting the crisis through his brilliant leadership.

At the end of a scripted introductory statement, Trump claimed that enormous progress had been made confronting both the virus and the economic devastation: "Our country is going to do fantastically well. You see what's going on. There is a pent-up demand in our country to get it back right where it was and maybe even better, and that's what's going to happen." It was an odd thing to say at a time when there had already been more than 40,000 deaths from the virus and the economy had lost roughly 20 million jobs. Then, after a statement on the effects that humidity, cleaners such as bleach, and sunlight had on how long the virus can survive on a surface of some kind, Trump suggested that treatments could be developed based on this research. First the president said, "So, supposing we hit the body with a tremendous—whether it's ultraviolet or just very powerful light—and . . . [bring] the light inside the body, which you can do either through the skin or in some other way." Alarmingly, but typical for a government with a strongman leader, the official who made the presentation felt the need to cater to the president and promised to have "the right folks" look into the obviously absurd potential treatment. Then, Trump suggested that household cleaners might be used to treat the virus: "And then I see the disinfectant, where it knocks it out in a minute. One minute. And is there a way we can do something like that, by injection inside or almost a cleaning," adding that "it would be interesting to check that." Late in the briefing, he returned to the subject: "I would like you to speak to the medical doctors to see if there's any way that you can apply light and heat to cure." He concluded, "I'm not a doctor. But I'm like a person that has a good you know what." Here, Trump implicitly claimed that he did not need expert advice to lead the nation. It is concerning that up to this point in the briefing, one of his chief medical advisors, Deborah Birx, sitting in a chair a few feet from the podium, had said nothing. Only when Trump looked at her directly did she state that his proposals could not function "as a treatment." The populist and outsider/strongman themes were also apparent when reporters attempted to question Trump on the dangerous suggestions that ingesting cleaners or irradiating organs with ultraviolet light might cure the disease. In response, Trump labeled the reporter asking the question a "total faker."

Following this exchange, Trump's war with the press escalated as he refused to take a question from a CNN reporter and at the end of the briefing claimed, "We've gotten very little credit for the great job we've done because of the media. Because the media is not an honest media." He also enacted the populist theme, labeling Biden "a sleepy guy in a basement of a house that the press is giving a free pass to who doesn't want to do debates because of COVID." As at his rallies, Trump drew on past grievances by complaining about the treatment his administration had received concerning "a fake Russia, Russia, Russia deal; an impeachment hoax—it was a total hoax; . . . [and] an illegal witch hunt." He also hit the populist theme and played up his leadership skills as an outsider/strongman when he downplayed the economic threats facing the nation by denying that economists had any special expertise: "I know a lot about economists, and the answer is they have no idea. I think I have as good an idea as anybody, and I think our economy will start to pick up very substantially, as soon as the states get open."

The outsider/strongman persona was also evident in Trump's boasting, which dominated the second half of the briefing, about his administration's tracing program and his claim that "we're very advanced in testing" despite the fact that experts agreed the nation lagged in testing.[64] On testing, he enacted the disdain for experts so typical of nationalist populism by stating his disagreement with Anthony Fauci, long-serving director of the National Institute of Allergy and Infectious Diseases, who had said that the nation must make more progress on testing. Trump responded, "No, I don't agree with him on that. No, I think we're doing a great job in testing." He then boasted that "we're doing phenomenally, in terms of mortality," despite leading much of the developed world in per capita deaths. He also claimed the administration had done "incredibly well" in supplying ventilators, masks, and other medical supplies to the states, and at the end of the briefing he said that without his administration's actions, "we would have lost millions of people." Pence's praise of the president for his strong leadership throughout the briefing also reflected the strongman persona. A strongman leader often expects such over-the-top praise from subordinates.

Trump's coronavirus briefing on April 23, 2020, functioned much more like a rally than a public health briefing. In it, he focused on the strongman and populists themes that dominated his rhetoric, expressing a disdain for experts, attacking the media and Democrats, and bragging shamelessly about his administration's responses despite rising death totals and massive economic losses. He combined the two messages when he directed medical researchers to consider using household cleaners or ultraviolet radiation to treat the disease. His message perfectly fit the atmosphere of a partisan rally at which his audience despised Democrats, blamed the media, and viewed experts as arrogant and out of touch. As a public health briefing, it was simply a disaster.

The response to the briefing was withering. Matt Flegenheimer noted that Trump's comments about "virus remedies . . . [produced] widespread condemnation as dangerous to the health of Americans," "inspiring a near-universal alarm" as well as "a flurry of backlash and ridicule."[65] State health officials responding to a significant increase in calls to poison hotlines were forced to issue warnings telling "people not to consume laundry detergent capsules," and even Lysol felt the need to make a statement urging "people not to ingest disinfectant."[66] Trump's comments also led to derisive criticisms from commentators and late-night talk show hosts.[67] Gerson labeled the briefing "arrogant ignorance" and predicted that it "may be remembered as the moment his schtick finally failed."[68] Gerson's point was that neither COVID-19 nor the economic collapse it caused could be confronted through Trump's rhetoric of bullying, bragging, and populist attacks on the media and experts. It would take real medical advances, not quack therapies, to control the virus. The toll of the virus was apparent to all. No attempt to blame China or accuse Democrats of hating the United States and no amount of bragging or bullying could obscure the reality of the situation. In this context, it is understandable that Trump largely stopped holding pandemic press briefings. They no longer served the function of rallies and revealed the failures of his administration's pandemic response.

Over summer 2020, although he sometimes labeled meetings with the press as briefings on the pandemic, he quickly reverted to his nationalist populist message; expressions of grievance against Democrats and the press; and a description of an imagined world in which the virus was controlled, the economy was rapidly rebounding, and Democrats were radical anti-American socialists who wanted to eliminate borders, defund the police, and destroy suburbs by filling them with dangerous Others.[69]

The weakness of Trump's nationalist populist message in response to a real emergency was also emphasized when he attempted to energize his supporters by holding his first rally since the pandemic began in Tulsa, Oklahoma, on June 20, 2020. The rally reflected the continued development of the nationalist populist and outsider/strongman message he expressed at CPAC and in the 2018 midterm rallies. It combined a "litany of racially offensive stereotypes" with "fearmongering," a strong attack on experts in which he even bragged about telling "my people [to] slow the testing down," and demonstrated a "near total absence of a positive agenda for reelection."[70] It did, however, demonstrate the limitations of what Gerson labeled his "schtick" in confronting a crisis, a point evident in the fact that only one-third of the 19,000 seats in the arena were filled.[71]

The same point was evident at the Republican National Convention (RNC), where at the height of the pandemic the president gave his nomination acceptance address to the national audience as well as 1,500 mostly maskless supporters crowded together on the White House lawn.[72] In his address, the president described the nation as a place where his outsider/strongman leadership had produced an economic boom and a pandemic response vastly superior to those of other developed nations.[73] In Trump's alternative reality, cities led by Democrats were a dystopia of crime and rioting, and Democratic nominee Biden was not a moderate liberal but both incredibly weak and a dangerous radical socialist who wanted to protect looters and criminal immigrants.[74] Trump presented no coherent policy agenda save an extension of the nationalist populism that had dominated his administration, along with a veneer of Reaganesque appeals to patriotism and unity. His speech functioned as "a tape loop" repetition of the message of both his rallies and his presidential addresses wrapped together, producing adulation from his most loyal supporters, derision from opponents, and a shrug of boredom from less loyal supporters and a small group of politically engaged but undecided voters.[75]

After the RNC, Trump again started holding rallies, although much smaller than before the pandemic and mostly in outdoor spaces such as airplane hangars, presenting the same nationalist populist and strongman appeals as in Tulsa and Phoenix and his RNC address. He continued this practice with a message "even uglier than in previous Trump rallies" until his imagined version of a nation that had triumphed over the virus ran up against the hard reality of his own diagnosis with the disease, and he was forced to stop holding rallies for ten days. His experience with the virus did not change his message when he returned to the rally stage and spoke to an audience in which "many . . . did not wear masks." Rather, he presented "his regular, factually challenged campaign stump speech, in which he brags about killing terrorists and building a wall along the southwestern border and accuses the news media of being 'frauds.'"[76] Even in a moment that demanded an expression of concern for all those who had died in the pandemic and for those who had not been able to receive the world-class care a president receives, he instead returned to the nationalist, populist, and strongman themes along with a vernacular style that dominated all his presidential rhetoric. It was the only message he had.

Conclusion

Trump's goal at presidential rallies was to create fear and anger to energize his supporters and to distract them from policy failures, ongoing investigations, and his own outrageous conduct. In discussing the earlier rally speech in Phoenix, I cited Trump's extremely defensive justification of his remarks following the march by white supremacists and neo-Nazis that resulted in violence that killed one counterprotester in Charlottesville. In this case, Trump refused to stick with a statement unequivocally attacking racism as "evil" that he had made two days after his initial infamous "very fine people on both sides" comment.[77] Instead, he bashed the media for treating him unfairly and continued to fan racial discord by attacking efforts to remove Confederate monuments from cities and towns across the South. In this and other rallies, he continued to pick a fight. The fights kept his core supporters energized and served as a distraction from real policy failures and ongoing investigations of his administration.

The same pattern would occur again and again in rally speeches, interviews, and on Twitter. It might seem that Trump's rhetoric often administered self-inflicted wounds to his administration. Based on polling about Trump, Perry Bacon Jr. and Dhrumil Mehta of FiveThirtyEight.com concluded, "Trump's popularity—and thus the GOP's midterm fortunes—is likely being dragged down by his personality characteristics and behavior. He should probably, say, stop tweeting. He would likely help his position if he stopped telling so many lies."[78] In this view, if Trump had spoken and acted in a more conventionally presidential manner, he would have been much more popular.

The view that Trump would have been more popular had his rhetoric been more traditional is misguided. Trump himself made this point in the rally in Wilkes-Barre I discussed earlier, at which he said it would be "easy . . . to be presidential, but you'd all be out of here right now" because "you'd be so bored." Trump's appeal was based on his status as an outsider. As president, he was the celebrity business strongman who would force change. If he had somehow rhetorically transformed himself into a normal Republican, someone like Jeb Bush or Marco Rubio, he would not have sounded authentic. Moreover, he was constrained by his promises to "drain the swamp," replace Obamacare with a much better health-care system, produce massive job and wage growth, and so forth. It was difficult to blame the elites for blocking his program when Republicans were in charge of both the Congress and the presidency. Moreover, by the midterm campaign, a number of senior figures in the Trump administration, including cabinet officers, had already left it after stories of questionable expenditures or other misconduct became public.[79] It appeared to some that rather than "draining the swamp," Trump had imported it to the White House.[80] These developments forced Trump to shift the populist portion of his message toward more and more strident attacks on the media and over time on the investigations of him, which in Wilkes-Barre he called the "Russia hoax."

Nor could Trump simply shift his rhetoric and focus on his administration's accomplishments. As he admitted, such an approach risked boring his supporters. In addition, he had demonstrated little facility with policy advocacy. For that reason, he addressed issues only in general terms during the campaign and his presidency, promising voters massive improvement, an argument that became increasingly difficult over time because no progress had been made on infrastructure and Obamacare had not been repealed. In addition, the effort to repeal the ACA informed the public about the law, and by spring 2018, 54 percent of the public viewed it favorably as opposed to 42 percent who viewed it unfavorably.[81] Although the economy continued to create new jobs, albeit at a pace slightly lower than at the end of Obama's second term, little else in economic trends aided Trump's core supporters in the white working class. In addition, by summer 2018, it was clear the tax bill was not going to produce a major jump in wages for the working class. In fact, between July 2017 and July 2018, hourly earnings adjusted for inflation decreased by .2 percent.[82] The failure of the tax bill to produce significant income gain for the middle and working classes created a situation in the midterm campaign in which Democrats focused much more heavily on attacking the law than Republicans did in defending it, and by a 38 to 33 percent margin voters were less likely to vote for Republicans because of the legislation.[83] Of course, it became still more difficult for Trump to tout his economic record when the failure to contain the COVID-19 virus led to a pandemic and economic collapse.

These dynamics gave Trump little option but to double down on the nationalist and strongman aspects of his message and shift the populist theme from attacking elites and draining the swamp to attacking the press, Democrats, and the Russia "hoax." The rhetorical situation also explains why Trump made outrageous statement after outrageous statement. Trump used these controversies to keep his followers engaged, maintain the us-versus-them message of his campaign, and distract supporters from the official investigations of him and the absence of real accomplishments helping the working class.

Trump also used this approach to account for a major difficulty with the nationalist portion of his message—it was largely untrue. Undocumented immigrants were not a major drag on the economy, and they were not committing a massive amount of crime, although as in any group, there were some criminals. Islamic terrorism was not a major threat. The same point could be made about refugees, NFL players protesting police violence against Black Americans, or any of the other groups Trump attacked. In addition, Trump's use of tariffs to produce a more favorable trading environment that would protect US manufacturing and agriculture had the effect of raising prices and limiting exports when other countries retaliated.[84] Given this situation, Trump used rallies, Twitter wars, and other controversies of the moment to divert his opponents and followers from the larger issues and the multiple political crises his administration experienced.[85] Creation of outrage became his core weapon for motivating his base. This explains why Trump stuck with his message even in cases in which his comments were widely criticized, such as after Charlottesville, or when his policies were deeply unpopular, as with family separation of undocumented immigrants and refugees in summer 2018. Trump knew that his core supporters responded strongly to rhetoric that activated their fear of declining white dominance in society. Thus, he had little choice but to emphasize the nationalist portion of his message.

Moreover, the sense of tribal loyalty among Republicans had become so strong that Trump could be confident they would stick with him even if some found his Twitter comments or other remarks distasteful. Tribal loyalty rather than genuine accomplishments made his approval rating "remarkably stable" over the first two years of his presidency. That stability reflected 84 percent approval among Republicans and "a wider gap between Republicans' and Democrats' views of Trump than for any other U.S. president in the modern era of polling."[86]

Trump's rally speeches as president reflected the same essential pattern as during the 2016 campaign, but they also represented radicalization of that pattern, particularly in attacks on political opponents and the press and in a vernacular style that constantly violated basic norms of political speech. At the rallies, particularly during and after the midterm campaign, Trump seemed more like the angry leader of an alt-right group or an authoritarian strongman such as Hugo Chavez than any other American president or any presidential candidate since Wallace.

This radicalization of Trump's rhetoric was quite evident in his response to largely peaceful protests that occurred following the death of George Floyd in police custody in Minneapolis, Minnesota. Floyd's murder by a police officer who suffocated him with his knee on Floyd's neck for more than eight minutes led to massive protests (and isolated cases of looting) in reaction to the ongoing crisis of police brutality experienced by Black Americans. Trump's response was to further radicalize the nationalist portion of his message with calls for "'shooting' looters," a vow "to call in troops to 'dominate' the streets," and consistent use of "Law and Order" as a slogan. His "combative pro-police, anti-protester platform" was similar, as Peter Baker noted, to "Wallace's inflammatory language" in 1968.[87] Conservative commentator Max Boot also compared Trump's rhetoric to that of Wallace, concluding, "The president is pouring gasoline on the flames of racial division."[88] In this crisis, even Trump's official remarks, such as a statement in the Rose Garden of the White House on June 1, 2020, echoed the harsh message of his rallies. Trump stated, "We are ending the riots and lawlessness that has spread throughout our country," instructed mayors and governors that they "must establish an overwhelming law enforcement presence," and warned them that if they did not take those actions, "then I will deploy the United States military and quickly solve the problem for them."[89] In statements such as this one as well as COVID-19 briefings, the rally message had supplanted formal presidential speeches and briefings.

The radicalization of Trump's rhetoric in rallies, press interviews, and other contexts similar to rallies, such as the contentious news briefings he held about the COVID-19 virus, enacted what rhetorical theorist Kenneth Burke described as the entelechial tendency to push any form of rhetoric to the "end of the line" by taking it to an extreme.[90] Burke sometimes explained entelechialization as motivated by the "perfection" principle, in this case the perfection of Trump's nationalist populist message by labeling opponents both un-American and a danger to the nation and the press both "fake" and the "enemy of the people." The outsider persona was entelechialized into that of a strongman who bragged about largely imaginary accomplishments, demonized opponents and Others who posed no threat to the nation, and threatened to overturn decisions by state governors about how to respond to COVID-19 or to send in the military to deal with protesters. The vernacular style of the campaign was perfected as Trump made more and more vulgar comments, enacting "a quasi-adult version of the playground bully's jeer."[91] As I explain in Chapter 6, a similar pattern was occurring in social media, especially on Twitter.

Rallies and contexts similar to rallies matter not only because of their role in a campaign because they sometimes drive public opinion but also because they reflect and enact democratic norms. Demonization of opponents is particularly dangerous because it can undercut grounds for compromise and lead to violence. At a crucial point in the 2008 campaign, Senator John McCain rejected entelechialization when he told a supporter that although he disagreed with Obama, his opponent was a good family man and not a threat to the republic.[92] In contrast, Trump's rally rhetoric was driven by the entelechial principle because he embraced a rhetoric of demonization, fear-mongering, threats, and bragging. As president, Trump used a nationalist populist message along with the strongman persona and associated vernacular style to create conflict in order to maintain a strong emotional connection with supporters. Press reporting on the rally in North Carolina made clear the emotional power of the bond. Karen Tumulty's description of those attending the rally as a "hateful crowd of Trump supporters" and of the rally itself as an expression of "poisonous sentiment" and "toxic" enthusiasm reflects the consensus view.[93] The same could have been said of any Trump rally.

When rhetoric produces such a strong emotional bond, attacks on the leader will be seen as fundamentally illegitimate and potentially as justification for action undercutting democratic norms. Writing in the *New York Times,* Miriam Beard described the emotional power of rallies and associated rhetoric as a situation in which, by tapping into the "small-town mentality," "the village had been mobilized as never before." Through the use of "Barnum and Bailey" techniques, the candidate produced the "biggest show ever offered," which tapped into "antifeminism" and appealed "readily to jobless men" in a campaign its leader called a "'revolt against reason.'"[94] The applicability to Trump rallies and his ongoing campaign is obvious. It is chilling, however, that Beard was writing about Adolf Hitler before he fully assumed power in Germany. Trump is not Hitler, but his rhetoric in rallies and the response it produces is similar enough to be terrifying.

6

Trump's Dystopian Twitterverse

Twitter was a perfect venue for Trump to reinforce his warnings about dangerous Others and attacks on elites, Democrats, those investigating him, and the press as well as to express praise for followers and especially himself.[1] In essence, Twitter enabled Trump to extend the rally atmosphere beyond the time and place of an actual event. Through this mechanism, as Shontavia Johnson noted, his "campaign successfully crowdsourced a message of anger and fear by leveraging the knowledge, contacts, and skills of his followers to disseminate his tweets widely," creating, according to a "political operative," "'a continuous Trump rally that happens on Twitter at all hours.'"[2]

After assuming the presidency, Trump continued to use Twitter to serve the same functions as it did during the campaign, creating a situation in which the "political universe [was] reshaped by Mr. Trump's Twitter feed."[3] In addition, Twitter also became a weapon he used against perceived enemies to undermine their accusations or investigations. Largely through Twitter and interviews with friendly media, such as *Fox News,* he conducted his war against Special Counsel Robert Mueller's investigation, the media, the impeachment inquiry, and congressional Democrats. Consequently, on Twitter and in interviews, the greatest evolution in his persona took place. He still was the celebrity business outsider, but especially in response to criticism or investigation, he increasingly manifested the persona of a strongman, often making strident attacks on his opponents, labeling them un-American in an attempt to delegitimize their criticism and create hate. In so doing, he shredded democratic norms for presidential behavior. His vernacular style was consonant with his evolving persona and helped him maintain a sense of authenticity.[4] In this way, his odd punctuation and almost random use of capitalization for emphasis, along with syntactical and grammatical errors, did not damage his campaign or presidency but instead made him seem more authentic than other politicians.[5]

In both the campaign and as president, Trump used Twitter to present the same nationalist populist message as at rallies and in more formal speeches but in more concentrated form. The character limit of Twitter did not permit Trump to present a complete version of the nationalist populist message, but it did provide him an invaluable means of extending the rally atmosphere into virtual space for core supporters, something they experienced each day. To accomplish this aim, Trump used Twitter to present a scene from the larger narrative, a vignette that reinforced his attack on elites, his warnings about a dangerous Other, and his claims of heroic achievements.

Via Twitter, Trump made himself present daily in the lives of his supporters and kept them involved in his war with the elites and the media and, after he assumed the presidency, those investigating his administration, including the Democrats. The work of Chaim Perelman and L. Olbrechts-Tyteca is helpful for understanding what Trump accomplished through Twitter. Perelman and Olbrechts-Tyteca noted the power of argument to create what they called a sense of "presence" that "acts directly on our sensibility" by making "something present to the consciousness."[6] Through Twitter, Trump literally made himself present in the lives of his followers and forced his opponents to respond, thus setting the bounds of political debate on a daily basis.[7] This enabled him "to center attention" on his dystopian worldview, place it in the "foreground" of the audience's "consciousness," and use "repetition" to create strong "emotion."[8]

One curious aspect of Trump's campaign and presidency is that his anti-immigrant message resonated most strongly in places where there are few immigrants and least powerfully in places such as California and New York that welcome immigrants of all kinds.[9] One factor, of course, is that Trump's anti-immigrant narrative was fundamentally inaccurate. Immigrants actually commit fewer crimes on average than native-born Americans.[10] Another factor is that Trump used rallies and Twitter to make his anti-immigrant message present in the lives of his followers. His nationalist populist narrative was not true, but it seemed that way to his followers. Perelman noted that "only by dwelling upon a subject does one create the desired emotions," and Trump used Twitter to make the threat posed by undocumented immigrants, Islamic terrorists, Black protesters, and others seem real.[11] Rhetoric can arouse strong emotions, such as fear or anger, even when there is little to be fearful or angry about, by making a topic seem ever present in people's lives. Thomas F. Mader noted that to achieve this reaction, something "must be overestimated," a rhetorical move that also "*distracts* the hearer from taking into account other matters" and can even be used "to conceal" the real issue.[12] Trump used Twitter to produce the vast overestimation of the danger posed by the various Others he demonized.

Most national political figures are extremely careful about what they say because they recognize that an unscripted comment could lead to ridicule or create outrage. Trump, in contrast, used the outrageous and the simply erroneous to create the sense he was not a normal politician and, therefore, authentic, in order to drive his political narrative. As David Smith noted in the *Guardian,* Trump used Twitter "to make the political weather," which permitted him both to focus the national narrative on nationalist populist themes and distract supporters, the press, and critics from gaffes, controversies of the moment, and later the Mueller and impeachment investigations.[13] Maggie Haberman, Glenn Thrush, and Peter Baker reported, "Before taking office, Mr. Trump told top aides to think of each presidential day as an episode in a television show in which he vanquishes rivals." They added that in his presidency, certainly the ultimate reality TV show, Twitter was "his Excalibur."[14]

Twitter is by nature of character limits not well adapted to presentation of a complex argument or a developed narrative. The strengths and limitations of Twitter were perfectly aligned with Trump's message and his outsider and later strongman persona. The contrast between Trump's approach and that of Barack Obama is striking. One of Obama's strengths (and weaknesses) was that he attempted to use rational argument to build strong support for his administration's policies. He made particular effort, for example, to make a strong case for the Affordable Care Act (ACA).[15] Twitter was of little help in this effort. The character limit of the medium was not sufficient for Obama to fully explain his argument. In contrast, Twitter as a medium was much better suited to Trump's purposes than those of Obama. Across his rhetorical practice, Trump's focus was not on policy but on presenting a nationalist populist message. Twitter was particularly helpful for making that narrative present in the lives of his supporters, settling scores with opponents and the media, and praising his own heroic character.

Trump used Twitter to support key themes in his nationalist populist message: the danger posed by immigrants, refugees, Islamic terrorists, and all of the various Others he depicted as threatening the lives of "real" (white) Americans; the complicity or responsibility of his opponents for these threats; the corruption of elites and their failure to care about real Americans; the danger posed by "fake news" (a synonym for negative press coverage of Trump); the illegitimacy of various investigations of his campaign and presidency; and his own greatness. That these themes dominated the Trump Twitterverse is clearly evident in two primary sources that compiled Trump tweets. The *New York Times* created a complete list of every person or organization Trump has insulted since his campaign began and a much shorter list of people he has complimented (mostly Trump, his family, and his supporters). In addition, the Trump Twitter Archive presents a searchable compilation of his more than 39,000 tweets.[16]

The Trump Twitterverse

From the announcement of his candidacy throughout his presidency, Trump used tweets to present a dystopian vision of a nation under siege. One common topic was the danger posed by undocumented immigrants. The Trump Twitter Archive includes more than three hundred tweets stating that the nation faced an immigration crisis. On August 10, 2015, Trump said, "We must stop the crime and killing machine that is illegal immigration. Rampant problems will only get worse. Take back our country!" On November 8, 2015, he said supporters should "fight illegal immigration it is destroying USA." On July 15, 2015, he issued a typically self-referential tweet, stating, "Trump is Right: Illegal Alien Crime is Staggering in Scope and Savagery." He returned to this theme repeatedly during the campaign and continued to restate it as president. For example, he tweeted about immigration twenty times in June 2019, blaming crime on undocumented immigrants, bragging about his administration's policies, and attacking Democrats for not funding a wall. A tweet on June 26, 2019, typifies his use of Twitter to reinforce his message about immigration: "The Democrats would save many lives if they would change our broken and very DANGEROUS Immigration Laws. It can be done instantly."

Trump took a similar approach to create fear about Islamic terrorism and crime committed by Black Americans. On November 15, 2015, he tweeted,

"When will President Obama issue the words RADICAL ISLAMIC TERROR-ISM? He can't say it, and unless he will, the problem will not be solved!" Not quite a month later on December 8, 2015, he again claimed terrorism was a major problem: "Our country is facing a major threat from radical Islamic terrorism. We better get very smart, and very tough, FAST, before it is too late!" As president, Trump not only warned of the danger of Islamic terrorism but sometimes took credit for fighting it. For example, on January 6, 2019, he tweeted, "Our GREAT MILITARY has delivered justice for the heroes lost and wounded in the cowardly attack on the USS *Cole*. We have just killed the leader of that attack, Jamal al-Badawi. Our work against al Qaeda continues. We will never stop in our fight against Radical Islamic Terrorism." Overall, the Trump Twitter Archive contains more than two hundred tweets that include the word *terror*, the vast majority of which reference the threat of Islamic terrorism.

Similarly to his tweets about terrorism, Trump used Twitter as a way to amplify fear of crime in cities. Here, he drew on a long history of advocating for tough action to confront urban crime that many thought was motivated by racial bias, including calling for the death penalty for five Black and Latino men (the Central Park Five) convicted of rape but later exonerated of the crime.[17] In a period in which crime had dropped substantially to a rate not seen since the early 1960s, Trump described a massive crime problem in thirty-two tweets during his presidential campaign. For example, on July 6, 2016, he said, "Crime is out of control, and rapidly getting worse. Look what is going on in Chicago and our inner cities. Not good!" On August 29, 2016, he claimed, "Inner-city crime is reaching record levels. African-Americans will vote for Trump because they know I will stop the slaughter going on!" Many similar examples exist. On the surface Trump appeared to be reaching out to Black voters, whereas, in fact, he was activating white fear of Black crime. After he became president, his political incentives shifted because high crime reflected on his presidency. As a consequence, this theme almost disappeared from his Twitter feed, except in instances when he took credit for helping Black Americans. On July 10, 2019, he retweeted a statement from Michael Brown that Trump had "done a great job of reducing crime in the African American Community because more African Americans are at work today. Trump is not a Racist, he's a Businessman. Because he's a great businessman, he's pushing for lives to be better." As these examples indicate, Trump was a master of using Twitter to create or reinforce fear of Others, especially immigrants, Islamic terrorists, and Black Americans.

Although Trump used Twitter to reinforce his dystopian narrative, he much more commonly used it to attack political enemies and the media, often "by challenging their honesty and integrity."[18] In this way, Twitter was a primary means of driving conflict in the campaign and after that during his presidency. Notably, Trump relied on Twitter to damage the image of his opponents, the media, and other elites by creating a dominant definition of them. Perelman noted that "definition" can function through "abbreviations" that "determine the choice of one particular meaning over others."[19] Trump used Twitter to create abbreviated definitions of his opponents (often in the form of petty name-calling) to label them weak, corrupt, and so forth. For example, the Trump Twitter Archive includes more than 325 tweets in which he accused Hillary Clinton of corruption by calling her "Crooked Hillary." The archive includes 80 tweets that mention Jeb Bush, almost all of which attack him as weak, or "low energy" (see December 22, 2015, and January 2, 2016). It includes almost 100 tweets during the 2016 primary campaign that mention Marco Rubio, most of which attack him as "weak" or worse. On May 12, 2015, Trump said, "Marco Rubio was a complete disaster today in an interview with Chris Wallace." On September 22, 2015, he referenced "Marco 'amnesty' Rubio" and two days later said Rubio was an "all talk, no action politician." Similar examples of his attacks on Ted Cruz, John Kasich, and many other political opponents could be cited from the campaign. Trump used a comparable tactic as president, especially after the 2018 midterm elections, as the 2020 presidential campaign was beginning. For example, from April 25, 2019, to mid-July 2019, he sent 16 tweets using the phrase "Sleepy Joe" to characterize former vice president Biden as old and tired. He used a similar tactic to attack Elizabeth Warren as inauthentic, labeling her "Pocahontas" because she had spoken of having a small percentage of Native American ancestry.

In addition to using Twitter to attack his opponents, often using an insulting nickname, Trump reinforced the conflict present in his dystopian narrative. He particularly focused on conflict with Obama and Clinton. The Trump Twitter Archive includes more than 1,000 tweets attacking Clinton and more than 2,500 tweets about Obama or his policies, almost all of which are attacks. Although all campaigns attack their opponents, Trump's Twitter attacks differed from normal politically oriented ones, which generally focus on perceived policy failures or mistakes of judgment. Trump's attacks were more personal, as his highly repetitive use of the label "Crooked Hillary" indicates.

Moreover, Trump used Twitter to tap into a sense of grievance among many of his core white supporters by activating their deep uneasiness about the changing identity structure of the nation. Trump both drew on that sense of grievance and tried to further activate it through his attacks on various people of color, especially women. In a related strategy, he often attacked women of color in Congress in order to define Democrats as communists, socialists, or simply extreme liberals. For example, he repeated a racial slur labeling Maxine Waters, a Black US representative from Los Angeles, "an extraordinarily low-IQ person [who] has become, together with Nancy Pelosi, the Face of the Democrat Party."[20] By attacking Waters, Trump both drew on racial anxiety and also attempted to literally make Waters and Pelosi "the face" of the party. A tweet attacking the "squad" (Representatives Ilhan Omar of Minnesota, Alexandria Ocasio-Cortez of New York, Ayanna Pressley of Massachusetts, and Rashida Tlaib of Michigan) as "'Progressive' Democrat Congresswomen who originally came from countries whose governments are a complete and total catastrophe" and encouraging them to "go back and help fix the totally broken and crime infested places from which they came" was both racist and of course wildly inaccurate because three of the four were born in the United States and the fourth was a naturalized citizen.[21] In this tweet and others, Trump drew on both racism and fear of demographic change and attempted to define the Democratic Party as typified by four of its most liberal members in the House. Trump reemphasized this theme in a tweet in summer 2019 in which he said, "The 'Squad' is a very Racist group of troublemakers who are young, inexperienced, and not very smart. They are pulling the once great Democrat Party far left, and were against humanitarian aid at the Border . . . And are now against ICE and Homeland Security. So bad for our Country."[22]

Especially after the midterm election, Trump again and again used Twitter to label the Democratic Party as extremist and unconcerned with real (white) Americans. The Trump Twitter Archive, for example, includes eleven tweets from May 2018 through mid-July 2019 attacking Democrats as socialists. These tweets did not engage in ideological argument. Rather, they functioned as the equivalent of a schoolyard taunt, labeling his opponents radicals, and often, un-American. Trump was not trying to win an argument in the way Reagan tried to convince the nation to support small-government conservatism but to persuade enough core supporters to hate the Democrats for Trump to win reelection in 2020.

Trump employed a similar strategy in attacking journalists. The Trump Twitter Archive and the *New York Times* compilation of groups and people attacked by Trump on Twitter include dozens of journalists. A typical example of a tweet attacking the media occurred on October 10, 2016, when Trump issued one of many attacks on CNN: "CNN is the worst—fortunately they have bad ratings because everyone knows they are biased." In this and many other tweets about CNN, almost every other network news organization (other than Fox, until he was offended by negative coverage and started attacking it as well), major newspapers, magazines, and individual reporters, Trump created conflict, reinforced his image as a populist outsider, and attempted to inoculate himself against critical reporting.

Trump's attacks on the media escalated after he became president. He made more than 640 attacks on "fake news" from his inauguration up to June 11, 2020. In contrast, he never used the term "fake news" in tweets in the campaign, during which his focus was on attacks on publications or individual reporters. Overall, attacks on the media became much more common after his election, when the focus shifted to the credibility of particular news organizations and of the media in general. This shift happened both because it was much harder for him to credibly attack elites during the first two years of his presidency, when Republicans were in charge of both houses of Congress and the presidency, and also because the media uncovered many contacts between the Trump campaign and Russia, numerous efforts by Trump to block the Mueller investigation, and various other cases of malfeasance or abuse by administration officials. Trump was quite candid in stating the goals behind his attacks on the media when he explained in an interview with Lesley Stahl of CBS, "You know why I do it? I do it to discredit you all and demean you so when you write negative stories about me, no one will believe it."[23]

The attacks on the media also reflected the evolution of his persona to include elements of the strongman, which happened most often on Twitter, at rallies, and in interviews or other unscripted settings. For example, in an unscripted meeting with President Vladimir Putin, Trump joked that the Russian leader did not have to put up with "fake news" the way he did. Conservative columnist Max Boot observed of this incident, "Trump seems jealous that Putin can censor the press and kill journalists. The First Amendment—what a nuisance!"[24] Trump reinforced a similar message in many tweets complaining about "fake news" or attacking individual journalists.

Trump also used Twitter to undercut the investigation led by Mueller and later the impeachment inquiry. During the 2016 campaign, Trump alleged Clinton's campaign had been guilty of collusion. On October 18, 2016, he tweeted, "Pay-to-play. Collusion. Cover-ups. And now bribery? So CROOKED. I will #DrainTheSwamp. https://t.co/FNzMit7mD8." This tweet was typical of many attacks on Clinton in rally speeches, tweets, and interviews for being corrupt. His view at that time was that Clinton should be fully investigated and prosecuted for her crimes.

His view of investigations changed after he became president. After it became clear the Russian government had intervened in the campaign to aid his election, Trump tweeted again and again denying any link between his campaign and Russia and attacking his accusers. The Trump Twitter Archive contains more than 900 tweets referencing Russia, hoax, witch hunt, Mueller, or collusion, the overwhelming majority of which denied his campaign had done anything wrong or attacked his accusers. From May 2017 through July 2019 he sent more than 140 tweets claiming there was no evidence of collusion or even that it had been demonstrated that no collusion occurred.[25] On ten occasions he referred derisively to what he called the "Collusion Delusion." He also claimed he was the real victim. On May 17, 2018, he tweeted, "Congratulations America, we are now into the second year of the greatest Witch Hunt in American History . . . and there is still No Collusion and No Obstruction. The only Collusion was that done by Democrats who were unable to win an Election despite the spending of far more money." On June 2, 2018, he claimed, "There was No Collusion with Russia (except by the Democrats). When will this very expensive Witch Hunt Hoax ever end? So bad for our Country. Is the Special Council [sic]/Justice Department leaking my lawyers [sic] letters to the Fake News Media? Should be looking at Dems corruption instead." From the beginning of his presidency to mid-November 2019, he labeled investigations of his campaign and presidency a "witch hunt" in more than 300 tweets. He also often claimed that not only was the investigation of him illegitimate but also that, in fact, his accusers were actually the guilty parties. For example, on August 6, 2018, Trump claimed that the real collusion had been between Russia and the Clinton campaign: "Collusion with Russia was very real. Hillary Clinton and her team 100% colluded with the Russians, and so did Adam Schiff who is on tape trying to collude with what he thought was Russians to obtain compromising material on DJT. We also know that Hillary Clinton paid through." In this and many other tweets, he accused Democrats and others investigating him of being unpatriotic and, often, un-American.

Trump adopted a similar strategy in responding to the allegation that he had obstructed justice by interfering in the investigation of his campaign. There were 58 tweets between June 2017 and mid-July 2019 in which he used the words "No Obstruction" and more than 100 total tweets denying that obstruction had occurred. Again, he often attacked his accusers, sometimes with the phrases "13 Angry Democrats" (21 tweets between May 2017 and mid-July 2019) or "conflicted" (33 tweets between June 2017 and mid-July 2019) to accuse the Mueller investigation of bias. A tweet from July 21, 2018, typifies his response: "No Collusion, No Obstruction—but that doesn't matter because the 13 Angry Democrats, who are only after Republicans and totally protecting Democrats, want this Witch Hunt to drag out to the November Election. Republicans better get smart fast and expose what they are doing!"

One of Trump's other responses was to allege that the investigation was part of an underlying government conspiracy against his campaign and presidency. He tweeted about a "deep state" conspiracy against him fifteen times between June 2017 and mid-July 2019. For example, on May 23, 2018, he tweeted, "Look how things have turned around on the Criminal Deep State. They go after Phony Collusion with Russia, a made up Scam, and end up getting caught in a major SPY scandal the likes of which this country may never have seen before! What goes around, comes around."

Trump's use of Twitter to respond to allegations of collusion and obstruction is typical of how he responded to claims of misconduct. He simply repeated again and again that there was no evidence of misconduct in the hope that simple repetition would convince supporters he was innocent of wrongdoing. This strategy clearly worked with many core supporters. He also shifted the blame to his accusers—a strategy consistent with his constant attacks on the press and the institutions investigating him. He labeled any investigation either by Mueller or state prosecutors illegitimate and stonewalled congressional investigations as well in what conservative commentator Jennifer Rubin labeled an "all-out assault on Congress."[26] After the impeachment inquiry started in the House, he attacked the investigation as a "witch hunt," using that phrase more than forty times in the six weeks after the investigation began in October 2019. He used the phrase "corrupt politician" more than a dozen times in late October and early November 2019 to attack Schiff for leading the investigation. His goal was clearly to delegitimize the investigation by labeling Democrats unpatriotic and un-American.

Trump's attacks on the press, democratic institutions, and the very idea of investigating him, his family, or his administration reflected the evolution of his persona to include elements of the strongman. As a candidate, he called for investigation and prosecution of Clinton. As president, he denied the legitimacy of efforts to hold him accountable and attacked basic democratic institutions. In addition to tweets about the "deep state," the Mueller investigation, Mueller himself, and former FBI director James Comey, the Trump Twitter Archive includes 280 Trump tweets or retweets about the FBI, many of which allege the agency unfairly targeted his campaign. For example, on May 12, 2019, he accused the FBI of acting illegally and claimed his campaign was the real victim when he tweeted, "FBI actions against the Trump Presidential Campaign do in fact meet the definition of spying."[27]

Trump's attacks on basic democratic institutions are consistent with the evolution of his presidential persona to become more like a strongman over time. This evolution and his willingness to challenge basic democratic principles were evident when on several occasions he spoke of serving more than two terms, which of course would violate the constitutional limit. In a tweet on June 16, 2019, he said, "The good . . . . news is that at the end of 6 years, after America has been made GREAT again and I leave the beautiful White House (do you think the people would demand that I stay longer?" He also made several other comments indicating he thought he deserved two extra years because of the Mueller investigation, a third term, a third and fourth term, or even to be "president for life."[28] Trump sometimes labeled such comments "jokes," but trial balloons might be more accurate. The key point is that over time he moved from labeling the political system corrupt because it was not investigating Clinton to actively doing and saying everything possible to undercut investigation of his campaign, business, family, and administration and delegitimize the FBI, other investigative bodies, the press, and the very idea of checks and balances. In that way, the role he created through his rhetoric evolved over time to be similar to that of a strongman who used the institutions of power to protect himself and go after his enemies.

Trump's approach had a measure of success. A *Politico*/Morning Consult poll found that in June 2018, 53 percent of Republicans had an unfavorable view of the Mueller probe.[29] Polling numbers after the final release of the Mueller report were similar, with a clear majority of Republicans disapproving of the findings and only 1 percent believing the report demonstrated that Trump had obstructed justice.[30] Nearly all Republicans seemed to believe of Mueller's findings that because numerous contacts between the Russian government and the Trump campaign, including direct offers of assistance from Russia and an exchange of polling information, did not rise to the level of a criminal conspiracy, no wrongdoing had occurred. It is important to recognize that this success in marshaling support occurred despite overwhelming evidence that the Trump campaign at minimum welcomed help from the Russian government in the 2016 election. In response to an email offering "very high-level and sensitive information [that was] . . . part of Russia and its government's support for Mr. Trump," Donald Trump Jr. responded, "If it's what you say I love it especially later in the summer."[31] He then attended a meeting with those offering this information, also attended by the campaign manager and by Trump's son-in-law, Jared Kushner. Rubin summarized the available evidence as constituting "airtight evidence of attempted conspiracy by the highest levels in the Trump campaign to obtain foreign help."[32]

On the question of obstruction, the Mueller report did not draw a conclusion about whether Trump obstructed justice because of a Department of Justice (DOJ) policy against indicting a sitting president, but it described a series of actions taken by Trump to block the investigation. More than a thousand former DOJ prosecutors signed a statement indicating that Trump's actions as detailed in the report would "result in multiple felony charges for obstruction of justice" if such prosecution were not banned by the DOJ policy.[33] This quite damning statement had no apparent effect on Trump supporters. Something similar happened in the House impeachment inquiry, in which despite overwhelming evidence that Trump had asked two foreign countries to investigate a political rival, Republicans continued to support Trump and deny the legitimacy of the investigation.[34]

The point is that despite strong evidence of misconduct with foreign powers by his campaign and as president and his obstruction of justice as president, Trump was able to convince a sizable majority of Republicans that the Mueller probe and impeachment inquiry were, in his words, a "partisan witch hunt." The argument that the Mueller probe was a partisan attempt by Democrats to unfairly attack Trump was made more difficult by the fact that Mueller was a registered Republican and a highly respected former FBI director whose investigation resulted in many indictments, in effect "find[ing] witches."[35] Similarly, the impeachment inquiry concerning Trump's request that Ukraine and China investigate Biden and his son Hunter was based on statements by the president and his aides.[36] However, Trump's constant repetition on Twitter and elsewhere of "no collusion," "witch hunt," "collusion delusion," "13 angry Democrats," "no obstruction," and other slogans, along with his attacks on his accusers and claim that he was the real victim, were apparently sufficient to undercut support for the investigations among almost all Republicans.

Trump's use of Twitter to respond to allegations of collusion and obstruction also indicates that, frankly, incredible claims can appear credible to supporters. Trump's claim that, in fact, Clinton's campaign colluded with Russia illustrates this point. Given the intelligence community's consensus that the Russian government intervened in the 2016 campaign to aid Trump, it should have been immediately clear that the claim Clinton colluded with Russia was on its face absurd. One would have thought no one would believe Clinton colluded with Russia against her own campaign. Yet, some Republicans supported Trump's claim that the Clinton campaign's actions should produce outrage.[37] Similarly, his claim repeated twenty-five times from September through November 2019 on Twitter that his call with the president of Ukraine had been "perfect," when the partial transcript released by the White House refuted that claim, is strong evidence that simple repetition can overwhelm facts, at least for partisan supporters.

To this point, I have focused on how Trump used Twitter to reinforce the nationalist and populist themes at the core of his message. Trump also used Twitter to depict himself as a celebrity business outsider and, as his presidency progressed, a strongman in the process of making the nation great again. Although vastly more tweets attacked opponents, elites, and the media or blamed a dangerous Other for threatening "real" (white) Americans than made positive statements, unsurprisingly the positive tweets were heavily focused on Trump's campaign, his abilities, his accomplishments, his family, and his properties.

One form of self-praise that became increasingly important as Trump's campaign progressed and that became still more important after he won the presidency was his use of the phrase "Make America Great Again" (MAGA). There are almost 1,000 tweets in the Trump Twitter Archive using this phrase in one form or another to praise some aspect of his campaign or presidency. Trump first used the slogan MAGA in a tweet on March 3, 2016, and used it 107 more times by Election Day. As president, he had used the term almost

400 times by mid-June 2020. Many campaigns use slogans to convey the essence of what they represent, but normally the slogans contain an ideological message of some kind. Obama spoke of the "audacity of hope" as a way of encapsulating policies that would represent a dramatic change away from the small-government domestic policy and interventionistic foreign policy of the George W. Bush administration. One of Ronald Reagan's slogans, "Let's Make America Great," was similar in some ways to Trump's MAGA.[38] But Reagan used the slogan to present a coherent small-government message. In contrast, MAGA had almost no ideological meaning. Rather, it was a shorthand phrase calling for a return to a time when the US industrial economy was preeminent, there had been many good jobs for those in Trump's base of support among the white working class, and the nation's population was whiter. The underlying message of the phrase was that Trump, through force of will, could resurrect that period of US economic and political dominance.

Bragging is a key component of the business outsider or strongman persona. Because nationalist populism does not focus on policy but on how the great leader will bring back a lost Golden Age, this theme was often reinforced through self-praise. Unsurprisingly, the Trump Twitter Archive contains dozens of self-referential tweets praising Trump, his companies, and his campaign. For example, the archive has compiled a long list of "personal superlatives," including the more than thirty times Trump claimed he was "key to solving issues." For example, on January 8, 2016, he predicted, "I will create jobs like no one else." On March 24, 2016, he said, "Just announced that as many as 5000 ISIS fighters have infiltrated Europe. Also, many in U.S. I TOLD YOU SO! I alone can fix this problem!" In neither of these tweets did he specify policy actions, explain how the policy would work, or provide any supporting evidence. Rather, the tweets indicated that the act of voting for Trump would be sufficient to "Make America Great Again." Similarly, on May 13, 2015, he made the amazing claim, "Our roads, airports, tunnels, bridges, electric grid—all falling apart. I can fix for 20% of pols, & better." Here, he bragged that he could fix bridges, dams, airports, and so on for one-fifth the cost that it would take another politician. There was no explanation of how this would occur, and it was obvious nonsense, but it reflected his use of Twitter to reinforce his image as an outsider who could achieve magical results. Many other examples could be cited. For example, on April 30, 2016, he said, "The economy is bad and getting worse—almost ZERO growth this quarter. Nobody can beat me on the economy (and jobs). MAKE AMERICA

GREAT AGAIN." He even commended himself when responding to attacks on his character. A tweet from March 10, 2016, is typical: "The media is so after me on women Wow, this is a tough business. Nobody has more respect for women than Donald Trump!" In this case, as was common, Trump ignored specific accusations about his behavior and simply asserted greatness.

During his presidency, Trump's pattern continued with more than 400 tweets that included the words "great job," almost always about his own performance or that of a member of his administration. For example, on May 13, 2019, he tweeted, "I am doing a great job—Also, Best Economy and Employment Numbers EVER!"[39] He also often bragged about nonexistent accomplishments, as when he claimed that the Republican plan would do a much better job of guaranteeing insurance coverage to those with preexisting conditions than the ACA would, despite the fact that his administration supported a court case to eliminate that provision of the ACA and his administration had no policy proposal to provide protection for those with preexisting conditions.

Trump's Twitter Use in a Pandemic

A national crisis can change a president and a presidency decisively. George W. Bush ran for president as a compassionate conservative, but after 9/11 he governed and talked as a war president. Similarly, after taking office in what was up to that point the worst recession since the Great Depression, Obama shifted from a message of audacious hope to focus on crisis management and reassurance. In contrast, when Trump faced the greatest public health crisis the United States had confronted since 1918 with the COVID-19 pandemic and resulting economic collapse, he did not shift his core message at all.

Rather, Trump used a similar approach on Twitter to respond to the pandemic as he had throughout his campaign and presidency. The nationalist portion of his message was most evident in tweets shifting blame to China. The Trump Twitter Archive includes thirty-seven tweets from late January 2020 to the end of May 2020 referencing both the virus and China. After a series of early tweets in which he claimed to be working closely with China, such as on January 27, 2020, when he said, "We are in very close communication with China concerning the virus," he shifted to blaming China. There are more than twenty-five tweets referencing the "China virus" or otherwise attacking China for failing to contain the virus. There are also ten tweets from February 25 to May 4, 2020, in which he linked the virus to open borders or praised his administration for restricting immigration from China and Mexico. On March 8, 2020, he combined the nationalist and populist aspects of his message and praised his administration's actions: "We have a perfectly coordinated and fine tuned plan at the White House for our attack on CoronaVirus. We moved VERY early to close borders to certain areas, which was a Godsend. V.P. is doing a great job. The Fake News Media is doing everything possible to make us look bad. Sad!"

Over time, Trump focused in particular on his decisions to close the border with China, then with Europe, and eventually other nations. This message allowed him both to displace blame for the growing pandemic and to claim credit for fighting it. It also was consistent with the nationalist thread in all of his rhetoric. On March 18, 2020, he said, "I always treated the Chinese Virus very seriously, and have done a very good job from the beginning, including my very early decision to close the 'borders' from China—against the wishes of almost all. Many lives were saved. The Fake News new narrative is disgraceful & false." In actuality, the *Washington Post* found that thirty-eight countries had established travel restrictions "before or at the same time the U.S. restrictions were put in place," but on Twitter Trump depicted himself as the brave president who had flouted expert opinion to protect the nation by closing down the border.[40] He also attempted to frame his decision to build a wall on the border with Mexico as somehow justified by the pandemic. On May 4, 2020, he said, "Mexico is sadly experiencing very big CoronaVirus problems, and now California, get this, doesn't want people coming over the Southern Border. A Classic! They are sooo lucky that I am their President. Border is very tight and the Wall is rapidly being built!" On April 18, 2020, he boiled this message down by saying, "Border is very strong!"

Trump expressed the populist theme by attacking the media for their coverage of the virus and Democrats for failing to support his approach to the virus. There are fifteen tweets between February 26 and May 11, 2020, in which he attacked the "Fake News" for their quite accurate coverage of the crisis that developed over this time. He also desperately attempted to shift blame to the Democratic Party for the growing death total and economic shutdown in seventeen tweets from February 25 to May 21, 2020. For example, on February 28, 2020, he expressed a nationalist message by claiming credit for shutting off international travel and then attacked Democrats:

"The Do Nothing Democrats were busy wasting time on the Immigration [impeachment] Hoax, & anything else they could do to make the Republican Party look bad, while I was busy calling early BORDER & FLIGHT closings, putting us way ahead in our battle with Coronavirus. Dems called it VERY wrong!" On March 23, 2020, he went as far as to state, "The Democrats want the Virus to win?" In this tweet, he essentially claimed that the Democratic Party was un-American.

Trump manifested the strongman persona with constant bragging. For example, between February 25 and the end of May 2020, he tweeted thirty-seven times about how his administration was doing a "great job" dealing with the virus, although more than 100,000 Americans died from it during this period. A tweet on May 25, 2020, contained several aspects of his message: "Great reviews on our handling of Covid 19, sometimes referred to as the China Virus. Ventilators, Testing, Medical Supply Distribution, we made a lot of Governors look very good—And got no credit for so doing. Most importantly, we helped a lot of great people." Here, he implicitly blamed China by labeling COVID-19 "the China Virus," praised his administration's actions, and even claimed credit for the successful actions of a number of governors, many of them Democrats, in slowing the spread of the virus. Similarly, on May 11, 2020, he combined the populist and strongman aspects of his message by bragging about his efforts and attacking the media: "Great credit being given for our Coronavirus response, except in the Fake News. They are a disgrace to America." Early in the crisis, on February 28, 2020, he combined all of the main themes of his message in a single tweet that also illustrated the vernacular style that typified his use of Twitter: "So, the Coronavirus, which started in China and spread to various countries throughout the world, but very slowly in the U.S. because President Trump closed our border, and ended flights, VERY EARLY, is now being blamed, by the Do Nothing Democrats, to be the fault of Trump."

Trump's response on Twitter to the pandemic and the economic collapse that followed was entirely predictable. He displaced blame on foreign Others, attacked his political opponents and the press, and claimed credit for what was widely viewed as a disastrous response.[41] Conservative columnist Michael Gerson's reference to "the horrendous reality of his pandemic response" and conclusion that "Trump's failures of leadership and character have increased the death toll" reflected the view of many.[42] On Twitter, however, Trump depicted himself as nothing short of heroic in defending the

nation against a deadly virus being spread because of the actions of dangerous Others and their enablers in the media.

Trump's response to the pandemic on Twitter is also notable for what is
absent. There are almost no tweets expressing concern or condolences for
those who lost their jobs in the economic crisis, were sickened by the virus,
or died without their family members present. Moreover, his tweets did not
link to Centers for Disease Control (CDC) or other guidelines. During a crisis, presidents normally use rhetoric to inform and console the public. In
response to the COVID-19 crisis, Trump used Twitter to displace blame onto
dangerous Others, attack his political opponents and the media, and brag
about what most experts thought was a failed response.

Conclusion

Trump used Twitter to present in concentrated form key portions of his nationalist populist message. His tweets were also often forwarded on other
forms of social media and broadly reflected his rhetoric on other platforms.
Trump himself recognized this point, saying, "Tweeting is like a typewriter"
to send messages across "his social media accounts," which according to the
president, "provide 'a tremendous platform'" and "drive the news cycle."
Trump added, "I doubt I would be here if it weren't for social media" because
many of his tweets took off "like a rocket ship."[43]

Nationalist populism with an outsider/strongman persona was the dis-
tillation of Trump's message; tweets were droplets of the message that he
transmitted to his followers to make himself present in their daily lives and to
keep them involved in the rally atmosphere of his campaign. It also allowed
him to circumvent the media filter and speak directly to supporters. Earlier,
I cited the view that Twitter was Trump's "Excalibur." Unlike Excalibur, the
sharp sword of King Arthur, Twitter was a blunt instrument Trump used to
make present his rally in the daily lives of supporters.

Many criticized Trump for what they saw as unprofessional behavior on
Twitter.[44] Yet, there is reason to believe he was quite successful in involving
core supporters in his campaign and presidency. Andrew Buncombe noted
that Trump's use of Twitter was "like nothing we've previously seen from
an elected politician" but also added that he was "remarkably effective" in
using "the tone of a schoolyard bully" to "dominate the news agenda," often

by diverting "attention" from something else. Buncombe cited the views of George Lakoff, who observed, "Trump uses social media as a weapon to control the news cycle."[45] One way he did this was through using Twitter to both avoid the media and change the subject by focusing on a new threat, a new enemy to despise, or a new media outrage. Nicholas Carr was on target when he observed, "Twitter has become the flywheel of a potent call-and-response feedback loop" that "heralds a politics of increasing fractiousness, irrationality, and risk."[46]

Trump did not use Twitter as a means of responding to opponents and moving forward a policy debate on his proposals. He could hardly have done so because he had few developed policy positions except for limiting immigration and building a border wall. Rather, as David Folkenflik observed, Trump's use of Twitter was "willfully divisive and often reflected a level of "estrangement from truth" that "is so complete that it defies belief."[47] In fact, as Mathew Ingram pointed out, Trump used Twitter not to maintain the argument but to avoid it. It enabled "him to state untruths with impunity, knowing that his tweets will be widely redistributed by his followers and the media, and to dodge follow-up questions or criticism."[48] Trump masterfully used Twitter to make himself, his campaign, and later his presidency a ubiquitous presence in the daily lives of his supporters. In so doing, he solidified his relationship with them and undercut the grounds for critique of his actions. His unconventional style also made him seem authentic.[49] As his opponents, commentators, and a legion of fact checkers discovered, rhetoric that creates a strong sense of presence can be difficult to undermine with refutation. Alan Gross's comment that "an absence of justification . . . cannot counteract the strong psychological tug that presence exercises" certainly applied to Trump's use of Twitter and more broadly his campaign and presidential rhetoric.[50]

After he became president, Trump's tweets reflected the same pattern of entelechial development that occurred in his rally speeches. This pattern was especially apparent in response to first the Mueller investigation and then the impeachment inquiry, when Trump attempted to undermine news organizations and those investigating him. Another factor pushing this entelechial development was that much of what Trump had promised during the campaign had not occurred. The combination of negative media coverage focused on policy failures, various misdeeds by cabinet officers and others, and investigations of Trump himself caused him to focus on ever more radical attacks on the press and his political opponents, often with the goal of undercutting democratic norms. For example, on October 23, 2019, Trump tweeted, "The Never Trumper Republicans, though on respirators with not many left, are in certain ways worse and more dangerous for our Country than the Do Nothing Democrats. Watch out for them, they are human scum!" The particular attack was on nonpartisan officials from the State Department and the National Security Council who testified about Trump's words and actions related to a demand that Ukraine investigate Biden and Biden's son Hunter. The underlying point was to delegitimize anyone who challenged Trump and to attempt to destabilize the very idea of truth, typical tactics used by strongmen throughout the world.

7

The Resonance of
Nationalist Populism

In one way, the explanation for the resonance of Trump's rhetoric of nationalist populism is obvious. He clearly activated and tapped into public fears about groups his supporters perceived as dangerous Others and more broadly societal change as well as their anger at elites who had prospered while most Americans in general, and the white working class in particular, lost ground. He offered himself as the outsider/celebrity/strongman hero to bring back what was remembered as the glory days of the 1950s and early 1960s. This message activated Trump's core supporters, and after he won the nomination, Republican leaders and the conservative media largely fell in line.

Although it is obvious Trump's message resonated for tens of millions of voters, the more fundamental issue is to explain why and how it resonated. One puzzle concerning Trump's campaign rhetoric in particular is that although it clearly delighted his "base," the "dismal picture of the American economy" he painted was "at odds with the economic reality of most Americans" because the nation as a whole was "in the midst of one of the longest sustained economic expansions in the nation's history" and was much closer to a Reaganesque "morning again in America" than to a national Youngstown.[1] Moreover, Trump's message was antithetical not just to what Democrats believed but also to everything conservatives had claimed to believe since the 1960s. Maureen Dowd's observation that "the shining city on a hill is an ugly pile of rubble" in Trump's United States was on target and got at the transformation in the Republican Party.[2] Ronald Reagan, the most important conservative hero of the second half of the twentieth century, combined a coherent small-government ideology with an optimistic retelling of the American dream. In terms of ideology, values, and narrative, Trump's version of "American carnage" represented a total rejection of Reagan's vision of the nation. Not only did he reject Reagan's vision but Trump violated every political norm, insulted his opponents and party leaders, failed to lay out a clear agenda, performed disastrously in the campaign (especially the debates), and continued to act in a decidedly unpresidential fashion after he won. What he said and did should have led to rejection at many points but instead produced an election victory in 2016 and near cult status with core supporters. The mystery is not to explain which message resonated but why.

One key to explicating Trump's success is his appeal among "among working-class white voters who have voted Democratic in the past."[3] An especially important group was Barack Obama supporters who voted for Trump. Diana Mutz reported that 92 percent of those who voted for Obama in 2012 supported Hillary Clinton in 2016.[4] The remaining voters concentrated in the white working class essentially determined the outcome of the election. Therefore, some explain Trump's success by arguing that he appealed to those experiencing economic hardship.[5] For Trump's core supporters "among white, working-class Americans," "poor job prospects" often led to "family dysfunction, social isolation, addiction, obesity, and other pathologies" and ultimately the creation of a "sea of despair."[6]

Although a sense of "despair" about lost opportunities clearly played a role in Trump's success, it is important to recognize that economic uncertainties were not central to his appeal. It is notable that the progressive populist rhetoric of Bernie Sanders strongly resonated with many in the working class. Sanders offered white working-class voters a way to reclaim some of the economic power they previously had when jobs in manufacturing were more plentiful and when labor unions were much more powerful. Trump's appeal to this group of Americans was different than that of Sanders. It was less about policy and more about group solidarity. After all, Trump hardly offered any policy arguments at all, just a promise that he would return the United States to an earlier time and cause the nation to start winning again, when the policies he actually supported primarily helped corporations and the rich.

There is strong evidence that Trump's appeal was not primarily based on his economic agenda. Notably, despite Trump's depiction of a dystopian

United States, "Throughout the year preceding the election unemployment was falling and economic indicators were on the upswing."[7] In addition, polls indicate that "financially troubled voters in the white working class were more likely to prefer Clinton over Trump."[8] For example, the Public Religion Research Institute (PRRI) found that "being in fair or poor financial shape actually predicted support for Hillary Clinton."[9] Economic distress was an important factor in Trump's electoral success, but it played an indirect rather than direct role.[10] Those experiencing unemployment or other immediate problems first supported Sanders and then voted for Clinton because both candidates had a detailed program that addressed their concerns. Something similar happened in 2008 when Obama built a significant margin over John McCain after the economic collapse highlighted the importance of policy action over cultural issues.[11]

The judgment that economic conditions did not put Trump in the White House is also supported by polling on issues Trump emphasized, particularly the finding that 59 percent of "white working-class Americans believe immigrants living in the country illegally should be allowed to become citizens provided they meet certain requirements."[12] Issue polling makes it clear that Trump's appeal was not based on his economic agenda.

Even though economic distress was not itself a strong predictor of support for Trump, it might have played an indirect role in creating the conditions that made Trump's nationalist populist message so effective. That message worked because it tapped into fear of the Other in particular and an authoritarian mind-set more generally. Karen Stenner explained that "political instability, economic decline, social disorder, and change can lower group esteem, frighten or frustrate individuals, and threaten their values, worldview, or way of life."[13] There is strong evidence that this has occurred within the white working class. Andrew Cherlin observed of the white working class that "when . . . prosperity is threatened they complain about blacks or immigrants, who are, in their minds, usurping their places in the economy."[14] Thus, the long-term economic decline experienced by the white working class helped create the situation in which Trump was able to activate a perceived "normative threat." This strategy was less effective for those in the throes of an economic reversal because, as Stenner noted, "personal threats actually distract authoritarians from" perceived "normative threat."[15] Those facing serious economic problems supported Clinton because she defended policies that actually would help them.

Rather than the immediate economic situation, the key was Trump's ability to activate perceived normative threats related to loss of status and a changing American society. Authoritarian personality structure played an essential role in this process. Amanda Taub cited the research of Matthew MacWilliams, who conducted two polls revealing that "authoritarianism . . . seemed to predict support for Trump more reliably than virtually any other indicator."[16] In explaining this finding, Mutz argued that "dominant group status threat" played a key role and added that anxiety about race was especially important. Mutz explained, "When confronted with evidence of racial progress, whites feel threatened and experience lower levels of self-worth. . . . [They] perceive greater antiwhite bias as a means of regaining those lost feelings of self-worth."[17] This group was crucial for Trump, whose election created what Thomas Edsall called "an authoritarian moment."[18] Edsall noted that "recent developments experienced by many voters as alarming—including the financial collapse of 2008, the surge of third-world immigration in the United States and Europe, and continuing fears among traditionalists that the social order is under assault have fueled authoritarianism."[19] In addition, as Denise Bostdorff astutely observed, "Change associated with Obama prompted a sense of loss and victimhood among a sizable number of Americans," many of whom undoubtedly had an authoritarian personality structure.[20] Trump's denigration of illegal immigrants, many racially insensitive or outright racist comments, attacks on the press, calls for harsh punishment of criminals, support for torture of terrorism suspects, defense of violence at his rallies, attacks on NFL players who knelt in protest during the National Anthem, opposition to equal rights for transgender people, and many other incendiary remarks all functioned as a form of threat activation that appealed to those with an authoritarian mind-set.

Trump activated not only anxiety (or outright fear) but also anger at elites, Democrats, and the media. Research on the political effects of emotions indicates that normally, anger and anxiety "have strikingly different political consequences." A study of attitudes on "political reactions to the Iraq War" found that whereas "anxiety heightens perceived risk," "anger reduces the intellectual effort put into thinking about politics."[21] Trump turned these varying emotional reactions to his advantage. He created anxiety by describing a nation threatened by crime, terrorism, and a host of other problems all tied to groups other than white Americans, a largely untrue narrative. But he also created anger at elites, especially the press, after he became president, which produced a situation in which "anger counteracted the negative impact of factual knowledge," thereby obscuring the falseness of his fearmongering.[22]

Trump's rhetoric of nationalist populism with an outsider and later strongman persona was perfectly adapted to appeal to the fear and anger of authoritarian voters. He used the nationalist portion of his message to activate fear of various Others, thereby making an us-versus-them mind-set the core of his campaign. He used the populist portion of his message blaming elites for the presence of the various dangerous Others in American life both to create villains to hate and to absolve his supporters of responsibility for the situation they faced. In this narrative, the white working class had lost status because elites had allowed the various dangerous Others to usurp their role. The decline in status was not caused by technological developments or changes in global markets, and it certainly was not caused by lack of education of the white working class. Rather, it occurred because elites such as Clinton cared more about protecting illegal immigrants and Black protesters and supporting unfair trade deals than they did about ordinary (white) working people. Finally, the celebrity outsider and then as president the strongman persona provided the magical answer to the threat posed by the dangerous Others. Trump would Make America Great Again through the force of his will. Undocumented immigrants would be deported on the first day of his presidency, and manufacturing jobs would return in droves as the nation started winning again. In this narrative, no difficult action was required, no major investment was needed, no trade-offs must be confronted because Trump would simply make it so. The emotional appeal of the three components of the narrative should be obvious. Trump created fear, stoked anger, and then presented himself as the outsider/strongman hero who would instantly return the nation to a lost Golden Age. In this way, his rhetoric activated authoritarian tendencies among core supporters.

Research on how triggering events activate authoritarian tendencies strongly supports this explanation for the power of Trump's rhetoric. Without a triggering event, authoritarian tendencies are not activated. Moreover, if political figures speak and act in a way that reduces the sense of threat, even those with an authoritarian mind-set might not support the nationalist populist messages of authoritarian candidates such as Trump. However, when activated by a perceived threat, authoritarian voters might demonize those they see as different and support drastic action against this group. Trump's rhetoric was not aimed primarily at persuading people to support his program. Rather, his rhetoric used the nationalist populist message and outsider/strongman persona with a vernacular rhetorical style to arouse and activate fear of the Other and of lost status, and that activation, in turn, fed support for his message and campaign.[23]

Research conducted by PRRI and the *Atlantic* demonstrated that Trump's strategy of using a nationalist populist message to produce threat activation was well adapted to his core audience. This analysis found that by a two-to-one margin, white working-class voters supported Trump over Clinton. Rather than policy, Trump's ability to tap into perceived threats to status played the key role in the election. The PRRI report revealed that 48 percent "of white working-class Americans say, 'things have changed so much that I often feel like a stranger in my own country,'" and 68 percent felt both that "the American way of life needs to be protected from foreign influence" and that "the U.S. is in danger of losing its culture and identity," with 52 percent believing that "discrimination against whites has become as big a problem as discrimination against blacks and other minorities."[24] It is also striking that almost half of the white working class (48 percent) believed that the American dream "was once but is no longer true."[25] The PRRI study clearly identified perceived threats to status as key factors motivating support for Trump in the white working class. Of those who felt that discrimination against white Americans was a serious problem, 74 percent supported Trump, and 79 percent of those who expressed "anxieties about cultural change" backed him.[26]

In particular, Trump's ability to tap into racialized resentment was central to his campaign victory. Edsall noted that Trump "capitalized on the increasing salience of race and ethnicity" as "millions of white voters began to see themselves more openly not as white supremacists but as white identified," a redefinition of identity that occurred as "whites perceive[d] their group's dominant status . . . [was] threatened." He added, "Trump has mobilized the white identity electorate, and in doing so has put the tenuous American commitment to racial and ethnic egalitarianism on the line."[27] Given that in 2016 Trump won white women by 9 percentage points, white men by 31 points, and white voters overall by 21 points, the power of his race-based appeal is indisputable.[28] Nate Cohn confirmed the power of Trump's threat activation, concluding that "racial resentment" was "the strongest predictor of whether voters flipped from Mr. Obama to Mr. Trump, and the biggest driver of Trump support among these voters."[29]

A closely related factor was perceived loss of status as white dominance in American society lessened both because of greater inclusion of people of color and because the percentage of Americans who identify as white gradually has declined. Ronald Inglehart and Pippa Norris concluded, "The proximate cause of the populist vote is anxiety that pervasive cultural changes and an influx of foreigners are eroding the cultural norms one knew since childhood."[30] Similarly, Taub observed that "authoritarians feel threatened by people they identify as 'outsiders' and by the possibility of changes to the status quo makeup of their communities," thus explaining why such voters "reject not just one specific kind of outsider or social change, such as Muslims or same-sex couples or Hispanic migrants, but rather . . . reject all of them."[31]

Political alienation also was an important factor in the appeal of the populist portion of Trump's message. David Brooks noted that "the Alienated long for something that will smash the system or change their situation, but they have no actual plan or any means to deliver it" and added that "alienation breeds a distrust that corrodes any collective effort" as well as "breeds a hysterical public conversation."[32] Political alienation also was related to fear of cultural change. Emma Green was on target when she observed, "Trump's most powerful message . . . was about defending the country's putative culture."[33] Voters experiencing such anxiety overwhelmingly supported Trump. Olga Khazan noted that "79 percent of white working-class voters who had anxieties about the 'American way of life' chose Trump over Clinton," and "several surveys showed many men supported Trump because they felt their status in society was threatened, and that Trump would restore it."[34]

Although researchers such as Karen Stenner and Marc Hetherington have focused on perceived normative threats in the society or threats to the social structure itself, they have not recognized that rhetoric itself can function as a trigger activating the perceived normative threat and, therefore, the authoritarian response. Although not writing about rhetoric, Stenner's explanation of threat activation is clearly applicable to someone such as Trump who stoked the fires of hatred and fear throughout his campaign and presidency. Stenner noted, "The greater the threat perceived by respondents, the greater the influence of authoritarian predispositions on intolerance; militarism; support for the death penalty; favoring order over freedom; derogative stereotyping and discriminating against out-groups; and cleaving to the in-group."[35] She also observed, "The authoritarian dynamic is set in motion (or set at rest) when those disposed to monitor the environment for threats to oneness and sameness detect conditions of normative threat (or reassurance)."[36] Trump's campaign and his nationalist populist message activated the sense of normative threat.

It is notable that Trump successfully activated fear of immigrants, Islamic terrorism, and other perceived threats to the identity of the white working class despite the absence of significant real threats from these groups. In fact, his message was most powerful in areas with few members of these groups. In contrast, states outside the deeply conservative American South that had large numbers of actual immigrants, both legal and undocumented, voted overwhelmingly for Clinton. California is the best example of this point. Trump's rhetoric was much less successful in creating fear of immigrants, people of Islamic faith, or Black Americans in areas with large populations of these groups because familiarity with each group reduced the sense of difference and threat, and of course none of these groups actually threatened American society.

Trump's rhetoric pointed to various dangerous Others and elite villains as a way of highlighting threats to the status of the white working class. His rhetoric, especially the name-calling and fearmongering at rallies and on Twitter played a crucial role in triggering the response. Stenner noted, "Authoritarian fears are alleviated by defense of the collective normative orders: positive differentiation of the in-group, devaluation of and discrimination against out-groups, obedience to authorities, conformity to rules and norms, and intolerance and punishment of those who fail to obey and conform."[37] This description helps explain the power of Trump's rhetoric and the functions fulfilled by his rallies and tweets. Trump provided core supporters an in-group to which they could pledge allegiance and several out-groups to jeer or hate. His call for violence against protesters at his rallies and his attacks on groups such as Black Lives Matter fit the typical pattern by which authoritarians express and then resolve their fears about the dangerous Others and elites they perceive as threatening.

Trump's rhetoric was not focused on actual solutions to problems afflicting the white working class, but it was shrewdly targeted at activating insecurity, fear, and hatred in the large proportion of this group scoring high on authoritarian personality indicators. It also created a sense that he was both one of them and their champion against dangerous Others and their enablers among elites. Hetherington and Elizabeth Suhay explained, "When authoritarians perceive threats to conformity or the existing moral order, they seek to enforce conformity, in part through obedience to authority and aggression toward outgroups."[38] In this way, "Trump's pitch to voters both created the sense of threat and promised a defense: a winning political strategy for the age of identity politics" that was "rooted in emotional attachments, not policy goals."[39] Taub cited Jonathan Haidt, who described a triggering event as "a button is pushed that says, 'In case of moral threat, lock down the borders, kick out those who are different, and punish those who are morally deviant.'"[40] Trump's rhetoric of nationalist populism pushed that button. His attacks on elites served a similar function, acting as what Hetherington and Jonathan Weiler called "*organic extensions*" of his authoritarian message.[41]

Trump's nationalist populism also helps explain how he was able to appeal so strongly to the evangelical community despite his failure to live by the standards of personal morality the group supports. Many evangelicals feel what Khazan calls an "unfounded sense of persecution" and "see more discrimination against Christians than Muslims in the United States."[42] Kristin Kobes Du Mez makes a similar point, noting, "Donald Trump appeared at a moment when evangelicals felt increasingly beleaguered, even persecuted" and appealed to their "embrace of militant masculinity" by presenting himself as a Christian warrior "who wouldn't let political correctness get in the way of saying what had to be said or the norms of democratic society keep him from doing what needed to be done."[43] Trump tapped into those feelings with both the nationalist and populist aspects of his message and presented himself as a champion for a community under siege.

Although the nationalist theme in Trump's rhetoric was extremely important to his success, the populist antielitist theme also was important. A key factor was that Trump's rhetoric satisfied "a deep craving for respect" among his core supporters, the importance of which was magnified by Clinton's reference to Trump supporters as a "basket of deplorables."[44] In this way, Trump's populist attack on elites was well adapted to working-class voters. Greg Sargent cited polling focused on voters who supported Obama in 2012 but shifted to Trump in 2016 that found, "A shockingly large percentage of these Obama-Trump voters said Democrats' economic policies will favor the wealthy—twice the percentage that said the same about Trump." These voters "are economically losing ground and are skeptical of Democratic solutions to their problems."[45] Despite the indisputable fact that Trump's policies would and then did aid the rich, Trump tapped into the feeling that Democrats had sold out the working class, demonstrating through his tweets and rallies that he was "a virtuoso at the politics of resentment."[46] This polling again illustrates how unimportant policy argument was to swing voters. Clinton favored policies similar to those of Obama, much more focused on helping the poor and working class than the economic deregulation and tax cuts for the rich favored by Trump. But Trump's populist attack on elites resonated with this group, whereas Clinton came across as out of touch to white working-class voters.

Trump was a master at tapping into what Jeremy Engels labeled "the politics of resentment," which "involves channeling civic resentment—engendered by economic exploitation, political alienation, and a legitimate sense of victimhood into a hatred of our neighbors and fellow citizens."[47] Engels commented that rhetoric creating resentment "does not provide solutions. It is a strategy of distraction that focuses attention on the grievance as an excuse to taunt and offend," precisely fist Trump's use of the approach.[48] Trump enacted a "politics of resentment" by creating hatred and fear of dangerous Others and placing blame on elites he depicted as uncaring and demeaning the "real people." Engels described how creation of a sense of resentment was used to block change that threatened economic elites, focusing on how Richard Nixon "worked to harness the resentment many middle-class white Americans felt for African Americans and student protestors by making it more respectable and rearticulating it in the language of liberal democracy." Such tactics define "political adversaries as 'enemies' and politics as war by other means to cultivate hatred in addition to fear," creating "toxicity for democracy."[49] Trump's nationalist populism with an outsider and later strongman persona and a vernacular style represented a kind of perverse perfection of Nixon's approach. Nixon's use of terms such as "silent majority" to create resentment were, in comparison with Trump's message, almost restrained. Trump was far more direct than Nixon in creating villains to fear and hate and shifting blame to elites. Moreover, for all his faults, Nixon had a domestic agenda of some breadth that was in some ways quite liberal, including support for a guaranteed income and a national health-care plan.[50] In contrast, Trump heaped scorn on liberal elites in order to block their efforts to help groups, especially in the white working class, who formed the core of Trump's base of support.

Trump also successfully drew on nationalist populist themes to create a strong sense of shared identity among core supporters. Taub cited Immo Fritsche, a political scientist at the University of Leipzig, who "has found that when people feel they have lost control, they seek a strong identity that will make them feel part of a powerful group."[51] Trump's call to join his crusade to Make America Great Again served this function. Similarly, Trump's attacks on the media and other elites created a strong affective bond with core supporters.[52] Sabrina Tavernise noted, "Much of what powers the love of Mr. Trump among his core supporters is his boxer's approach to the political class in Washington and to the news media."[53] He captured the rage of many who felt that they had lost ground and that elites did not care. Eduardo Porter commented that Trump's "diagnosis of the raw anger and disillusionment among white working-class Americans" was "brilliant." He added of the description of "American carnage" in Trump's Inaugural Address that it "struck a nerve with millions of voters who feel left behind by a country buffeted by demographic, technological, and social change."[54]

Trump's enactment of the outsider (and later strongman) who could "drain the swamp" also played a role. A PRRI study revealed, "Nearly half [of the American people] (49%) say things have gotten so far off track that we need a strong leader who is willing to break the rules if that is what it takes to set things right." The figure supporting such an authoritarian leader is 60 percent for the white working class and 67 percent for those in the white working class who say "immigrants are a burden on society."[55] The outsider persona was also particularly adapted to the high percentage of his core supporters who possessed an authoritarian personality. They have "a greater need for order" and "often imbue authorities with transcendent qualities, not subject to questioning and doubt"—a perfect description of the response Trump received at rallies.[56] In this way, "Trump's strongman rhetoric" "struck a chord" with a large group, including according to a 2016 survey "almost half—44 percent—of U.S. non-college graduates [who] approved of having a strong leader unchecked by elections and Congress."[57] There is also substantial research indicating that a significant portion of the population would support a "domineering leader" who could respond to risks present in a dangerous world.[58]

A similar point can be made about what on first glance is a style of political rhetoric totally unlike that of any other modern American political leader. In fact, the stylistic pattern associated with nationalist populism was well adapted to appealing to Trump's core audience. Trump used a "vernacular style" combining "an unholy tangle of lies, misapprehensions, disinformation and personal insults" as well as "schoolyard nicknames for opponents" to exercise his "great gifts in the art of vengeance and humiliation."[59] This style was based in "the idea that political authenticity means spontaneity."[60] Trump's creation of perceived authenticity through his vernacular style partially explains why his many gaffes did not destroy his campaign. Joshua Green explained, "Trump's willingness to flout any norm was a powerful source of his appeal."[61] As Jan-Werner Müller noted, "revelations of corruption" and other gaffes "rarely seem to hurt populist leaders" because, "in the eyes of their followers, 'they're doing it for us,' the one authentic people."[62] In fact, criticism often led Trump supporters to redouble their support. Jeremy Peters reported, "Republican voters repeatedly described an instinctive, protective response to the president."[63]

Social scientific studies, polling, ethnographic studies of Trump supporters (especially the subgroup attending rallies), and press interaction with individual Trump voters all support the conclusion that Trump's message of nationalist populism, with an outsider/strongman persona along with an associated vernacular style, was well adapted for tapping into and magnifying fear of social change; anger at elites in the political, media, and expert communities; and a desire for a strong leader who could immediately and easily return the nation to a Golden Age that never existed. There is no question about the emotional resonance of Trump's message for strong supporters. The comment of veteran *Washington Post* reporter Phillip Bump that "I've seen a good number of political rallies, and the audience response at a Trump rally is unlike anywhere else" reflects the consensus of commentators and researchers, who often used expressions such as "frenzied crowd of die-hard supporters" to describe Trump rallies. Bump ascribed this response to the fact that Trump "is telling the elites who've run the country where they can shove it" and cited as evidence the fact that "people in the audience will turn toward the assembled media and raise their middle fingers." Rallygoers loved "to hear Trump disparage the people they hate and . . . reflect that disparagement back" at elites.[64] As Republican strategist Steve Schmidt, a longtime adviser to John McCain, observed, "Central to the [Trump] show is the idea of shared victimization."[65] Evidence of this sense of victimization that Trump taps into and activates among supporters is found in polling that "nearly two-thirds of Trump voters say they're at least somewhat concerned about 'reverse racism' . . . the idea that whites are the focus of discrimination."[66]

A review of thirty postpresidential Trump rallies, based on interviews with Trump supporters, also revealed the strong emotional resonance of Trump's message. The review described how "the crowd goes wild" when Trump claims "our country is respected again" or says the border wall is being built; boos when Trump mentions "the fake news," says that Democrats represent "radical socialism," or attacks leading Democrats; and exults in chanting "CNN sucks!"[67] These responses are driven by fear, anger, and resentment, not ideology. Additional evidence of the appeal of Trump's nationalist populism can be found in the way it is reflected in statements by leading Trump supporters, including members of the Republican leadership in Congress, labeling Democrats "anti-American."[68]

Ethnographic research by Arlie Russell Hochschild also supports the power of Trump's message. For her book *Strangers in Their Own Land*, Hochschild interviewed a wide range of people in the white working class in Louisiana who "feel like a besieged minority" that is "culturally marginalized," making them "afraid, resentful, displaced, and [feeling] dismissed."[69] She reported that everyone she had "profiled" and "most of their kin, friends, and" others they knew "had voted for Trump" and explained how he tapped into their "regional pride" and "resentment" and the sense that they "are the real patriots; respect us for that."[70] Hochschild described the response of people at a Trump rally, how it produced "an ecstatic high" of "a united brother- and sisterhood of believers" who "revile and expel members of out-groups."[71] Trump supporters at the rally had "been in mourning for a lost way of life. . . . They yearn to feel pride but instead have felt shame. Their land no longer feels their own." At the rally they "seemed in a state of rapture. As if magically lifted, *they are no longer strangers in their own land*." One even spoke of the joy of being "in the *presence of such* a man."[72] The power of the nationalist, populist, and outsider/strongman persona, along with the associated vernacular style, is obvious in Hochschild's reporting of the feelings of Trump supporters.

Trump's Rhetoric and the Republican Establishment

Trump's rhetoric of nationalist populism with an outsider/strongman persona not only helps explain the resonance of his campaign and his almost unchanging approval rating as president but also how he could achieve those results without having any kind of coherent policy platform and while facing the opposition of virtually all of the Republican establishment early in the

2016 primary season. In the primary campaign, Trump's initial appeal was among those voters whose fear of loss of status was strongly activated by his nationalist populist message. In the general election campaign, he ultimately received support from almost all Republicans, even though most principled conservatives initially opposed his candidacy. The early opposition of mainstream conservative elites to Trump can be traced to their commitment to free-market and small-government ideological principles. Hetherington and Weiler noted that conservatives focused on defense of the status quo and market-friendly policies often lack authoritarian tendencies.[73] This explains why a number of conservative intellectuals and a few political figures, notably Governor John Kasich of Ohio, refused to support Trump even after his nomination and eventual election. They found his ideas and his rhetoric repellent.

Trump's ideological incoherence and the opposition of the Republican establishment did not doom his campaign early in the primary campaign because his main appeal was to voters with a high level of authoritarianism. Stenner noted that authoritarianism "is not a desire to preserve the status quo, whatever that may be. It does not preclude support for social change, so long as we are changing together in pursuit of common goals. And it is not preference for laissez-faire economics. It does not necessitate opposition to government interventions that might serve to enhance oneness and sameness."[74] Trump's appeal was not that he presented a coherent conservative ideological vision in the way Reagan did. Rather, he drew upon and also triggered a sense of fear and then provided a release from that fear through support for him as the hero who had the guts to break up the system in order to bring back the society and economy of the fabled past.

In her groundbreaking work on authoritarianism, Stenner argued, "Status quo conservatives . . . can be a liberal democracy's strongest bulwark against the dangers posed by intolerant social movements."[75] Principled conservatives did not provide that "bulwark" against the Trump campaign in part because the sheer number of candidates in the Republican primary allowed Trump to defeat them one at a time. If there had been fewer candidates, a Kasich or a Marco Rubio might have overwhelmed Trump early in the primaries. In addition, several candidates, notably Rubio and Ted Cruz, made the mistake of responding to Trump with a pointed and personal rhetoric that reinforced his message attacking elites. Ultimately, Trump was able to win the nomination despite the fact that his core group of supporters was roughly one-third of Republican primary or caucus voters. For example, on

Super Tuesday, Trump received more than 40 percent of the vote in only two of eleven states. His vote total was under 30 percent in three states and was in the low 30s in most of the remaining states.[76] However, in the divided primary field, that level of support allowed him to win nearly all of the early primaries. After the nomination was assured, most Republicans fell into line behind him out of loyalty to the party or in the hope that Trump might be transformed into a traditional conservative.

The tribal nature of early twenty-first-century American politics was a crucial factor in Trump's eventual transformation of the Republican Party into the party of Trump. Edsall noted, "For many Republicans partisan identification is more a tribal affiliation than an ideological commitment."[77] A recent study of a national sample from Survey Sampling International concluded, "The power behind the labels 'liberal' and 'conservative' to predict strong preferences for the ideological in-group is based largely in the social identification with those groups, not in the organization of attitudes associated with the labels."[78] As this research indicates, issue positions and support for a coherent ideology might be much less important than group identity. After Trump was the Republican nominee, loyalty to the Republican "tribe" became paramount for many voters.

In addition, Trump had little difficulty effectively consolidating Republican support after he won the nomination because his core message of nationalist populism was a good fit for many ordinary Republican voters. Although not scoring as high on authoritarian scales as the white working class, a high percentage of Republicans has attitudes consistent with authoritarianism. One study revealed that more "than 55 percent of surveyed Republicans scored as 'high' or 'very high' authoritarians." This also helps explain why Trump was so appealing to conservative Christians and others who espoused quite traditional values.[79]

Conclusion

Trump used a rhetoric of nationalist populism with an outsider and later strongman persona and an associated stylistic pattern to tap into the perception of many in the white working class that their way of life was under siege and to activate an authoritarian personality structure possessed by many of these voters. The function of Trump's rhetoric of nationalist populism with an outsider/strongman persona was to provide supporters villains to fear and hate as well as a hero who could save them by doing and saying things that others would not say or do in order to bust up the system. Trump's use of this rhetorical pattern was highly effective first in gaining strong support from roughly one-third of Republican primary supporters, next in consolidating support among remaining Republican voters or Republican-leaning voters whose identity as "Republican" was more tribal than ideological, then in appealing to enough members of the white working class who had supported Obama in 2008 and 2012 to win the election, and finally in maintaining the support of slightly more than 40 percent of the people as president.

Trump's reliance on this rhetorical pattern also explains his continuing focus on the dangers posed by immigration, terrorism, inner-city crime, groups such as Black Lives Matter, and NFL players kneeling during the National Anthem as well as unfair trade deals as means of threat activation. Trump needed to activate a sense of threat to keep core supporters engaged. This explains what on the surface appeared an inexplicable development in the aftermath of hearings that ultimately resulted in the confirmation of Brett Kavanaugh to the Supreme Court. One might have expected that at the conclusion of hearings, which many thought did not fully look into Kavanaugh's record or allegations that he had attempted sexual assault while in high school, liberals would have been enraged and Republicans would be satisfied. In fact, Republicans were "elated" by liberal protest and "cast the Trump resistance movement as 'an angry mob'" in order to evoke "fear of an unknown and out-of-control mass people" and tap "into grievances about the nation's fast-moving cultural and demographic shifts."[80]

The fact that the most threatening things this "mob" did were march, chant, and on occasion yell at Republican leaders in Congress made little difference. Trump and other Republicans could cast them as threatening to activate a sense of normative threat. The complete absence of any actual threat did not undercut this strategy. More broadly, the falseness of his rhetoric in general did not limit his ability to sow hate and fear and therefore produce threat activation. With his core audience, as Gerson observed, Trump was quite successful in using "political rallies" and other venues "to whip up a right-wing mob into frothing anger."[81] At the end of the 2018 midterm campaign, when Trump faced strong opposition not only from liberals but also from college-educated voters and many suburban women, he doubled down on this approach and "settled on a strategy of fear—laced with falsehoods and racially tinged rhetoric" in describing "an apocalyptic vision of the country" under siege from a liberal "mob" and a "caravan" of undocumented immigrants from Central America that he claimed without evidence of any kind included "Middle Easterners." Trump was trying to rile "up his most avid supporters, often through frightening and emotional appeals" in order to "re-create the 2016 playbook."[82] In feeding anger with attacks on the media or chants to "lock her [Clinton] up," Trump's rhetoric activated a sense of threat among "illiberal and authoritarian forces that constitute the real danger to civil peace and democracy."[83]

Limitations of the rhetorical pattern also help explain why his support rarely exceeded the low 40s in national polling despite continuation of strong job creation (until the pandemic struck in 2020) that began during the Obama administration and why it failed so badly in the 2018 midterm election. Trump's message was particularly adapted to activating voters with authoritarian personality structures. Studies show "44 percent of white respondents nationwide scored as 'high' or 'very high' authoritarians, with 19 percent as 'very high.'"[84] Most of these voters are concentrated in the working class, and many of them already identified with the Republican Party. Although there are undoubtedly Democrats who score high on authoritarianism, tribalism makes it difficult for Trump to appeal to those who strongly identify with the Democratic Party. Similarly, the nature of Trump's message limits its appeal to people of color. In addition, Trump's history of making sexist comments, along with allegations by a large number of women that he had either harassed them or committed sexual violence against them, the *Access Hollywood* tape in which he seemed to brag about committing such violence, and his opposition to social and medical programs of particular importance to women limited his potential support. Trump had many female supporters among women with strong identities as Republican and those who scored high on authoritarianism, but his record and rhetoric sharply limited his appeal beyond those groups.

It is also important that the very factors that made Trump's message resonate strongly for authoritarian voters in the white working class also made it repellent for those who scored low on authoritarianism. Hetherington and Suhay note, "While diversity is threatening to authoritarians, it is often welcomed by nonauthoritarians," who find it "a cause for celebration."[85] The authoritarian underpinning for Trump's rhetoric of nationalist populism and an outsider/strongman persona also illuminates the fury Republican intellectuals and traditional conservatives, such as Jeff Flake, Gerson, Kasich, McCain, George Will, and others expressed toward Trump. The intellectuals and principled Republican political figures backed conservative economic and social policies and a strong defense along with support for alliances such as the North Atlantic Treaty Organization (NATO). They were not afraid of diversity in ideas or people. They supported small-government conservatism in a Reaganesque manner, but they rejected Trump's nativism on policy grounds and his personal demeanor on moral ones. Although conservative intellectuals consistently attacked Trump's approach, few officeholders did so, and many of them, including Flake and Kasich, soon left office. The failure of so many to speak up against and vote against policies they had opposed in some cases for decades speaks to both the power of political tribalism and the stranglehold Trump had on the Republican Party.

The upshot is that Trump's message was well adapted to activating slightly more than 40 percent of voters but ill adapted to reach groups that would push his support much higher. He was able to defeat a weak candidate such as Clinton because he strongly activated his core supporters, and enough other voters either wanted major change in politics or were put off by Clinton or her husband. Questionable decisions by her campaign, such as largely ignoring the industrial Midwest, also undoubtedly played a role. In addition, it is important to recognize that although Trump's message as president continued to excite his base, it also energized millions of men and especially women to become involved in politics to oppose him.

The strengths and limitations of Trump's message of nationalist populism with an outsider/strongman persona were evident in the results of the 2020 presidential election. In that election, activating Trump's base of core supporters was not enough to win reelection. Without the pandemic, the result might have been very different.

The explanation for Trump's appeal during the campaigns and for how he maintained support in polling as president in a range from the middle 30s to the low 40s also suggests an answer to what at first glance appears to be the inexplicable fact that a significant number of Obama supporters, roughly 8 to 13 percent, shifted support to Trump, a shift essential to Trump's election.[86] Mutz asked, "How is it that the same American public that elected an African American to two terms as US President subsequently elected a president known to have publicly made what many consider to be racist and sexist statements?"[87] However, when the role of voters with authoritarian personality structures is considered, along with the somewhat different ways in which Obama and Clinton spoke of issues related to race and diversity, an explanation emerges.

Research on authoritarianism indicates that a perceived threat can be either activated or deactivated. Hetherington and Weiler noted, "An authoritarian disposition lies dormant in the absence of threat."[88] At the same time, although as Trump's campaign and presidency demonstrated, rhetoric can activate authoritarian tendencies, it also can be used to tamp down on those tendencies by minimizing perceived threat. Stenner observed that in some circumstances, "latent predispositions to authoritarianism are deactivated as the classic fears are calmed."[89] She explained that "talk of our 'common goals and values' and trustworthy leaders could dramatically diminish, even reverse, the impact of authoritarianism on intolerance, although it did prove much easier to threaten than to reassure, that is, to activate than to deactivate those fundamental predispositions."[90] Stenner went on to note that "if different races and ethnicities within a particular society could *seem* less different . . . then those who are innately intolerant of difference would generally be more 'tolerant'" and added that "nothing inspires greater tolerance from the intolerant than an abundance of common and unifying beliefs, practices, rituals, institutions, and processes."[91]

It is clear Obama recognized the potential of race to undermine his campaign and presidency. However, Obama's rhetorical focus was always on shared values, what all Americans had in common, as opposed to what divided them. Famously, in the "Race" speech, he spoke movingly of all the problems both people of color and the white working class had to overcome and called for the groups to work together.[92] In the speech that introduced him to the national stage, the keynote at the 2004 Democratic National Convention, he made the crowd and nation roar with approval as he spoke of the nation as not composed of "red" states or "blue" states but as the United States of America. He also said that there was not a "black America" or "white America" or "Latino America" but rather "the United States of America."[93] Obama defended liberal policies based on commonality rather than difference. His rhetoric provided a picture of a community in which everyone counted, everyone did their fair share, and everyone received the support they needed. It was and is a powerful message that clearly tamped down the fears of enough Americans who possess a disposition toward authoritarianism in order for him to win the presidency twice.

Obama's inclusive message was not enough to tamp down intolerance among a large group of Republican partisans, many of whom undoubtedly had strong authoritarian tendencies. A sizable proportion of this group viewed Obama as socialist or anti-American or even doubted that he had been born in Hawaii despite incontrovertible evidence to the contrary. For these voters, his inclusive message was either ignored or could not overcome frankly racist attitudes. But his message was powerful enough to create a coalition of Americans of every race, religion, and ethnicity—a group not threatened by diversity—and to reassure a small but crucial group of voters with an authoritarian mind-set.

Although candidate Clinton's policy positions were close to those of Obama, her rhetorical practice was different. The Clinton campaign was defined by a "forthright championing of racial, religious, and sexual diversity well beyond any tried by presidential candidates heretofore—accompanied by a blistering ad campaign highlighting Trump's insults against all kinds of minority groups."[94] Unfortunately, "talking about difference, and applauding difference . . . are the surest ways to aggravate those who are innately intolerant and to guarantee the increased expression of their predispositions in manifestly intolerant attitudes and behaviors."[95] One unfortunate side effect of Clinton's commitment to diversity was to provide an opening for Trump's rhetoric of nationalist populism. Trump responded with nativist and racially coded messages that strongly tapped into fear of social change, especially among voters with an authoritarian personality structure. In addition to a message that highlighted difference much more than that of Obama, Clinton lacked Obama's gifts for appealing to shared American identity and recasting the American dream. Stenner's research makes it clear that it is easier to stir up fear and hate of Others than it is to tamp down those feelings. Obama had a gift for talking in an inspiring way about American identity and the need for shared sacrifice to move the entire community forward. Clinton lacked that gift. In addition, although it was entirely appropriate for Clinton to address the wrongs committed against various groups, such liberal rhetoric had the effect of activating people who feared their group would lose its status. This group's support for Trump decided the 2016 election.

8

Nationalist Populism and the
Threat to American Democracy

In the previous chapters, I explained how Trump employed a rhetoric of nationalist populism with an outsider/strongman persona and a vernacular rhetorical style to activate voters with an authoritarian personality structure as well as gain support by drawing upon and tapping into a sense of Republican tribal identity. Explaining how Trump's message worked with a portion of the audience and how it failed to resonate with a larger group also can inform our understanding not only of his campaign and administration but more broadly of how rhetoric functions in contemporary American democracy and about dangers posed by a rhetoric espousing nationalist populism.

Trump, Rhetoric, and American Politics

Trump's ability to create and maintain support from a bit more than 40 percent of the populace with his rhetoric of nationalist populism is immensely revealing concerning contemporary American rhetorical practice and American democracy. First, the Trump campaign shattered norms that had guided presidential campaigns for decades.[1] He did more than simply commit gaffe after gaffe. Prior to Trump, serious presidential candidates laid out an ideological vision for the nation. Although candidates often pointed to major problems facing the nation, they also were careful to present a picture of a better future that could be achieved. Additionally, although campaigns leveled sharp and sometimes personal attacks, candidates avoided mere name-calling and made an effort to defend statements as truthful. On occasion, candidates violated these norms, notably Sarah Palin in 2008, but in the main they observed them as important to American democracy and also because of fear of voter backlash. Trump did not just violate but obliterated these norms.

Both as a candidate and as president, Trump had "no detailed governing agenda" and was "incapable of using policy details in the course of political persuasion."[2] As I have demonstrated, the purpose behind Trump's nationalist populism was not to build support for policies that would improve the life of the working class but to serve as a primal scream expressing the anger of this group at the system. Trump also violated norms by constantly attacking opponents, often referring to them with demeaning nicknames, such as "Crooked Hillary" in reference to Hillary Clinton. Rather than producing backlash from voters, these childish attacks often drew cheers. Michael Kazin's comment that "populism . . . too often allows the malicious to overshadow the hopeful" was certainly accurate about the Trump campaign.[3] In fact, norm violation was a crucial part of his rhetoric of nationalist populism. It was a means of creating controversy and fanning hatred against elites and the dangerous Other. It is disquieting that after 2016, rather than rejecting a rhetoric based in lies, fear, and name-calling, many campaigns chose to model their approach on Trump's.[4]

The Trump campaign and presidency also made it clear that the small-government ideology espoused by Ronald Reagan and so many others no longer dominated conservatism in general or the Republican Party in particular. From 1980 until 2016, Reagan's ideological vision of small-government conservatism and a strong defense dominated the party, although his vision was general enough that there was considerable disagreement on how much government was needed and how aggressive the nation should be in using its military power. Even more than ideology, Republicans were defined by an individualist narrative vision of the American dream that animated Reagan's rhetoric.[5] With Trump's election, the Republican Party endorsed an ideology and a narrative different than the optimistic and at least rhetorically inclusive message of Reagan. R. R. Reno explained that for a generation, "Ronald Reagan was the party's North Star" but that what elected Trump was antithetical to Reagan's worldview: "The America First, antiglobalist themes won him the election, not freedom-oriented anti-government ones."[6] In his Farewell Address, Reagan spoke of the nation as a "shining city on a hill" that was "teeming with people of all kinds living in harmony and peace" and added that it was "open to anyone with the will and the heart to get here."[7] Whereas Reagan saw a triumphant celebration of freedom, Trump saw a dystopian vision of "American carnage." In this context, E. J. Dionne Jr. was quite correct when he said, "It's possible to imagine that, somewhere, Ronald Reagan is weeping."[8] The contrast between Trump's and Reagan's vision of the nation created a situation in which Corey Robin rightly observed that the Republican Party faced an "existential crisis" and was "headed for a showdown with itself."[9]

The crisis facing the party was not only about ideology but also about something more fundamental, the defining values of conservatism itself. Michael Gerson, who wrote speeches defending democratic values for George W. Bush, defined "Trumpism" as "some mix of protectionism, nativism, and bitter resentment of elites" and added that the core question facing Republican leaders was: "Will conservatives so easily abandon conservatism for white identity politics?"[10] *New York Times* columnist David Brooks also noted that the conflict within conservatism was about values when he said, "At his essence Trump is an assault on the sacred order that conservatives hold dear" and then added that "today you can be a conservative or a Republican, but you can't be both."[11] Other leading conservative intellectuals focused on Trump's role in the conservative movement. Max Boot emphasized the dangers posed by the cult of personality that Trump's use of the outsider/strongman persona fostered.[12] He observed, "The entire Republican platform can now be reduced to three words: whatever Trump wants," a development that led former House speaker John Boehner to observe, "There is no Republican Party. . . . There's a Trump party. The Republican Party is kind of taking a nap somewhere."[13] Similarly, George Will, a leading conservative intellectual for a generation, labeled "today's GOP . . . the president's plaything" and called for the people to "vote against his party's cowering congressional caucuses . . . to affirm the nation's honor."[14] Gerson, Brooks, Boot, Will, and other leading conservative intellectuals viewed Trump's message of nationalist populism with an outsider/strongman persona as so antithetical to the core values of conservatism that in several cases they called upon all citizens to vote for Democrats.

Republican leaders in the House and the Senate clearly attempted to paper over the sharp contrast between the Reaganesque ideological and narrative vision that had dominated the party for thirty-five years and that of Trump by focusing on those areas in which they could make common cause with

Trump's nationalist populism, notably a tax cut heavily tilted toward the rich, the nomination of very conservative federal judges, and steps that limited social programs serving people living in poverty and women. However, the conflict between the two visions of the world was still present. The party and most conservative activists had chosen to support a vision of "American carnage" rather than one of it being "morning again" in the "shining city on the hill." There is substantial risk that Trump and those who succeed him could transform the Republican Party into a far-right cult of personality similar to far-right parties in Europe.

A third implication relates to the power of public reason. The resonance of Trump's fundamentally false nationalist populist message speaks to the limited power of reason in our public life. Voters did not choose Trump because he made a stronger argument. Rather, Trump used his narrative of threatened identity, nostalgia for an entirely imaginary Edenic past, and promise to return the nation to that past through force of will to create a political "universe in which facts, logic, reason, and the laws of political gravity do not apply."[15] He appealed to "supporters . . . who are terrified they are losing their country," when in fact their country is not under threat but simply adapting to a changing demography.[16] In defending the fundamentally false nationalist populist narrative, Trump "tapped into what Richard Hofstadter identified in 1966 as 'anti-intellectualism' in American life," in large part because in a "popular cultural world" defined by reality television, he "reigned supreme."[17] The limited power of reason was especially evident in the presidential debates, in which Trump struggled to make anything like a coherent case for his views. In the debates, Trump made dozens of apparently irrelevant comments as well as many patently false statements.[18] No one could have watched the exchanges between Trump and Clinton or Trump and Joe Biden and thought Trump was more knowledgeable or had a clearer grasp of how his program might work. The public clearly saw the flaws in Trump's performance, and various polls showed that he lost badly.[19] Yet, Trump supporters influenced by Trump's nationalist populist message saw this failure to present a coherent defense of his agenda as being of little import. These supporters resided in a "Trump bubble," in which fact checks "provide[d] no effective check."[20] Trump's presidential rhetoric continued this pattern.

Authoritarianism, in part, explains the failure of reasonable criticism of Trump to make much difference. Marc Hetherington and Jonathan Weiler noted, "A tendency to rigid thinking and an unwillingness or inability to process new information that might challenge such thinking also appears to be characteristic of authoritarians' mode of political understanding."[21] Moreover, expert refutation of Trump merely reinforced his antielitist message and created greater resentment against those he claimed did not respect hardworking, ordinary Americans. Stephen Reicher and Alexander Haslam noted that refuting Trump and calling him a liar might have "reinforce[d] the dynamics which led to Trump's ascendancy in the first place" and made critics come across "as part of the sneering elite."[22] Moreover, when activated, and Trump clearly did that, "authoritarians . . . [were] much more interested in pursuing one-sided information that reinforced existing beliefs," a goal the conservative media and social media easily filled.[23]

Trump was a master at tapping into "antipathy toward intellectual know-it-alls."[24] In addition, he used techniques common in reality TV to create an easy-to-understand, compelling narrative. David Friend noted that whereas Clinton's speeches and other "outreach efforts felt like a PBS fund drive," Trump created a reality TV campaign that for eighteen months "the nation [watched] compulsively."[25] The difficulty was that Clinton's dull narrative was mostly true, whereas Trump's compelling reality TV narrative was almost entirely false. In Trump's campaign, status as a celebrity was more important than governing experience or having a developed ideological vision.[26] Paul Krugman's observation that Trump's constant lying "suggests that politicians can get away with telling voters just about anything that sounds good" was exactly right and immensely disquieting.[27]

Cultural critics often bemoan the pernicious effects of what they call hegemonic reason. Trump's successful use of a rhetoric of nationalist populism in the 2016 presidential campaign suggests a different conclusion. Trump's campaign and presidential rhetoric demonstrate that reason is hardly hegemonic in American politics and is sometimes almost powerless to confront a nationalist narrative that feeds our basest fear and hatred despite being false.

How Trump's Rhetoric of Nationalist Populism Threatens American Democracy

The dramatic changes in presidential rhetoric reflected in Trump's nationalist populist message pose severe dangers for American democracy.[28] The first danger flows from the obliteration of norms governing how political

figures should talk and act.[29] Trump's rhetoric acted as a "contagion of divisive and at times violent language" that "filters down to other politicians and
to partisan media," creating a situation in which "demonization has become
mainstream."[30] Boot was on target when he argued that Trump's rhetoric was
"normalizing bigotry and conspiracy-mongering," a development so dangerous that Boot argued it would "take a generation to clean up the toxins he
has released."[31]

To activate core supporters, nationalist populists such as Trump "want
confrontation and conflict."[32] Governor John Kasich of Ohio observed during
the Republican primaries, "Donald Trump has created a toxic environment"
by preying "on the fears of people."[33] One of the pernicious effects of norm
violation is that it encourages the opposition to respond in kind. Frank Bruni
was getting at this problem when he noted, "For more and more Americans,
the other side isn't merely misguided in the extreme. It's evil in the absolute,
and virtue is measured by the starkness with which that evil is labeled and
reviled," a rhetorical practice that produces "emotional satisfactions" at the
"terrible price" of "dehumanization."[34]

Norms matter for another reason; democracy itself is constituted through
our words. As Bruni noted, "Words, like monuments, matter. They nudge.
They shape. That's true when they elevate what shouldn't be elevated, encouraging complacency or evil, and that's just as true when they show us
a better way and help us get there."[35] The irony of moving from Barack
Obama's audacious hope to Trump's angry nationalist populism should be
apparent to all. By undercutting rhetorical norms that have shaped American
politics for decades, Trump created fear and hatred and sowed division. In a
political system in which partisans view their political opponents not as misguided but as dangerous or evil, winning at all costs will become the norm.
This could lead to the gradual loss of basic democratic institutions or in a
crisis threaten the democratic system itself.

Trump's nationalist populist message also threatens American democracy
by undercutting the very idea of truth itself. One way in which Trump violated political norms was by lying constantly about his record, proposals, actions, and especially those who opposed him. In fact, as David Leonhardt observed, "He lies in ways that no American politician ever has before" and "sets
out to deceive people."[36] The lies were so prevalent that the *New York Times*
allocated a full page with very small print to reprint a summary of all the
lies in the first 100 days of the Trump administration.[37] The *Washington Post*

fact checker labeled him "the most fact-challenged politician" and added that "he earned 59 Four-Pinocchio ratings during his campaign" and made 488 "false or misleading claims" in his first 100 days as president; he reached 1,000 false or misleading claims in the first week of August 2017.[38] The *Washington Post* even introduced a new label, "the Bottomless Pinocchio," to account for Trump's penchant for repeating lies dozens of times, thereby "purposely injecting false information into the national conversation."[39] All politicians exaggerate or bend the truth, and some occasionally tell outright lies, but as Dionne observed, the essence of Trump's approach to politics is "indifference to verifiable facts" because "a lie is as good as the truth as long as you can get your base to believe it."[40] Similarly, Sheryl Gay Stolberg concluded, "The glaring difference between Mr. Trump and his predecessors is the sheer magnitude of falsehoods and exaggerations," leading scholars to fear that "in elevating the art of political fabrication," he might have "forever changed what Americans are willing to tolerate from their leaders."[41]

Trump's narrative of the heroic outsider/strongman fighting against weak elites in the thrall of the "deep state" to protect the people from the Others who threaten the security and identity of ordinary people was the underlying force behind Trump's predilection to lie. To create the anger, hatred, and fear essential to activating authoritarian voters, Trump had to depict an American dystopia in which ordinary white working-class voters were losing their jobs to unfair trade deals, undocumented immigrants, and reverse discrimination, a dystopia that faced an epidemic of crime coming from inner cities and terrorism from undocumented and radicalized immigrants. In this narrative, elites were weak and cared more about protecting undocumented immigrants and terrorism suspects than they did about ordinary citizens, and a deep state opposed his heroic efforts at reform. The difficulty with the narrative was that every part of it was untrue except that working-class Americans lacked the same opportunity for upward mobility present for earlier generations. The key point is not merely that as a candidate and then as president Trump lied constantly but that his entire campaign and presidency rested on a big lie that the nation itself faced a crisis of "American carnage."[42]

Trump's willingness to lie about almost anything also undermined the idea of reasoned policy change. Greg Sargent observed that the Trump "administration has regularly shown contempt for the very idea that consequential policy decisions require serious justification or a weighing of their consequences."[43] Trump's advocacy for tax cuts was a good example of this problem. Trump's core supporters in the white working class received only a modest tax cut from the legislation, at best.[44] However, Trump could hardly sell his tax plan by honestly admitting that the vast majority of the benefits would flow to the rich and to corporations, whose stock, of course, is disproportionately owned by the rich. So, he again and again exaggerated the size of the tax cuts for the middle and working classes.[45] This point can be generalized. Trump's core narrative that the nation was under siege was clearly false, as was his claim that undocumented immigrants committed a massive number of violent crimes or that Islamic terrorism threatened all Americans. Lying was not merely a strategy for puffing up his credentials or dodging a political controversy. It was the only way he could develop the core themes of nationalist populism and the outsider/strongman hero. One consequence, as Leonard Pitts noted, was that "the idea of principled debate got run over by the Trump Train."[46]

Public reason plays a key role in American democracy. Roger Cohen was exactly right when he argued that "the frivolous blurring of truth and untruth, fact and falsehood, is the most grave" threat to the nation because "liberty depends on facts. When the distinction between truth and lies disappears, there is no basis for the rational discourse on which the organization of a free society, governed by laws, depends."[47] One could not have an honest debate with Trump because he routinely said untrue things and rejected criticism as evidence of partisanship. The net effect was to undercut the very idea of sensible policymaking. As E. J. Dionne, Norman Ornstein, and Thomas Mann concluded, "Lies and untruths are the enemy of honest democratic deliberation. Policymaking needs to be taken seriously because government matters."[48]

The quantity of lies also had the effect of devaluing any specific falsehood, which quickly became old news. Charles M. Blow concluded, "Trump is quite literally overwhelming our human capacities with his mendacity," and Michelle Goldberg added, "The scale of dishonesty can be destabilizing. It's a psychic tax on the population."[49] Previously, presidents and other political figures viewed accusations they had lied as attacks on their honor that merited the strongest response. In contrast, over the course of the first three years of his presidency, Trump told more and more lies over time. At the beginning of his presidency, the *Washington Post* reported that Trump averaged roughly 5 lies per day, but by August 2018, he was averaging 7.6 lies per day.[50] Shortly before his thousandth day in office, he was averaging almost 14 lies for every day of his presidency, and over the previous two months had lied "almost 22" times a day.[51] The escalation was a natural result of his rhetorical strategy and political situation. Given that his administration had not produced the magical results he had promised, and there were few signs of "American carnage," he had little choice but simply to lie about the state of the nation.

American democracy is built on the premise that over time the give-and-take of ideas will both reflect the competing views of all citizens and lead to sensible policy change. That battle of ideas was at the heart of what in *Federalist 10* James Madison called the "republican remedy for the diseases most incident in a republican form of government." Madison had faith in the "republican remedy" despite being quite aware of the dangers posed by partisanship and self-interest because he believed that over time better ideas had a way of winning out. In *Federalist 41*, he explained, "A bad cause seldom fails to betray itself."[52] Trump's rhetoric of nationalist populism with an outsider/strongman persona and an associated rhetorical style threatened democracy by undercutting the idea of truth. In Trump's United States, the "Republican remedy" was to blindly support Trump and ignore his many falsehoods and other provocative statements. If truth is purely partisan and depends only on party affiliation or loyalty to the leader, then public reason has no role to play, and all issues will be decided based on power alone. Such a politics leads to extremism, mistreatment of minorities and political opponents, and blind loyalty to the leader.

The third danger Trump's rhetoric posed for American democracy flowed from his recurrent use of conspiracy theories. Gerson cited a host of conspiracies Trump championed and concluded that in defending Trump, "Republicans are lowering their standards of sanity to defend an administration seized by conspiracy thinking," in effect "defining lunacy down."[53] It was not merely that Trump often embraced conspiracy theories but that Trump's nationalist and populist narrative itself included a strong component of conspiracy, notably Trump's claims that Obama was not born in the United States and that the "deep state" was out to destroy his own campaign and later his presidency.[54] The conspiracy theory about Obama was crucial to Trump's development of a national following, and the conspiracy theory about the "deep state" was a key aspect of Trump's message and response to criticism flowing from both Robert Mueller's investigation and the impeachment inquiries. Despite its obvious absurdity, the "deep state" conspiracy theory had considerable resonance on the right.[55] Trump's reliance on conspiracy theories was inevitable given the fundamentally false nature of his nationalist populist narrative. Jan-Werner Müller explained, "Conspiracy theories . . . are rooted in and emerge from the very logic of populism itself." He cited Trump "reacting to every loss in the primaries with the charge that his opponents were committing fraud" as a perfect example of the nonfalsifiability of the populist worldview. If Trump does not win, "there must be something going on behind the scenes that allows corrupt elites to continue to betray the people."[56]

Trump's reliance on conspiracy theories undercut support for democracy. If one believes that in fact there is a "deep state" out to thwart the agenda of the president, then there is little reason for supporters to abide by the rules governing campaigns, elections, and the administration of government essential to democracy. Belief in a deep state conspiracy provides justification for words and actions that violate democratic norms, such as attempting to undercut the Mueller investigation, encouraging Russian interference in the 2016 election, the unprecedented refusal to allow government officials to testify in front of congressional committees chaired by Democrats, and firing inspectors general at government agencies to limit oversight. More fundamentally, claiming that opponents are members of the deep state labels them unpatriotic, un-American, and even treasonous.[57] It is a short step from labeling one's opponents treasonous to concluding that the rules of democracy need not apply when confronting such villains.

The fourth danger posed by Trump's rhetoric is that it risks undercutting the crucial role played by the media in informing the American people and serving as a check on abusive government. I noted in discussion of Trump rallies and also his use of Twitter that Trump attacked the media to create anger in core supporters, and these attacks occurred more frequently after he became president. He also used this tactic to undercut criticism of his actions and words. Critical stories about his policies, revelations about his campaign's connections to Russia, or any other damaging disclosure were routinely labeled "fake news," and he frequently called the media "the enemy of the people."[58] In fact, Trump answered a question from a friendly *Fox News* interviewer by saying that about "80 percent" of the media fell into the "fake news" category.[59] With his attacks on the media, Trump was "riling up his supporters" and "actively stoking the anger" at that 80 percent. His goal was "to provoke as much rage and division as he can" to prevent the media from fulfilling the crucial role of informing the public about abuses of power or failed policy.[60]

Notably, Trump held few traditional press conferences until the advent of the COVID-19 pandemic, when he substituted briefings for campaign rallies and used them not to inform the nation but to claim credit, shift blame, and inflame his base with attacks on the press. Prior to the COVID crisis, rather than having real press conferences or interviews with the mainstream media in which he would be pressed to defend policies and back up assertions with actual evidence, Trump restated his message in an endless series of interviews with friendly media from outlets such as Fox. He used these sessions to repeat his nationalist populist message and undermine news organizations focused on gathering and reporting the best available information about issues of the day.

By labeling critical reporting "fake news" and referring to the media as "the enemy of the people," Trump accomplished two aims. He aroused anger to keep his core supporters engaged and also undercut criticism by categorizing journalists as enemies of ordinary people. In Trump's political universe, you are a valued journalist only if you report positive news about him. David Frum explained, "President Trump has made it his supreme and highest priority to defame those who responsibly and accurately report his tenure of high office" and added that "what he demands from the media is not objectivity but complicity."[61] A similar rhetoric has been used by "totalitarian regimes . . . to justify assassinations and purges," and there is certainly a real risk that his angry attacks on the media are "going to get somebody killed."[62] It is shocking that at a rally on the evening of the day the FBI had captured a fervent Trump supporter who sent fourteen pipe bombs to prominent Democrats, including former presidents Obama and Bill Clinton, and two of the packages containing the bombs were sent to CNN, Trump continued to make sharp attacks on both Democrats and the media.[63]

There is also a danger that basic democratic norms could be threatened by the attacks on the media. Frum warned that "restrictions on media freedom are an early warning sign of de-democratization."[64] One signal of this danger is that polling found that "more than half" of Republicans thought that as a whole the press were the "enemy of the people," and "nearly 9 in 10 disapprove of the media coverage."[65] It seems clear that for many of his supporters, Trump successfully used a rhetoric of nationalist populism to undercut the role of media as watchdogs safeguarding democratic norms. The media play a crucial role in any democratic society by facilitating debate on the issues, exposing misleading or false claims about issues, and revealing questionable or simply corrupt dealings. That is why freedom of the press is included in the first amendment to the US Constitution. There is a reason that in recent years right-wing governments in Hungary and Poland took steps to restrict independent media.[66] Such media serve a crucial function in any democracy, and actions to restrict or undercut their role threaten democracy itself. The resonance of Trump's rhetoric of nationalist populism suggests that tens of millions of Americans could support similar restrictions in the United States.

Trump's rhetoric threatened democracy in a fifth way by reinforcing already dangerously high levels of polarization and alienation. This result was an inevitable by-product of Trump's core message. Hetherington and Weiler noted strong evidence for "greater polarization . . . on issues that are structured in part by authoritarianism" and then added that "polarization may be persistent and sustain an increasingly intense and acrimonious political divide" in which parties are "more distant from one another than they have been in nearly 100 years."[67] Polarization increased after Trump was elected precisely because his rhetoric fueled it.

In the political universe Trump's rhetoric helped create, "Whether voters support or oppose a policy may simply not be all that important to their vote," and their support for a given policy might be determined primarily by their party allegiance rather than ideological leanings.[68] Extreme partisanship is a major part of this situation. Amanda Taub and Brendan Nyhan referred to "a core truth of modern politics: that voters tend to seek out information that fits the story they want to believe, usually one in which members of the other party are the bad guys."[69] The situation is so serious that some believe "Americans live in alternate worlds, with different laws of gravity, languages, and truths. Politics is raw, more about who you are than what you believe. Even democracy feels fragile."[70] More than anything else, Trump's rhetoric created that sense of fragility. This increased partisanship was on display when the House Judiciary Committee debated impeachment. Again and again, Republican committee members defended Trump by strongly supporting claims falsified by the evidentiary record, including the president's own words in a phone transcript with the Ukrainian president in which he asked for a favor that involved launching an investigation of Biden and his son Hunter.[71] The arguments of these Republicans were shaped not by the actual evidence but by the partisan need to defend Trump. The similarity to the politics in an authoritarian or totalitarian society, where the leader cannot be criticized, is obvious.

Trump's rhetoric also drew on and reinforced a sense of alienation that undercut citizen engagement essential to democracy. Trump's rally speeches during the 2016 campaign described a dystopian American landscape, and after winning the presidency, he claimed he was rapidly transforming it into a new/old paradise. In this universe, the press was part of the "deep state," out to get him, and his opponents were weak tools of special interests who cared more about protecting undocumented immigrants or terrorists than about the American people. Only Trump cared for ordinary people and had the courage to take decisive action. He used Twitter to spread this narrative in virtual space and make it continually present in the lives of his supporters. Trump's entire approach was to use his nationalist populist narrative to create fear and anger. Political alienation and polarization were not unfortunate side effects of his rhetoric; they were essential aims of it.

One effect of this rhetorical pattern was to make crafting policy to solve actual problems extremely difficult. Lilliana Mason observed, "Even uninformed Americans . . . know the name of their ideological team. But team names without issue knowledge can generate political conflict that is unmoored from distinct policy goals. This is likely to lead to a less compromise-oriented electorate. After all, if policy outcomes are less important than team victory, a policy compromise is a useless concession to the enemy."[72] A good example is the Affordable Care Act (ACA), which implemented an individual mandate as a way to move closer to universal coverage. The individual mandate was originally a conservative reform proposal authored by Stuart M. Butler of the Heritage Foundation.[73] Obama believed that basing his national health insurance plan on a market-based conservative proposal created the preconditions for compromise that could yield bipartisan health legislation.[74] However, conservative opposition to anything Obama proposed was so strong that Republicans in Congress and the conservative media routinely labeled the ACA socialism. The fact that the legislation had been the conservative reform proposal in the late 1980s and the early 1990s made no difference. Because Obama was for it, the proposal was "evil." Trump's rhetoric of nationalist populism worsened this situation, as did his efforts to reverse other accomplishments of the Obama administration.

These problems were obvious in the debate about the ACA that occurred during the first year of Trump's presidency. Since its passage, Republicans had labeled the ACA a catastrophe destabilizing the American health-care system and harming countless millions. The call to "repeal and replace" was not just a theme of the Trump campaign but reflected the views of nearly every important figure in the Republican Party. In Trump's and the dominant Republican narrative, the ACA was a disaster. However, when Trump and Republicans began an effort to repeal the ACA in Congress, their narrative depicting the law as a disaster ran up against the reality that more than 20 million people were receiving health care through the program, and it also provided protection for tens of millions of other Americans with preexisting conditions.[75] This led to strong grassroots opposition to repeal of the ACA.[76] Republicans were caught between their highly polarized dystopian narrative and the reality that the law, although imperfect, had dramatically cut the number of uninsured Americans and protected the insurance coverage of many millions of others. The polarizing nature of the narrative made compromise and policy reform all but impossible. The absence of a conservative reform proposal that would provide coverage and protect insurance benefits largely explains why even with Republican control of both houses of Congress and the presidency, they were unable to repeal the ACA.

Continued demonization of the media worsens this problem by making it difficult to inform the public about issues facing the nation and policy options for dealing with them. The tribal nature of American politics has created a situation in which, according to a University of Virginia Center for Politics poll of Trump voters, "Nearly nine in 10 respondents (88%) said that media criticism of Trump reinforces that the president is on the right track, and the same percentage agrees with Trump's assertion that the press is 'the enemy of the American people.'"[77] One cannot have a reasonable debate in this political climate. The increased polarization and alienation Trump's nationalist populist message produced made crafting policies and seeking compromise solutions almost impossible. At a time when the nation faces genuine crises related to global warming, a pandemic, a failing infrastructure, and a host of other problems, Trump's rhetoric undercut the nation's capacity to address those issues. Democracies sometimes devolve into authoritarianism when they are unable to confront the real problems facing the society. Trump's rhetoric made such failure more likely.

A sixth threat to democracy is that a skillful leader could use a rhetoric of nationalist populism to mobilize voters to support authoritarian policies. Trump used his nationalist populist message to drive support for his effort to undercut the Mueller probe and the impeachment inquiry, labeling the attempt to use the constitutionally mandated process a "coup."[78] Given that the process for impeachment is laid out in the Constitution itself, and there was substantial discussion of impeachment in both the Constitutional Convention and *The Federalist Papers,* the coup claim is obviously nonsense. But the evident resonance of the claim among Trump supporters was a sign of the weakness of democratic norms. It is clear that many Trump supporters would have supported action inconsistent with basic principles of American democracy if that action aided Trump.

It is also important to recognize that Trump demonstrated the power of a rhetoric based in nationalist populism with an outsider/strongman persona and an associated rhetorical style but not its maximum potential. Trump's many weaknesses as a candidate and political leader explain why he so often failed to accomplish his particular political objectives. In part, he simply was not disciplined enough to stick to his message. Moreover, his rhetoric, although emotionally powerful, lacked eloquence. His stream-of-consciousness style and constant egocentric comments constrained the influence of his rhetoric. A political leader who possessed greater rhetorical skill could use the same message to much greater effect. In addition, Trump's personal life, his family, and his business all created baggage that limited his appeal. Another problem limiting his approval ratings as president was that rather than "draining the swamp" of corruption in Washington, his administration was defined by what conservative commentator Peter Wehner labeled "full-spectrum corruption," with a number of cabinet officers and the president himself accused, indicted, and/or convicted of financial or other misdeeds.[79]

The disquieting implication is that a more disciplined authoritarian leader who kept on message and lacked the personal, business, and political baggage Trump possessed could be much more effective in using the rhetoric of nationalist populism with an outsider/strongman persona than was Trump. The greatest weakness in Trump's core message was his enactment of the outsider/strongman persona. Given his long history of failed business ventures, bankruptcies, unpaid bills, personal scandals, and lack of personal accomplishment, other than being a rich builder and reality television star, Trump's outsider/strongman appeal rested in his many statements that as a master dealmaker, under his leadership the nation would start winning again. One suspects that even many strong supporters knew that would not happen, but they supported him anyway because he seemed to be on their side. The difficulty became more significant as his presidency progressed and the economic miracle he promised did not occur. Dionne, Ornstein, and Mann were on target when they noted that "a limiting factor to Trump's authoritarian bent" was "his sheer incompetence in fulfilling the basic functions of his office."[80]

Trump demonstrated the power of a rhetoric of nationalist populism and associated rhetorical style but not the full potential of that rhetoric. If the leader enacting that message were a person of genuine accomplishment, a former general or admiral perhaps, or a business leader with real credentials and not the checkered history of Trump, that person could use the nationalist populist message to build a stronger base of support and more effectively attack opponents than did Trump. If that person also had the ability to craft a coherent message, in contrast with Trump's stream-of-consciousness ranting, that rhetoric could be still more powerful.

Research on authoritarian personality structures supports this claim. Marc Hetherington and Elizabeth Suhay stated that "levels of threat appear to powerfully condition the preference of the less authoritarian" and added "that perceptions of threat cause those low in authoritarianism to adopt more 'authoritarian' policy views." They concluded, "When people perceive grave threats to their safety, most individuals are susceptible to 'authoritarian thinking.'"[81] A more skillful leader could consistently enact the rhetoric of nationalist populism with an outsider/strongman persona to create the perception that the American way of life itself was under attack. That kind of rhetoric of authoritarian activation poses a grave threat to democracy because "a wide range of Americans will potentially support antidemocratic policies during threatening times."[82]

In the aftermath of 9/11, many Americans supported the use of torture to gain information from terrorism suspects despite strong evidence that torture was not just immoral but also ineffective.[83] They did so because they were afraid. A skillful leader could tap into and magnify such fear through a message of nationalist populism. The dangers associated with such a development are obvious.

Trump and Authoritarianism

A skeptic might respond to the claim that Trump's rhetoric of nationalist populism with an outsider/strongman persona threatened democracy by saying that the threat was exaggerated and emphasizing the strength of

American democratic institutions. The skeptic might add that there is a big difference between having an authoritarian personality structure and actually supporting authoritarianism. In fact, there is a real risk that nationalist populist rhetoric such as that used by Trump could create pressures moving the nation over time toward an authoritarian form of government. Writing about the "authoritarian dynamic," Karen Stenner described the "very different world" that would be produced by a rhetoric that activated the authoritarian mind-set. In that world, the:

> aggregate result . . . will be deeply intensified value conflict across the tolerance domain, sharply polarized politics, and enormously increased demands upon the polity: for greater *and* lesser discrimination against minorities and restrictions on immigration; for more *and* fewer limits on free speech, assembly, and association; for stricter *and* softer policies on common rites, abortion, censorship, and homosexuality; for harsher *and* more lenient punishment.[84]

The "very different world" was Trump's United States.

Trump's election and steady approval rating as president together can be seen as a "warning sign of a political crisis."[85] Nationalist populism can result in what Cas Mudde and Cristóbal Rovira Kaltwasser called "democratic erosion," creating "a real danger to democracy."[86] One obvious concern is the relationship between Trump and the alt right. Matthew Lyons noted, "The Alt Right helped Donald Trump get elected president."[87] Trump's nationalist populism clearly "inspired white supremacist and anti-Semitic groups, including remnants of the Ku Klux Klan. They embraced him with enthusiasm and without reservation—and he avoided nearly every opening to criticize their behavior and their corrosive rhetoric."[88] After Charlottesville, where an alt-right group clashed with counterprotesters and a white supremacist drove into the crowd, killing one person, Trump went out of his way to avoid offending those on the far right who supported him. He said there were "some very fine people on both sides" in Charlottesville.[89] In response, notorious white supremacist David Duke responded on Twitter, "Thank you President Trump for your honesty & courage to tell the truth about #Charlottesville."[90] In this incident, Trump violated a political norm supported by presidents of both parties for decades—that explicit racism is not acceptable in American life.

The contrast with how Reagan responded to a cross burning is telling. After reading a report about the cross burning and other harassment of a

Black family in the Washington area, Reagan took a presidential motorcade to visit the family and express his horror at the event and support for them. He said at the time, "I thought maybe I might just call attention to how reprehensible something of this kind is."[91] Reagan's record on civil rights has been sharply criticized, but he strongly embraced the norm that explicit racism has no place in American life and in his rhetoric supported a diverse vision of the American dream.[92] No president, not even Lyndon B. Johnson, Clinton, or Obama, who made real efforts to change policy, has been able to adequately confront systemic racism. But at least since Richard Nixon, explicit racism was banished from presidential rhetoric. That changed with Trump. The rhetoric of nationalist populism that Trump along with his followers and many imitators on the right used has risked magnifying the problem of racial hatred and more broadly undermining norms of behavior and rhetoric essential in a humane liberal democracy. One result is that Trump's rhetoric, much of it based in "overt bigotry," "normalize[ed] . . . racism."[93]

Trump's willingness to violate democratic norms, to simply lie when challenged, to demean his opponents, and to traffic in conspiracy theories led a number of commentators to note the similarities between him and authoritarian and totalitarian leaders, including Benito Mussolini, a comparison Mabel Berezin labeled "apt."[94] Chip Berlet added, "There are parallels to" [the Weimar Republic] in "our current political climate," and he observed that the "examples of Trump's fascist-sounding rhetoric are numerous."[95] The danger is not that there might be a sudden transition to authoritarianism but that over time the various threats associated with Trump's rhetoric and governance might gradually undercut democratic principles. Max Fisher and Amanda Taub explained, "Populism is a path that, at its outset, can look and feel democratic. But followed to its logical conclusion, it can lead to democratic backsliding or even outright authoritarianism."[96] Ruth Marcus commented that "some of the president's deviations from democratic and political norms slap you in the face" and then added ominously that "authoritarianism does not announce itself. It creeps up on you."[97] In a way, Marcus is wrong. Trump announced his authoritarian worldview in tens of thousands of tweets and rally speeches that bear a resemblance with rhetoric used by far-right political parties in Europe today and in past decades going back to the 1930s. It is disquieting, to say the least, how positively tens of millions of Americans reacted to this rhetoric. The fear of creeping authoritarianism seems warranted given a poll indicating that if

Trump claimed that "the 2020 presidential election should be postponed until the country can make sure that only eligible American citizens can vote," "roughly half of Republicans . . . would support postponing the 2020 election."[98] This situation and the actions of Republican-dominated legislatures restricting the power of newly elected Democratic governors, in effect changing the rules after the election had occurred to block Democrats from governing, led both liberal commentators such as Dionne and neoconservatives such as Boot to worry that Republicans "are becoming an authoritarian party."[99] It is clear many Republicans in Congress have been unwilling to criticize actions that if a Democrat had committed them they would have excoriated and called for impeachment. The danger of creeping authoritarianism is real.

The warnings of commentators about the risk that nationalist populism could gradually lead to authoritarian government action are supported by research on authoritarian personality structure. Hetherington and Suhay noted that research on authoritarianism and how it can be activated among nonauthoritarian voters indicates that "antidemocratic preferences can quickly become popular, mainstream positions under the right circumstances."[100] Stenner made the same point when she observed, "The seemingly sudden and unexpectedly venomous civil dissolution that may attend this 'inauguration' of the authoritarian dynamic must be considered a consequence, not a cause, of the dis-integration of the populace." Such dis-integration can occur quite rapidly because "many citizens support democratically elected leaders only when confident they are committed to 'people like me.'"[101] Similarly, based on the research of Hetherington and Suhay, Taub noted, "If social change and physical threats coincided at the same time, it could awaken a potentially enormous population of American authoritarians who would demand a strongman leader and the extreme policies necessary . . . to meet the rising threats."[102]

The system of checks and balances that is the basis of American democracy and the institutions that have developed in this system provide strong protection against the dangers posed by authoritarianism. The risk is that gradual erosion of democratic norms could weaken those protections. Trump's many attacks on the press, including his labeling of any anti-Trump reporting as "fake news" and calling the press the "enemy of the people," are glaring signs of that erosion. The strong support on the right for these attacks on the media is another sign. Similarly, Trump's attacks on the FBI, his actions and words that "repeatedly undermined his own Justice Department," and his interference in the Russia investigation and impeachment inquiry represented erosion of norms of presidential behavior related to the justice system and the democratic principle that no one is above the law.[103] With his words and actions, Trump demonstrated that he was "increasingly impatient with structures of democratic accountability."[104] He also seemed to suggest that the Department of Justice should not prosecute Republicans when he tweeted on September 4, 2018, "Two long running, Obama era, investigations of two very popular Republican Congressmen were brought to a well-publicized charge, just ahead of the Mid-Terms, by the Jeff Sessions Justice Department. Two easy wins now in doubt because there is not enough time. Good job Jeff."[105] It also was alarming that Trump claimed "the absolute right to PARDON myself," "joked" about serving more than the two terms allowed by the Constitution, and shortly before the 2020 election "called on William P. Barr, the attorney general, to take action before Election Day against his Democrat opponent . . . , an extraordinary attempt to pressure the government's chief law enforcement to help him politically."[106] Trump also broke democratic norms when he suggested the protest against the nomination of Brett Kavanaugh to the Supreme Court should not be legal. He said, "I think it's embarrassing for the country to allow protesters," a comment that echoed statements during the 2016 campaign when he said that "demonstrators should lose their jobs or be met with violence for speaking out."[107] Trump also undercut democratic norms when he used divisive and sometimes outright insulting language to attack people of color, which "immersed the nation in a new wave of fraught battles over race."[108] It also was concerning that both a Pew Research Center and a *Washington Post*/ABC poll found that the close connection Trump established with core supporters was primarily based on personality, not policy or ideology.[109] Such polling results indicate the continuing appeal of the strongman persona. Paul Krugman observed that Trump's base supporters "love" him "not for his policies but for the performative cruelty he exhibits toward racial minorities and the way he sticks his thumb in the eyes of 'elites.'"[110] This is not a recipe for appropriate presidential leadership, congressional oversight, or bipartisan action for the good of the nation.

The danger is that the erosion of democratic norms could lead to what Steven Levitsky and Daniel Ziblatt called a democratic "breakdown," in which "a veneer of democracy" remains but authoritarian actions undermine "its substance."[111] Based on a study of "how democracies now die" around the world, they noted that violation of basic norms can be a major threat: "Without robust norms, constitutional checks and balances do not serve as the bulwarks of democracy we imagine them to be. Institutions become political weapons, wielded forcefully by those who control them against those who do not. This is how elected autocrats subvert democracy."[112] Levitsky and Ziblatt described "Four Key Indicators of Authoritarian Behavior" and fifteen specific tests of these indicators and concluded that Trump violated a large proportion of them in his campaign or the first two years of his presidency.[113] Many of the indicators of authoritarian behavior relate to violation of rhetorical norms, such as attacking rivals as subversive, questioning the legitimacy of elections, labeling critics as criminals or foreign agents, endorsing violence during rallies, praising authoritarian leaders, and threatening legal action against critics or the press.[114]

Perhaps the most basic threat of all was Trump's divisive rhetoric, animated by a "politics of rage" that labels some Americans "real" and others criminals or un-American subversives, a rhetorical practice that has the effect of "stirring and normalizing bigotry."[115] Gerson's comment that "Trump is urging Americans to drink at a poisoned well of intolerance" that "desensitizes some people to the moral seriousness of prejudice" was exactly right.[116] From Lincoln through Obama, the most influential presidents and other political leaders provided an optimistic vision of the American dream in which the ideals shared by all Americans defined the nation. In his last important political speech, Reagan expressed this faith by saying, "But the United States is unique because we are an empire of ideals. For two hundred years we have been set apart by our faith in the ideals of democracy, of free men and free markets, and of the extraordinary possibilities that lie within seemingly ordinary men and women." The faith in American ideals of which Reagan spoke was more important than group or personal identity. At the end of the same speech, Reagan said:

> Whether we come from poverty or wealth; whether we are Afro-American or Irish-American; Christian or Jewish; from big cities or small towns, we are all equal in the eyes of God. But as Americans that is not enough; we must be equal in the eyes of each other. We can no longer judge each other on the basis of what we are, but must, instead, start finding out who we are. In America, our origins matter less than our destinations, and that is what democracy is all about.[117]

In many ways, Reagan's vision of the United States as an "empire of ideals" was similar to Obama's audacious hope for a time in which the nation might live up to those ideals. Although different in their ideology, Reagan and Obama each spoke of a nation defined not by identity or power or wealth but by fundamental democratic principles in which as Obama stated in his 2012 State of the Union Address, "everyone gets a fair shot, and everyone does their fair share, and everyone plays by the same set of rules." Obama added that these ideas "aren't Democratic values or Republican values, but American values."[118] The antidote to the division, hate, and fear created by nationalist populism might lie in such an optimistic rhetoric of shared identity as a means of reclaiming the American dream.

Reagan and Obama and other presidents who embraced an American identity that transcended group or ethnic status often failed to live up to that optimistic and universalist message in the policies they advocated, but their vision of the United States as an "empire of ideals," in Reagan's lovely phrase, pointed the nation toward a better future.

Trump's rhetoric of nationalist populism undermines the ideals on which American identity and that better future are based and therefore threatens democratic principles.[119]

The rhetorical pattern described in this book; the unsettling devotion of Trump supporters to their leader despite constant lies, gaffes, and other misdeeds; and the research on authoritarian voters yield a similar conclusion. In undercutting rhetorical norms for public talk in the world's oldest democracy, Trump threatened basic ties that bind the people of this nation together and American democracy itself.

At the same time, support for the basic principles of democracy remains strong, and there were many principled conservatives who consistently opposed Trump, although only a few elected Republican figures remained constant in their opposition to his rhetoric and policies. There is, however, a danger that in a crisis traditional conservatives might acquiesce to authoritarian or even totalitarian actions. It is unsettling that precisely that kind of acquiescence led to the rise of Adolf Hitler.[120]

Another sign of danger is the erosion of democracy in Eastern Europe, especially in Hungary and Poland. Using a rhetoric much like Trump's, Viktor Orban transformed Hungary into an "illiberal democracy."[121] It is notable that Trump's rhetoric of nationalist populism lessened pressure on Orban and others to follow democratic norms.[122] In the right circumstances, democratic erosion could occur in the United States as well. Thomas Edsall cited figures "from a recent EuroPulse survey showing that authoritarianism is stronger in the United States than it is in the European Union: In the E.U., 33 percent of the electorate can be described as authoritarian, while in the United States it is 45 percent."[123]

Yet, the resistance to Trump's rhetoric also speaks to the power of democratic ideals and the resilience of the system devised by James Madison to protect the world's oldest democracy. Commentators have sometimes underestimated the strength of the democratic system. In 1980, Bertram Gross warned of risks Reagan posed to the American democratic system in his book *Friendly Fascism*.[124] In fact, Reagan, rather than threatening democracy, would become one of the most eloquent defenders of what in the Westminster Address he called the "not-at-all-fragile flower" that is democracy.[125] The arc of American history also speaks to the power of reasoned argument based on a positive vision of the American dream. All who fundamentally changed this nation have enacted a version of that optimistic narrative, from Lincoln's appeal to the better angels of our nature to Franklin Delano Roosevelt's confident statement that the only thing we have to fear is fear itself, to Martin Luther King Jr.'s vision of a time when his little children would be judged based on the content of their character, to Reagan's city on a hill, to Obama's audacious hope. As Obama said in 2008, "In the unlikely story that is America, there has never been anything false about hope."[126]

Moreover, although he ran as the savior of the working class, the economic policies of the Trump administration resulted in "an unambiguous transfer of income and power . . . from the public to the rich."[127] His actions as president demonstrated strong support for "the GOP's corporate agenda" and "indifference to working-class interests."[128] In the long, run, as John Adams observed, "Facts are stubborn things," and ultimately Trump will be judged by his core supporters based on his ability to produce the magical results he promised, something that clearly began to happen as the COVID-19 pandemic and associated economic collapse occurred.[129]

Despite the safeguards built into the American system, the difficulty of maintaining support for a fundamentally false narrative, and the power of the optimistic vision at the heart of the American dream, there is still cause for concern. The unfortunate truth is that in Trump's United States, facts seem considerably less stubborn than in the past and the power of a rhetoric based in fear and hate quite evident.

NOTES

INTRODUCTION: DONALD TRUMP—
A RHETORICAL ENIGMA

1. See Kurt Eichenwald, "A People's History of Donald Trump's Business Busts and Countless Victims," *Newsweek*, October 28, 2016, https://www.newsweek.com/2016/10/28/donald-trump-business-busts-victims-511034.html; David A. Graham, "The Many Scandals of Donald Trump: A Cheat Sheet," *Atlantic*, January 23, 2017, https://www.theatlantic.com/politics/archive/2017/01/donald-trump-scandals/474726.

2. David Axelrod, "How Hillary Clinton Could Win," *New York Times*, September 25, 2016, SR1, SR7.

3. Michael Kruse and Taylor Gee, "The 37 Fatal Gaffes That Didn't Kill Donald Trump," *Politico*, September 25, 2016, https://www.politico.com/magazine/story/2016/09/trump-biggest-fatal-gaffes-mistakes-offensive-214289.

4. Michael Gerson, "Trump Spirals into Ideological Psychosis," *Washington Post*, October 17, 2016, https://www.washingtonpost.com/opinions/trump-spirals-into-ideological-psychosis/2016/10/17/91bf4366-948d-11e6-bc79-af1cd3d2984b_story.html.

5. Joshua Green, *Devil's Bargain: Steve Bannon, Donald Trump, and the Nationalist Uprising* (New York: Penguin, 2017), 40.

6. J. Michael Hogan, "George Wallace, Speech at Serb Hall (26 March 1976)," *Voices of Democracy* 11 (2016): 64. See also Lloyd Rohler, *George Wallace: Conservative Populist* (Westport, CT: Praeger, 2004), 96–99.

7. Hogan, "George Wallace, Speech at Serb Hall," 64.

8. David Brooks, "The Crisis of Western Civilization," *New York Times*, April 21, 2017, A25.

9. Katy Tur, the first national correspondent for a major network to be assigned to Trump, noted, "Trump is a candidate without a campaign." See Tur, *Unbelievable: My Front-Row Seat to the Craziest Campaign in American History* (New York: HarperCollins, 2017), 172.

10. Lilliana Mason, "Ideologues Without Issues: The Polarizing Consequences of Ideological Identities," *Public Opinion Quarterly* 82 (2018): 867.

11. Green, *Devil's Bargain*, 170.

12. Brooks, "Crisis of Western Civilization."

13. See Nate Silver, "First Debate Often Helps Challenger in Polls," *New York Times*, October 3, 2012, https://fivethirtyeight.blogs.nytimes.com/2012/10/03/first-debate-often-helps-challenger-in-polls/; Robert

C. Rowland, "The 1980 Carter-Reagan Debate: Style vs. Substance," *Southern Speech Communication Journal* 51 (1986): 142–165; Rowland, "The First 2012 Presidential Debate: The Decline of Reason in Presidential Debates," *Communication Studies* 64 (2013): 528–547.

14. In a study of the arguments produced by the two candidates in the debate, I found that Trump's violation of the norms of presidential debates and his lack of coherent statements made his debate performance unique in the presidential debates held since the Kennedy/Nixon debates. See Robert C. Rowland, "The 2016 Presidential Debates as Public Argument," in *Televised Presidential Debates in a Changing Media Environment*, vol. 1: *The Candidates Make Their Case*, ed. Edward A. Hinck (Santa Barbara, CA: Praeger, 2019), 228–248. For polling and typical commentator reaction, see Kathleen Parker, "Trump's Night of Sniffles and Screw Ups," *Washington Post*, September 27, 2016, https:// www.washingtonpost.com/opinions/trumps-night-of-sniffles-and-screw-ups /2016/09/27/38c18574-84ef-11e6-a3ef-f35afb41797f_story.html. Polls indicated that Trump had lost decisively. See Jennifer Agiesta, "Post-Debate Poll: Hillary Clinton Takes Round One," CNN, September 27, 2016, https://www.cnn.com/2016 /09/27/politics/hillary-clinton-donald-trump-debate-poll/index.html; Andrew Prokop, "Early Polls and Focus Groups Suggest Hillary Clinton Won the Debate," Vox, September 27, 2016, http://www.vox.com/2016/9/27/13069088/hillary -clinton-won-first-presidential-debate.

15. Jonathan Capehart, "Donald Trump Bombs on the Ultimate Reality TV Show," *Washington Post*, September 27, 2016, https://www.washingtonpost.com /blogs/post-partisan/wp/2016/09/27/donald-trump-bombs-on-the-ultimate -reality-tv-show/?utm_term=.2e8a04cb77d7.

16. Trip Gabriel, "Trump Is Given Thumbs Down in the Suburbs," *New York Times*, September 28, 2016, A17; see also Jenna Johnson, "Trump Starts Subdued, Then His Cool Quickly Melts," *Washington Post*, September 26, 2016, https://www .washingtonpost.com/politics/trump-yells-and-sniffs-his-way-through-the-first -2016-presidential-debate/2016/09/26/c990f05e-8403-11e6-a3ef-f35afb41797f _story.html?utm_term=.6a3cbcf7e40.

17. Patrick Healy, "Debacle: What Al Gore's First Debate Against George W. Bush Can Teach Hillary Clinton," *New York Times*, September 25, 2016, https:// www.nytimes.com/interactive/2016/09/25/us/politics/george-w-bush-al-gore -2000-presidential-debate.html.

18. Charles Krauthammer, "When Facts, Logic, and History Don't Matter," *Washington Post*, September 29, 2016, https://www.washingtonpost.com/opinions /when-facts-logic-and-history-dont-matter/2016/09/29/8fa91cc0-8680-11e6-a3ef -f35afb41797f_story.html?utm_term=.a7fa51e50773.

19. Michael Gerson, "Our Republic Will Never Be the Same," *Washington Post*, August 16, 2018, https://www.washingtonpost.com/opinions/our-republic-will

-never-be-the-same/2018/08/16/c85266e8-a178-11e8-8e87-c869fe70a721_story
.html?utm_term=.315754571bb9.

20. Jake Flanagin, "Marco Rubio Looks Like a Beaten Man as He Apologizes
for His Anti-Trump Insults," Quartz, March 10, 2016, https://qz.com/636152
/watch-marco-rubio-looks-like-a-beaten-man-as-he-apologizes-for-his-anti
-trump-insults.

21. "What You May Have Forgotten about the Hillary Clinton Email Controversy," CBS News, June 14, 2018, https://www.cbsnews.com/news/what-you-may
-have-forgotten-about-the-hillary-clinton-email-controversy; David M. Hers-
zenhorn, "House Benghazi Report Finds No New Evidence of Wrongdoing by
Hillary Clinton," New York Times, June 28, 2016, https://www.nytimes.com/2016
/06/29/us/politics/hillary-clinton-benghazi.html.

22. Eric Levitz and James D. Walsh, "Trump's Greatest Worst Hits of 2017," New
York Magazine, January 7, 2018, http://nymag.com/daily/intelligencer/2018/01
/donald-trump-greatest-worst-hits-of-2017.html.

23. Although the president is required to report to Congress on the state of
the union, it is not required that this report take the form of a speech. However,
since Woodrow Wilson every president has fulfilled the requirement through a
speech to Congress.

24. Amina Dunn, "Trump Approval Ratings So Far Are Unusually Stable—
and Deeply Partisan," Pew Research Center, August 1, 2018, http://www.pew
research.org/fact-tank/2018/08/01/trumps-approval-ratings-so-far-are-unusually
-stable-and-deeply-partisan/.

25. See for example, Anand Giridharadas, "Donald Trump Breaks with Tradition, and It's Paying Off," New York Times, March 15, 2016, https://www.nytimes
.com/2016/03/15/us/politics/donald-trump-surprise-over-substance.html; Pippa
Norris, "It's Not Just Trump: Authoritarian Populism Is Rising Across the West—
Here's Why," Washington Post, March 11, 2016, https://www.washingtonpost.com
/news/monkey-cage/wp/2016/03/11/its-not-just-trump-authoritarian-populism
-is-rising-across-the-west-heres-why/; David Neiwert, "Trump and Right-Wing
Populism: A Long Time Coming," Political Research Associates, June 21, 2016,
https://www.politicalresearch.org/2016/06/21/trump-and-right-wing-populism
-a-long-time-coming; Declan Walsh, "Fearful and Flummoxed: Watching the
Presidential Race from Abroad," New York Times, September 14, 2016, https://www
.nytimes.com/2016/09/14/world/americas/hillary-clinton-donald-trump.html
?mcubz=3; Amanda Taub, "The Rise of American Authoritarianism," Vox, March
1, 2016, https://www.vox.com/2016/3/1/11127424/trump-authoritarianism; Eugene
Robinson, "Our #FakeHero President Is an Insult to Our Founders," Washington Post, July 3, 2017, https://www.washingtonpost.com/opinions/our-fake-hero
-president-is-an-insult-to-our-founders/2017/07/03/c0bc0402-6024-11e7-a4f7
-af34fc1d9d39_story.html; Jennifer R. Mercieca, "Afterword: Trump as Anarchist

and Sun King," in *Faking the News: What Rhetoric Can Teach Us about Donald J. Trump*, ed. Ryan Skinnell (Exeter, UK: Imprint Academic, 2018), 174; Mary E. Stuckey, "American Elections and the Rhetoric of Political Change: Hyperbole, Anger, and Hope in U.S. Politics," *Rhetoric and Public Affairs* 20 (2017): 667.

26. Stephen Reicher and Alexander Haslam, "What Psychology Can Teach Us about Trump's Victory—and What Trump's Victory Can Teach Us about Psychology," European Association of Social Psychology, June 6, 2017, https://www.easp.eu/news/itm/-452.html.

27. Walsh, "Fearful and Flummoxed."

28. David Frum, *Trumpocracy: The Corruption of the American Republic* (New York: HarperCollins, 2018), ix.

29. Denise Bostdorff makes a similar observation. See "Obama, Trump, and Reflections on the Rhetoric of Political Change," *Rhetoric and Public Affairs* 20 (2017): 698.

CHAPTER 1. THE ELEMENTS OF TRUMP'S RHETORIC

1. Katy Tur, "The Trump Fever Never Breaks," *New York Times*, September 1, 2017, SR4.

2. Amanda Taub, "The Rise of American Authoritarianism," Vox, March 1, 2016, https://www.vox.com/2016/3/1/11127424/trump-authoritarianism.

3. Lilliana Mason, "Ideologues Without Issues: The Polarizing Consequences of Ideological Identities," *Public Opinion Quarterly* 82 (2018): 867.

4. Arlie Russell Hochschild's labeling of Trump as the "emotions candidate" is exactly right. See *Strangers in Their Own Land: Anger and Mourning on the American Right* (New York: New Press, 2016), 225.

5. Karen Stenner, *The Authoritarian Dynamic* (Cambridge, UK: Cambridge University Press, 2005), 322–323.

6. Emma Green, "It Was Cultural Anxiety That Drove White, Working-Class Voters to Trump," *Atlantic*, May 9, 2017, https://www.theatlantic.com/politics/archive/2017/05/white-working-class-trump-cultural-anxiety/525771.

7. See Jenny Edbauer Rice, "The 'New': Making a Case for Critical Affect Studies," *Quarterly Journal of Speech* 94 (2008): 200–212; Debra Hawhee, "Rhetoric's Sensorium," *Quarterly Journal of Speech* 100 (2015): 5, 10; Jeff Pruchnic and Kim Lacey, "The Future of Forgetting: Rhetoric, Memory, Affect," *Rhetoric Society Quarterly* 41 (2011): 483.

8. Jamie Landau and Bethany Keeler-Jonker, "Conductor of Public Feelings: An Affective-Emotional Rhetorical Analysis of Obama's National Eulogy in Tucson," *Quarterly Journal of Speech* 104 (2018): 167, 169, 177.

9. "Bringing War Down to Earth: The Dialectic of Pity and Compassion in *Doonesbury*'s View of Combat Trauma," *Quarterly Journal of Speech* 101 (2015): 398.

10. Erin J. Rand, "An Inflammatory Fag and a Queer Form: Larry Kramer, Polemics, and Rhetorical Agency," *Quarterly Journal of Speech* 94 (2008): 302, 303.

11. Catherine Chaput, "Rhetorical Circulation in Late Capitalism: Neoliberalism and the Overdetermination of Affective Energy," *Philosophy and Rhetoric* 43 (2010): 8, 14, 15.

12. Callum Borchers, "The 'Nasty Effect,' and Why Donald Trump Supporters Mistrust the Media," *Washington Post,* April 24, 2016, https://www.washington post.com/news/the-fix/wp/2016/04/24/the nasty effect-and-why-donald-trump -supporters-mistrust-the-media/?utm_term=.5cce9e397391.

13. Celeste M. Condit, "Pathos in Criticism: Edwin Black's Communism-as-Cancer Metaphor," *Quarterly Journal of Speech* 99 (2013): 1–26; Emily Winderman, "S(anger) Goes Postal in *The Woman Rebel:* Angry Rhetoric as a Collectivizing Moral Emotion," *Rhetoric and Public Affairs* 17 (2014): 381–420.

14. Condit, "Pathos in Criticism," 6, 7, 13, 14.

15. Condit, 21.

16. Winderman, "S(anger) Goes Postal in *The Woman Rebel,*" 386.

17. Winderman, 390, 409.

18. Michael Lee, "The Populist Chameleon: The People's Party, Huey Long, George Wallace, and the Populist Argumentative Frame," *Quarterly Journal of Speech* 92 (2006): 356, 357. The difficulty of defining populism is evident in the useful but quite different approaches rhetorical scholars have taken regarding various populist leaders and social movements. See, for instance, Cat Duffy, "States' Rights vs. Women's Rights: The Use of the Populist Argumentative Frame in Anti-Abortion Rhetoric," *International Journal of Communication* 9 (2015): 3494–3501; Kristy Maddux, "Fundamentalist Fool or Populist Paragon? William Jennings Bryan and the Campaign Against Evolutionary Theory," *Rhetoric and Public Affairs* 16 (2013): 489–520; Howard S. Erlich, "Populist Rhetoric Reassessed: A Paradox," *Quarterly Journal of Speech* 63 (1977): 140–151; Lloyd Rohler, "Conservative Appeals to the People: George Wallace's Populist Rhetoric," *Southern Communication Journal* 64 (1999): 316–322; Gary C. Woodward, "Reagan as Roosevelt: The Elasticity of Pseudo-Populist Appeals," *Central States Speech Journal* 34 (1983): 44–58; Michael Serazio, "Encoding the Paranoid Style in American Politics: 'Anti-Establishment' Discourse and Power in Contemporary Spin," *Critical Studies in Media Communication* 33 (2016): 181–194; Mark Rolfe, *The Reinvention of Populist Rhetoric in the Digital Age: Insiders and Outsiders in Democratic Politics* (London: Palgrave Macmillan, 2016).

19. Rolfe, *Reinvention of Populist Rhetoric in the Digital Age,* 24; Cas Mudde and Cristóbal Rovira Kaltwasser, *Populism: A Very Short Introduction* (New York: Oxford University Press, 2017), 1.

20. Jan-Werner Müller, *What Is Populism?* (Philadelphia: University of Pennsylvania Press, 2016), 2. Müller later argues that progressive figures such as Senator

Bernie Sanders should not be considered populists because they present a coherent ideological vision and defend a pluralist worldview. Although his view that progressives such as Sanders are not populists is not universally shared, his approach to populism is quite consistent with my analysis of nationalist populism.

21. Michael Kazin, quoted in Isaac Chotiner, "Is Donald Trump a Populist?" *Slate,* February 24, 2016, https://slate.com/news-and-politics/2016/02/is-donald-trump-a-populist.html.

22. Lee, "Populist Chameleon," 358, 359, 361, 362. Similar to Lee, Woodward refers to populist discourse as a "vocabulary" and a "style" that was "evident in the presidencies of Teddy Roosevelt, Franklin Roosevelt, Jimmy Carter, and Ronald Reagan," a conclusion that emphasizes the ideological flexibility of the frame. See Woodward, "Reagan as Roosevelt," 44, 45, 48. Rolfe also identifies similar characteristics. See Rolfe, *Reinvention of Populist Rhetoric in the Digital Age,* 25, 27.

23. Lee, "Populist Chameleon," 356, 361.

24. Maddux, "Fundamentalist Fool or Populist Paragon?" 511.

25. Müller, *What Is Populism?,* 21, 93.

26. Erlich, "Populist Rhetoric," 142, 148, 150.

27. Michael Kazin, "How Can Donald Trump and Bernie Sanders Both Be 'Populist'?" *New York Times,* March 27, 2016, https://www.nytimes.com/2016/03/27/magazine/how-can-donald-trump-and-bernie-sanders-both-be-populist.html. Douglas Kellner makes a similar argument in labeling Trump an "authoritarian populist." See Douglas Kellner, *American Nightmare: Donald Trump, Media Spectacle, and Authoritarian Populism* (Rotterdam: Sense Publishers, 2016), 22.

28. Michael Kazin, *The Populist Persuasion: An American History,* rev. ed. (Ithaca, NY: Cornell University Press, 1998), 2. John Judis makes a similar argument in *The Populist Explosion: How the Great Recession Transformed American and European Politics* (New York: Columbia Global Reports, 2016), 19–29, 59–64.

29. Charles Postel, "If Trump and Sanders Are Both Populists, What Does Populist Mean?" *American Historian,* February 2016, https://www.oah.org/tah/issues/2016/february/if-trump-and-sanders-are-both-populists-what-does-populist-mean/.

30. Mudde and Kaltwasser, *Populism,* 6, 11.

31. Müller, *What Is Populism?,* 1.

32. Mudde and Kaltwasser, *Populism,* 5; Müller, *What Is Populism?,* 19.

33. Müller, *What Is Populism?,* 20; Judis, *Populist Explosion,* 26.

34. Populist Party, "Populist Party Platform of 1892," July 4, 1892, American Presidency Project, http://www.presidency.ucsb.edu/ws/index.php?pid=29616.

35. See J. Michael Hogan, "Conclusion: Memories and Legacies of the Progressive Era," in *Rhetoric and Reform in the Progressive Era: A Rhetorical History of the United States,* vol. 6, ed. J. Michael Hogan (East Lansing: Michigan State University Press, 2003), 472, 473, 474, 480. Although the Progressive movement was more inclusive than the larger society, that inclusiveness was quite limited

in relation to Black Americans. See Brian R. McGee, "Rhetoric and Race in the Progressive Era: Imperialism, Reform, and the Ku Klux Klan," in Hogan, *Rhetoric and Reform in the Progressive Era,* 311–338.

36. Bernie Sanders, "Text of Bernie Sanders' Wall Street and Economy Speech," MarketWatch, January 5, 2016, https://www.marketwatch.com/story /text-of-bernie-sanders-wall-street-and-economy-speech-2016-01-05.

37. The distinction between heuristic and ontological genres is developed in Robert C. Rowland, "On Generic Categorization," *Communication Theory* 1 (1991): 128–144. For a discussion of how situation and purpose produce an identifiable "constellation of forms," see Karlyn Kohrs Campbell and Kathleen Hall Jamieson, "Form and Genre in Rhetorical Criticism: An Introduction," in *Form and Genre: Shaping Rhetorical Action,* ed. Karlyn Kohrs Campbell and Kathleen Hall Jamieson (Falls Church, VA: SCA, 1978), 20, 21, 22. For similar perspectives, see Rowland, "On Generic Categorization," and Carolyn R. Miller, "Genre as Social Action," *Quarterly Journal of Speech* 70 (1984): 151–167.

38. Campbell and Jamieson, "Form and Genre in Rhetorical Criticism," 22; see also Rowland, "On Generic Categorization," 141.

39. Robert C. Rowland and Kirsten Theye, "The Symbolic DNA of Terrorism," *Communication Monographs* 75 (2008): 52–85.

40. Stenner, *Authoritarian Dynamic,* 24.

41. Stenner, 1.

42. Stenner, 29.

43. Daniel Cox, Rachel Lenesch, and Robert P. Jones, *Beyond Economics: Fears of Cultural Displacement Pushed the White Working Class to Trump,* PRRI, May 9, 2017, https://www.prri.org/research/white-working-class-attitudes-economy-.

44. Stenner, *Authoritarian Dynamic,* 17, 269.

45. Stenner, 17.

46. See Salvador Rizzo, "Trump's Claim That Immigrants Bring 'Tremendous Crime' Is Still Wrong," *Washington Post,* January 18, 2018, https://www.washing tonpost.com/news/fact-checker/wp/2018/01/18/trumps-claim-that-immigrants -bring-tremendous-crime-is-still-wrong/?utm_term=.7fab45b96c25; Nicole Lewis, "Comparing the 'Trump Economy' to the 'Obama Economy,'" *Washington Post,* December 14, 2017, https://www.washingtonpost.com/news/fact-checker /wp/2017/12/14/comparing-the-trump-economy-to-the-obama-economy/?utm _term=.6aefdda8fb82; Miriam Valverde, "A Look at the Data on Domestic Terrorism and Who's Behind It," PolitiFact, August 16, 2017, https://www.politifact .com/truth-o-meter/article/2017/aug/16/look-data-domestic-terrorism-and -whos-behind-it/.

47. Marc J. Hetherington and Jonathan D. Weiler, *Authoritarianism and Polarization in American Politics* (Cambridge, UK: Cambridge University Press, 2009), 7.

48. Hetherington and Weiler, *Authoritarianism and Polarization in American Politics*, 86–90.

49. For a similar argument, see Ronald Inglehart and Pippa Norris, "Trump, Brexit, and the Rise of Populism: Economic Have-Nots and Cultural Backlash," HKS Faculty Research Working Paper Series RWP16-026, August 6, 2016, https:// www.hks.harvard.edu/publications/trump-brexit-and-rise-populism-economic -have-nots-and-cultural-backlash.; E. J. Dionne Jr., Norman J. Ornstein, and Thomas E. Mann, *One Nation after Trump: A Guide for the Perplexed, the Disillusioned, the Desperate, and the Not-Yet Deported* (New York: St. Martin's, 2017), 123.

50. Amanda Taub, "Trump's Victory and the Rise of White Populism," *New York Times*, November 10, 2016, https://www.nytimes.com/2016/11/10/world/americas /trump-white-populism-europe-united-states.html.

51. Pippa Norris, "It's Not Just Trump: Authoritarian Populism Is Rising Across the West—Here's Why," *Washington Post*, March 11, 2016, https://www.washington post.com/news/monkey-cage/wp/2016/03/11/its-not-just-trump-authoritarian -populism-is-rising-across-the-west-heres-why/."

52. Taub, "Trump's Victory and the Rise of White Populism."

53. Berlet and Lyons are cited in Chip Berlet, "'Trumping' Democracy: Right-Wing Populism, Fascism, and the Case for Action," Political Research Associates, December 12, 2015, 3, http://www.politicalresearch.org/2015/12/12/trumping -democracy-right-wing-populism-fascism-and-the-case-for-action/#sthash.7Lk 503sn.dpbs.

54. Müller, *What Is Populism?*, 3, 21.

55. Although not focused on populist discourse, Rita Kirk Whillock shows how former Ku Klux Klan member David Duke tapped into race-based fear of societal change. See "The Subversion of Argument: Lessons from the Demagogic Rhetoric of David Duke," *Political Communication* 11 (1994): 217–231.

56. Cas Mudde, "The Populist Zeitgeist," *Government and Opposition* 39 (2004): 544.

57. Kazin, *Populist Persuasion*, 225; Paul Krugman, "Coal Country Is a State of Mind," *New York Times*, March 31, 2017, A23.

58. Historian Walter Russell Mead is quoted in Thomas B. Edsall, "The Peculiar Populism of Donald Trump," *New York Times*, February 2, 2017, https://www .nytimes.com/2017/02/02/opinion/the-peculiar-populism-of-donald-trump.html.

59. Thomas Greven, "The Rise of Right-Wing Populism in Europe and the United States: A Comparative Perspective," May 2016, 2, http://www.fesdc.org /fileadmin/user_upload/publications/RightwingPopulism.pdf.

60. Greven, "Rise of Right-Wing Populism in Europe and the United States," 2.

61. Müller is interviewed in Francis Wilkinson, "Why Donald Trump Really Is a Populist," *Bloomberg*, February 16, 2017, https://www.bloomberg.com/opinion /articles/2017-02-16/why-donald-trump-really-is-a-populist.

62. Greven, "Rise of Right-Wing Populism in Europe and the United States," 7.

63. Mudde, "Populist Zeitgeist."

64. Müller, *What Is Populism?*, 93.

65. Mudde and Kaltwasser, *Populism*, 42, 43. Kellner makes a similar argument about Trump. See *American Nightmare*, 21.

66. Müller, *What Is Populism?*, 3, 4.

67. Kathleen Parker, "Republicans Would Rather Have a King Than a President," *Washington Post*, March 28, 2017, https://www.washingtonpost.com/opinions /republicans-would-rather-have-a-king-than-a-president/2017/03/28/a6b8dd9a -13ef-11e7-9e4f-09aa75d3ec57_story.html.

68. Mudde and Kaltwasser, *Populism*, 64.

69. Müller is interviewed in Wilkinson, "Why Donald Trump Really Is a Populist."

70. Mudde and Kaltwasser, *Populism*, 70.

71. Quoted in Wilkinson, "Why Donald Trump Really Is a Populist."

72. Taub, "Trump's Victory and the Rise of White Populism." See also Mudde and Kaltwasser, *Populism*, 18.

73. For a similar argument, see J. Eric Oliver and Wendy M. Rahn, "Rise of the Trumpenvolk: Populism in the 2016 Election," *Annals of the American Academy of Political and Social Science* 667 (2016): 191.

74. Michael Wolfe, *Fire and Fury: Inside the Trump White House* (New York: Henry Holt, 2018), 249.

75. Brian L. Ott and Greg Dickinson, *The Twitter Presidency: Donald J. Trump and the Politics of White Rage* (New York: Routledge, 2019), 2, 72. Ott and Dickinson note that "the style that he performs is rooted by pervasive sentiments (anxiety and fear) about race" and also argue that Trump "performs his rage" (28, 41).

76. Ott and Dickinson, *Twitter Presidency*, 74.

77. This argument is clearly developed in Ott and Dickinson, *Twitter Presidency*.

78. Taub, "Rise of American Authoritarianism."

79. Taub, "Rise of American Authoritarianism."

80. Quoted in Taub, "Rise of American Authoritarianism."

81. I presented a less-developed version of this argument in Robert C. Rowland, "The Populist and Nationalist Roots of Trump's Rhetoric," *Rhetoric and Public Affairs* 22 (2019): 343–388.

82. Donald J. Trump, "Here's Donald Trump's Presidential Announcement Speech," *Time*, June 16, 2015, http://time.com/3923128/donald-trump-announcement-speech/. Future references will be made by paragraph number.

83. Trump later made still more outrageous claims about the unemployment rate. See Louis Jacobson, "Donald Trump Repeats Pants on Fire Claim That Unemployment Rate Could Be 42 Percent," *PolitiFact*, February 11, 2016, https:// www.politifact.com/truth-o-meter/statements/2016/feb/11/donald-trump /donald-trump-repeats-pants-fire-claim-unemployment/.

84. Joshua Green, *Devil's Bargain: Steve Bannon, Donald Trump, and the Nationalist Uprising* (New York: Penguin, 2017), 161.

85. Michelle Ye Hee Lee, "Donald Trump's False Comments Connecting Mexican Immigrants and Crime," *Washington Post,* July 8, 2015, https://www .washingtonpost.com/news/fact-checker/wp/2015/07/08/donald-trumps-false -comments-connecting-mexican-immigrants-and-crime/?utm_term=.15708 a71c093.

86. Ben Terris, "Donald Trump Begins 2016 Bid, Citing His Outsider Status," *Washington Post,* June 16, 2015, https://www.washingtonpost.com/politics /donald-trump-is-now-a-candidate-for-president-of-the-united-states/2015 /06/16/5e6d738e-1441-11e5-9ddc-e3353542100c_story.html?utm_term=.4ef97007 d319.

CHAPTER 2. TRUMP'S RHETORIC OF NATIONALIST
POPULISM IN 2016 CAMPAIGN RALLIES

1. Olga Khazan, "People Voted for Trump Because They Were Anxious, Not Poor," *Atlantic,* April 23, 2018, https://www.theatlantic.com/science/archive/2018 /04/existential-anxiety-not-poverty-motivates-trump-support/558674/.

2. Thomas F. Pettigrew, "Social Psychological Perspectives on Trump Supporters," *Journal of Social and Political Psychology* 5 (2017): 112.

3. Nate Cohn and Alicia Parlapioano, "How Broad, and How Happy, Is the Trump Coalition?" *New York Times,* August 9, 2018, https://www.nytimes.com /interactive/2018/08/09/upshot/trump-voters-how-theyve-changed.html.

4. I rely on reports from both the 2016 campaign and rallies during Trump's presidency. Although, as I note later, his message became more extreme after his election, the emotional functions fulfilled in rallies remained much the same in both periods.

5. Jenna Johnson, "Chants, Cheers, Boos, and the Man at the Center of It All," *Washington Post,* June 22, 2018, https://www.washingtonpost.com/graphics/2018 /politics/trump-crowd-sound/.

6. Gwynn Guilford, "Inside the Trump Machine: The Bizarre Psychology of America's Newest Political Movement," Quartz, April 1, 2016, https://qz.com /645345/inside-the-trump-machine-the-bizarre-psychology-of-americas-newest -political-movement/.

7. Maggie Koerth, "Donald Trump Incites His Crowds—and His Crowds Incite Him," FiveThirtyEight, March 15, 2016, https://fivethirtyeight.com/features /donald-trump-incites-his-crowds-and-his-crowds-incite-him/.

8. Guilford, "Inside the Trump Machine."

9. Stephen D. Reicher and S. Alexander Haslam, "Trump's Appeal: What Psychology Tells Us," *Scientific American,* March 1, 2017, https://www.scientific american.com/article/trump-rsquo-s-appeal-what-psychology-tells-us, 4, 17.

10. Katy Tur, *Unbelievable: My Front-Row Seat to the Craziest Campaign in American History* (New York: HarperCollins, 2017), 244.

11. Charles Homans, "The Post-Campaign Campaign of Donald Trump," *New York Times Magazine,* April 9, 2018, https://www.nytimes.com/2018/04/09 /magazine/donald-trump-rallies-campaigning-president.html.

12. Johnson, "Chants, Cheers, Boos, and the Man at the Center of It All."

13. Tur, *Unbelievable,* 273.

14. David Frum, *Trumpocracy: The Corruption of the American Republic* (New York: HarperCollins, 2018), 111.

15. Guilford, "Inside the Trump Machine."

16. Eric Niiler, "The Psychology Behind the Violence at Trump Rallies," *Wired,* March 18, 2016, https://www.wired.com/2016/03/psychology-behind-violence -trump-rallies/.

17. Reicher and Haslam, "Trump's Appeal," 5.

18. Johnson, "Chants, Cheers, Boos, and the Man at the Center of It All."

19. Guilford, "Inside the Trump Machine."

20. Niiler, "Psychology Behind the Violence at Trump Rallies."

21. Reicher and Haslam, "Trump's Appeal," 11, 12–13.

22. Guilford, "Inside the Trump Machine."

23. Reicher and Haslam, "Trump's Appeal," 14.

24. Reicher and Haslam, 16.

25. Bobby Azarian, "The Psychology Behind Donald Trump's Unwavering Support," *Psychology Today,* September 13, 2016, https://www.psychologytoday.com /us/blog/mind-in-the-machine/201609/the-psychology-behind-donald-trumps -unwavering-support.

26. Guilford, "Inside the Trump Machine." Guilford also notes that "the *content* of their [Trump and Hitler] speeches" is not similar.

27. Reicher and Haslam, "Trump's Appeal," 6.

28. Donald J. Trump, "Full Transcript of Donald Trump's Jobs Speech," *Fortune,* June 28, 2016, https://fortune.com/2016/06/28/transcript-donald-trump-speech -jobs/; Donald Trump, "Transcript of Donald Trump's Immigration Speech," September 2, 2016, *New York Times,* https://www.nytimes.com/2016/09/02/us /politics/transcript-trump-immigration-speech.html.

29. See Nick Corasaniti, Alexander Burns, and Binyamin Appelbaum, "Donald Trump Vows to Rip Up Trade Deals and Confront China," *New York Times,* June 29, 2016, A1; Ben Jacobs, "In Arizona We Saw the Real Donald Trump: The One We Already Knew," *Guardian,* September 1, 2016, https://www.theguardian.com/us-news /2016/sep/01/in-arizona-we-saw-the-real-donald-trump-the-one-we-already-knew.

30. Donald J. Trump, "Full Transcript of Donald Trump's Speech in Akron, Ohio," August 8, 2016, https://heavy.com/news/2016/08/read-full-transcript -donald-trump-rally-speech-akron-ohio-text/.

31. Donald Trump, "Full Transcript: Donald Trump NYC Speech on the Stakes of the Election," June 22, 2016, https://www.politico.com/story/2016/06/transcript-trump-speech-on-the-stakes-of-the-election-224654.

32. Donald Trump, "Donald Trump Gives First Campaign Speech Since Hiring Bannon and Conway," August 18, 2016, RealClear Politics, https://www.realclearpolitics.com/video/2016/08/18/watch_live_donald_trump_gives_first_campaign_speech_since_hiring_stephen_bannon.html.

33. Pettigrew, "Social Psychological Perspectives on Trump Supporters," 109.

34. E. J. Dionne Jr., Norman J. Ornstein, and Thomas E. Mann, *One Nation after Trump: A Guide for the Perplexed, the Disillusioned, the Desperate, and the Not-Yet Deported* (New York: St. Martin's, 2017), 82. Conservative columnist Jennifer Rubin drew precisely the same conclusion. See Rubin, "Republicans Make Trump's Racist and Incendiary Language Possible," *Washington Post,* August 6, 2018, https://www.washingtonpost.com/blogs/right-turn/wp/2018/08/06/republicans-make-trumps-racist-and-incendiary-language-possible/?utm_term=.0613 6377e17b.

35. Amanda Taub, "The Rise of American Authoritarianism," Vox, March 1, 2016, https://www.vox.com/2016/3/1/11127424/trump-authoritarianism.

36. See Ronald Reagan, "Televised Address by Governor Ronald Reagan: A Strategy for Peace in the 80s," October 19, 1980, Ronald Reagan Presidential Library and Museum, https://www.reaganlibrary.gov/10-19-80; Reagan, "Televised Campaign Address: A Vital Economy—Jobs, Growth, and Progress for Americans," Ronald Reagan Presidential Library and Museum, October 24, 1980, https://www.reaganlibrary.gov/10-24-80.

37. Speeches on immigration, health care, the war in Iraq, and a host of other topics are archived at "Best Speeches of Barack Obama Through His 2009 Inauguration," http://obamaspeeches.com/.

38. Aaron Blake, "Trump's Forbidden Love: Single-Payer Health Care," *Washington Post,* May 5, 2017, https://www.washingtonpost.com/news/the-fix/wp/2017/05/05/trumps-forbidden-love-single-payer-health-care/?utm_term=.codde890a9d3.

39. Homans, "Post-Campaign Campaign of Donald Trump."

CHAPTER 3. NATIONALIST POPULISM IN DEBATES, THE REPUBLICAN NATIONAL CONVENTION, AND THE INAUGURAL

1. "Annotated Transcript: The Aug. 6 GOP Debate," *Washington Post,* August 6, 2015, https://www.washingtonpost.com/news/post-politics/wp/2015/08/06/annotated-transcript-the-aug-6-gop-debate/?utm_term=.5974e356229c; "The *Fox News* GOP Debate Transcript, Annotated," *Washington Post,* March 3, 2016, https://www.washingtonpost.com/news/the-fix/wp/2016/03/03/the-fox-news-gop-debate-transcript-annotated/?utm_term=.3d6de13a26ae.

2. David A. Fahrenthold, "Trump Was Center of Attention and Attacks in GOP Debate," *Washington Post*, March 3, 2016, https://www.washingtonpost.com /politics/trump-to-face-three-rivals-and-his-media-nemesis-in-thursdays-gop -debate/2016/03/03/a3d24eda-e0de-11e5-9c36-e1902f6b6571_story.html?utm _term=.12c0356431aa.

3. Trump is quoted in Ezra Klein, "Donald Trump's Fight with *Fox News* and Megyn Kelly, Explained," Vox, August 9, 2015, https://www.vox.com/2015/8/8 /9121377/donald-trump-megyn-kelly.

4. Trip Gabriel, "Donald Trump and the G.O.P. Debate: Policy Is Not His Point," *New York Times*, August 6, 2015, A1.

5. Andrew Prokop, "The Ratings for the First Republican Debate Were Massive and Unprecedented," Vox, August 7, 2015, https://www.vox.com/2015/8/7/9117381 /republican-debate-ratings.

6. Karen Tumulty and Phillip Rucker, "Trump Roils First Debate among GOP Contenders," *Washington Post*, August 6, 2015, https://www.washingtonpost.com /politics/donald-trump-dominates-raucous-republican-debate/2015/08/06/b8 a5f0e6-3c79-11e5-8e98-115a3cf7d7ae_story.html?utm_term=.ce9d8de64bf9.

7. Ezra Klein, "Donald Trump Is an Embarrassment Who Is Impossible to Embarrass: It's His Superpower," Vox, August 6, 2015, https://www.vox.com/2015 /8/6/9114505/donald-trump-honey-badger-gop-debate.

8. "The Debate's Biggest Winners—and Losers," *Politico*, August 7, 2015, https://www.politico.com/magazine/story/2015/08/republican-debate-2015 -winners-losers-121139_Page2.html.

9. Luntz is quoted in Glenn Thrush, "5 Takeaways from the GOP Debate," *Politico*, March 4, 2016, https://www.politico.com/story/2016/03/five-takeaways -from-the-gop-debate-220246; Frank Bruni, "Five Big Questions after a Vulgar Republican Debate," *New York Times*, March 3, 2016, https://www.nytimes .com/2016/03/03/opinion/five-big-questions-after-a-vulgar-republican-debate .html; David A. Graham, "Motor City Meltdown," *Atlantic*, March 3, 2016, https:// www.theatlantic.com/liveblogs/2016/03/republican-debate-detroit/472245/.

10. Patrick Healty and Jonathan Martin, "In Republican Debate, Ted Cruz and Marco Rubio Wage Urgent Attacks on Donald Trump," *New York Times*, March 4, 2016, A1.

11. Karen Tumulty, "Trump Throws the GOP into an Identity Crisis," *Washington Post*, March 4, 2016, https://www.washingtonpost.com/politics/trump -throws-the-gop-into-an-identity-crisis/2016/03/04/d9a6477c-e233-11e5-846c -10191d1fc4ec_story.html?utm_term=.7685924e4c38.

12. Chris Cillizza, "Winners and Losers from the 11th Republican Presidential Debate," *Washington Post*, March 3, 2016, https://www.washingtonpost.com /news/the-fix/wp/2016/03/03/winners-and-losers-from-the-11th-republican -presidential-debate/?utm_term=.5dc309027fe8.

13. "Transcript of the First Debate," *New York Times*, September 27, 2016, https://www.nytimes.com/2016/09/27/us/politics/transcript-debate.html.

14. Patrick Healy and Jonathan Martin, "His Tone Dark, Donald Trump Takes G.O.P. Mantle," *New York Times*, July 22, 2016, A1.

15. Alex Altman, "Midnight in America: Donald Trump's Gloomy Convention Speech," *Time*, July 22, 2016, http://time.com/4418398/donald-trump-convention-speech/.

16. "Critics: Trump Convention Speech Signals Shift to Coded Race Language," *Chicago Tribune*, July 22, 2016, https://www.chicagotribune.com/nation-world/ct-trump-coded-race-language-20160722-story.html.

17. For a description of typical themes present and functions served in successful and unsuccessful convention speeches, see William A. Galston, "What's the Purpose of an Acceptance Speech?" Brookings Institution, July 21, 2016, https://www.brookings.edu/blog/fixgov/2016/07/21/whats-the-purpose-of-an-acceptance-speech/; Henry Z. Scheele, "Ronald Reagan's 1980 Acceptance Address: A Focus on American Values," *Western Journal of Communication* 48 (1984): 51–61, Roderick P. Hart, *Campaign Talk: Why Elections Are Good for Us* (Princeton, NJ: Princeton University Press, 2000), 106–116.

18. Donald Trump, "Transcript: Donald Trump at the G.O.P. Convention," *New York Times*, July 22, 2016, https://www.nytimes.com/2016/07/22/us/politics/trump-transcript-rnc-address.html, 53. References will be made by paragraph number. Note, the *New York Times* essentially turned every sentence into a separate paragraph.

19. See Glenn Kessler and Michelle Ye Hee Lee, "Fact-Checking Donald Trump's Acceptance Speech at the 2016 RNC," *Washington Post*, July 22, 2016, https://www.washingtonpost.com/news/fact-checker/wp/2016/07/22/fact-checking-donald-trumps-acceptance-speech-at-the-2016-rnc/.

20. See Ronald Reagan, "Republican National Convention Acceptance Speech," July 17, 1980, Ronald Reagan Presidential Library and Museum, https://www.reaganlibrary.gov/7-17-80; Barack Obama, "Barack Obama's Acceptance Address," August 28, 2008, *New York Times*, https://www.nytimes.com/2008/08/28/us/politics/28text-obama.html.

21. Jeff Shesol, "Dark Rhetoric in Washington," *New York Times*, January 21, 2017, A27.

22. Thomas L. Friedman, "Road Trip Through Rusting and Rising America," *New York Times*, May 24, 2017, A25; Peter Baker and Michael D. Shear, "Trump, Sworn In, Issues a Call: 'This American Carnage Stops,'" *New York Times*, January 21, 2017, A1; Mark Landler, "A Broadside for Washington," *New York Times*, January 21, 2017, A1; David E. Sanger, "A Harder Line: 'America First,'" *New York Times*, January 21, 2017, A1; Maggie Haberman and Glenn Thrush, "A Brand-Conscious Trump Embraces the Look of the Presidency," *New York Times*, January 21, 2017, A11.

23. Karlyn Kohrs Campbell and Kathleen Hall Jamieson, *Presidents Creating the Presidency: Deeds Done in Words* (Chicago: University of Chicago Press, 2008), 31.

24. Donald J. Trump, "Inaugural Address," January 20, 2017, https://www.white house.gov/inaugural-address, 2–5. Further references will be cited by paragraph number.

25. See Campbell and Jamieson, *Presidents Creating the Presidency.*

26. Carl Hulse, "Opening Message: Ask What Your Government Has Done to You?" *New York Times,* January 21, 2017, A17.

27. Marc Fisher, "Trump's Inaugural Speech Was a Sharp Break with Past—and His Party," *Washington Post,* January 20, 2017, https://www.washingtonpost .com/politics/trump-inaugural-speech-sharp-break-with-past-and-his-party /2017/01/20/bcfc06d6-de7a-11e6-918c-99ede3c8cafa_story.html.

28. Michael Gerson, "Trump's Funeral Oration at the Death of Reaganism," *Washington Post,* January 21, 2017, https://www.washingtonpost.com/opinions /trumps-funeral-oration-at-the-death-of-reaganism/2017/01/21/4fc8bef6-dffb -11e6-918c-99ede3c8cafa_story.html.

29. Bush is cited in Yashar Ali, "What George W. Bush Really Thought of Donald Trump's Inauguration," *New York Magazine,* March 29, 2017, https://nymag .com/intelligencer/2017/03/what-george-w-bush-really-thought-of-trumps -inauguration.html.

30. George Will, "Trump's Dreadful Inaugural Address," *Lawrence Journal-World,* January 21, 2017, 7A.

31. Commentators and anchors are cited in Michael M. Grynbaum, "Inaugural All Its Own Brings Astonishment and Awe to Television," *New York Times,* January 21, 2017, A22; James Poniewozik, "Inauguration Watch: Mr. Reality TV Goes to Washington," *New York Times,* January 21, 2017, A22.

32. "President Trump's Dark Vision," *New York Times,* January 21, 2017, A26.

33. Leonard Pitts Jr., "Trump Promises Magical Solutions," *Lawrence Journal-World,* January 22, 2017, 7A.

CHAPTER 4. THE TRANSITION FROM OUTSIDER TO
STRONGMAN IN TRUMP'S FORMAL PRESIDENTIAL RHETORIC

1. The classic statement of this view can be found in Jeffrey K. Tulis, *The Rhetorical Presidency* (Princeton, NJ: Princeton University Press, 1987). For a number of essays discussing the rhetorical presidency, see Martin J. Medhurst, ed., *Beyond the Rhetorical Presidency* (College Station: Texas A&M University Press, 1996).

2. Karlyn Kohrs Campbell and Kathleen Hall Jamieson, *Presidents Creating the Presidency: Deeds Done in Words* (Chicago: University of Chicago Press, 2008), 6, 7.

3. Campbell and Jamieson, *Presidents Creating the Presidency,* 8.

4. Campbell and Jamieson, 9, 12.

5. Vanessa Beasley, *You the People: American National Identity in Presidential Rhetoric* (College Station: Texas A&M University Press, 2004), 149, 150.

6. As one example, see my discussion of Barack Obama's speech to a Joint Session of Congress on health care. Robert C. Rowland, "Barack Obama and the Revitalization of Public Reason," *Rhetoric and Public Affairs* 14 (2011): 693–725.

7. "President Obama Takes Questions at GOP House Issues Conference," January 29, 2010, Whitehouse.gov, https://obamawhitehouse.archives.gov /photos-and-video/video/president-obama-takes-questions-gop-house-issues -conference#transcript.

8. Ronald Reagan Presidential Library and Museum, https://www.reagan library.gov/speeches/major-speeches-1964-1989.

9. Amos Kiewe and Davis W. Houck, *A Shining City on a Hill: Ronald Reagan's Economic Rhetoric, 1951–1989* (New York: Praeger, 1989), 136.

10. Kiewe and Houck, *Shining City on a Hill*, 136.

11. Peter Baker, "Trump's National Address Escalates Border Wall Fight," *New York Times,* January 8, 2019, https://www.nytimes.com/2019/01/08/us/politics /donald-trump-speech.html.

12. All of the short speeches or remarks cited in what follows are available under briefings and statements on health care; see Whitehouse.gov, https://www .whitehouse.gov/briefings-statements/page/14/?issue_filter=healthcare.

13. Donald J. Trump, "Remarks by President Trump in Joint Address to Congress," February 28, 2017, Whitehouse.gov, https://www.whitehouse.gov /briefings-statements/remarks-president-trump-joint-address-congress/; Donald J. Trump, "President Donald J. Trump's State of the Union Address," January 30, 2018, Whitehouse.gov, https://www.whitehouse.gov/briefings-statements /president-donald-j-trumps-state-union-address/ (future references will be made in the text by paragraph number); Donald J. Trump, "Remarks by President Trump to the 72nd Session of the United Nations General Assembly," September 19, 2017, https://www.whitehouse.gov/briefings-statements/remarks -president-trump-72nd-session-united-nations-general-assembly/; Donald J. Trump, "President Donald J. Trump's Address to the Nation on the Crisis at the Border," Whitehouse.gov, January 8, 2019, https://www.whitehouse.gov/briefings -statements/president-donald-j-trumps-address-nation-crisis-border/.

14. Maggie Astor, "Longest State of the Union? Not Quite, but Trump's Was Long," *New York Times,* January 30, 2018, https://www.nytimes.com/2018/01/30 /us/politics/trump-state-of-the-union-long.html.

15. Campbell and Jamieson, *Presidents Creating the Presidency,* 139.

16. Campbell and Jamieson, 158. See also Jeffrey P. Mehltretter Drury, "Beyond 'Rhetorical Agency': Skutnik's Story in the 1982 State of the Union Address," *Western Journal of Communication* 82 (2018): 40–58.

17. The discussion of monuments and the enumeration of ordinary American heroes are so similar to passages in Ronald Reagan's First Inaugural Address that it seems likely it served as the model for these passages. See Reagan, "First Inaugural," January 20, 1981, https://www.reaganlibrary.gov/research/speeches/inaugural-address-january-20-1981. For a discussion of Reagan's use of narrative and value appeals in the address, see John M. Jones and Robert C. Rowland, "Redefining the Proper Role of Government: Ultimate Definition in Reagan's First Inaugural," *Rhetoric and Public Affairs* 18 (2015): 691–718.

18. Louis Nelson and Tara Palmieri, "Trump Moves to Get Base 'Stirred Up' with NFL Attacks," *Politico*, September 25, 2017, https://www.politico.com/story/2017/09/25/trump-nfl-fight-nascar-243091.

19. Trump Twitter Archive, http://www.trumptwitterarchive.com/.

20. Max Book, "Protest Is as American as Football: Why Doesn't Trump Get It?" *Washington Post*, September 10, 2018, https://www.washingtonpost.com/opinions/protest-is-as-american-as-football-why-doesnt-trump-get-it/2018/09/10/8ffb8c58-b522-11e8-94eb-3bd52dfe917b_story.html?utm_term=.dbed5f65b000.

21. Linda Qiu, "Out of Context, Out of Proportion, Out of the Realm of Possibility," *New York Times*, January 31, 2018, A14.

22. Jim Tankersley, "Trump Owns the Booming Economy: Republicans on the Trail Barely Mention It," *New York Times*, July 27, 2018, https://www.nytimes.com/2018/07/27/us/politics/economy-politics-midterms.html.

23. Glenn Kessler, "How President Trump Twists Government Data to Suit the Political Moment," *Washington Post*, December 5, 2018, https://www.washingtonpost.com/politics/2018/12/05/how-president-trump-twists-government-data-suit-political-moment/?utm_term=.8b65fac93fab.

24. "Contraception and Religious Liberty," *New York Times*, October 4, 2012, A34.

25. E. J. Dionne Jr., "Instead of Seeking 'Common Ground,' Trump Gives a Flabby, Divisive Speech," *Washington Post*, January 30, 2018, https://www.washingtonpost.com/blogs/post-partisan/wp/2018/01/30/the-only-support-holding-up-trumps-speech-stories-of-american-heroes.

26. George Ingram, "Myths about U.S. Foreign Aid," Brookings Institution, April 7, 2017, https://www.brookings.edu/blog/unpacked/2017/04/07/myths-about-u-s-foreign-aid/.

27. See Julie Hirschfeld Davis and Rick Gladstone, "Trump Cites 'Great Progress' in North Korea Nuclear Talks," *New York Times*, July 12, 2018, https://www.nytimes.com/2018/07/12/world/asia/north-korea-kim-jong-un-trump-letter-nuclear.html. The report largely refutes Trump's claim of "great progress."

28. Quoted in Phillip Rucker, "Trump Praises Kim's Authoritarian Rule, Says 'I Want My People to Do the Same,'" *Washington Post*, June 15, 2018, https://

www.washingtonpost.com/politics/trump-praises-kims-authoritarian-rule-says
-i-want-my-people-to-do-the-same/2018/06/15/cea20aa2-70a5-11e8-bf86-a2351
b5ece99_story.html?utm_term=.ea91b21bac18.

29. There is consensus among mainstream experts that the deal included strict
constraints limiting Iran's capacity to produce nuclear weapons. See Zachary
Lamb, "The Impact of the Iran Nuclear Agreement," Council on Foreign Relations,
May 8, 2018, https://www.cfr.org/backgrounder/impact-iran-nuclear-agreement.

30. Karen Tumulty and Phillip Rucker, "Trump Calls for Unity, Pushes GOP
Agenda in State of the Union Speech," *Washington Post,* January 30, 2018, https://
www.washingtonpost.com/politics/trumps-steep-challenge-in-his-first-state
-of-the-union-address-uniting-a-fractured-country/2018/01/30/ecb51258-05c7
-11e8-b48c-b07fea957bd5_story.html; Marc A. Thiessen, "Trump's Speech Nailed
It: Let's See What He Does Now," *Washington Post,* January 31, 2018, https://www
.washingtonpost.com/opinions/trumps-speech-nailed-it-lets-see-what-he-does
-now/2018/01/31/eb513a1c-060e-11e8-94e8-e8b8600ade23_story.html.

31. Marc Fisher, "Best Behavior: How Trump Alters His Tone to Suit the Occasion," *Washington Post,* January 30, 2018, https://www.washingtonpost.com
/politics/best-behavior-how-trump-alters-his-tone-to-suit-the-occasion/2018
/01/30/7a7791f8-05df-11e8-b48c-b07fea957bd5_story.html.

32. James Hohmann, "The Daily 202: State of the Union Underscores Why
Trump Is His Own Worst Enemy," *Washington Post,* January 31, 2018, https://
www.washingtonpost.com/news/powerpost/paloma/daily-202/2018/01/31/daily
-202-state-of-the-union-underscores-why-trump-is-his-own-worst-enem/5a710
80230fb041c3c7d7528/?utm_term=.0aa05e4bf0d.

33. Dionne, "Instead of Seeking 'Common Ground,' Trump Gives a Flabby,
Divisive Speech."

34. "A Divisive and Misleading State of the Union," *Washington Post,* January
30, 2018, https://www.washingtonpost.com/opinions/a-divisive-and-misleading
-state-of-the-union/2018/01/30/a52694c4-060e-11e8-94e8-e8b8600ade23_story
.html; Dana Milbank, "A Uniquely Depressing State of the Union," *Washington Post,* January 30, 2018, https://www.washingtonpost.com/opinions/a
-uniquely-depressing-state-of-the-union/2018/01/30/d3ec3642-060e-11e8-94e8
-e8b8600ade23_story.html.

35. Hohmann, "Daily 202."

36. Donald J. Trump, "Remarks by President Trump in Joint Address to Congress," February 28, 2017; Trump, "Remarks by President Trump to the 72nd Session of the United Nations General Assembly," September 19, 2017.

37. David Ignatius, "The Most Surprising Thing about Trump's U.N. Speech,"
Washington Post, September 19, 2017, https://www.washingtonpost.com/opinions
/global-opinions/trumps-strikingly-conventional-un-speech/2017/09/19/876cb
41a-9d75-11e7-9c8d-cf053ff30921_story.html.

38. David Rothkopf, "Trump's First Speech to the United Nations Was a Disastrous, Nationalistic Flop," *Washington Post,* September 19, 2017, https://www.washingtonpost.com/news/global-opinions/wp/2017/09/19/trumps-first-speech-to-the-united-nations-was-a-disastrous-nationalistic-flop/?utm_term=.21a482270d74.

39. Phillip Bump, "Trump's Frustrated Sales Pitch on the Border Wall Reverts to His Oldest Political Tactic: Fear," *Washington Post,* January 9, 2019, https://www.washingtonpost.com/politics/2019/01/09/trumps-frustrated-sales-pitch-border-wall-reverts-his-oldest-political-tactic-fear/?utm_term=.d852cb66d937.

40. Trump, "President Donald J. Trump's Address to the Nation on the Crisis at the Border."

41. Jennifer Rubin, "Trump's Nothingburger Speech," *Washington Post,* January 8, 2019, https://www.washingtonpost.com/opinions/2019/01/09/trumps-nothingburger-speech/?utm_term=.1e86d85d6ee.

42. *Politifact* introduced an article naming campaign misstatements by Donald Trump the "2015 Lie of the Year," with a discussion of the idea of truthful hyperbole, implicitly making the point that Trump's policy rhetoric was almost always hyperbolic but almost never truthful. See Angie Drobnic Holan and Linda Qui, "2015 Lie of the Year: The Campaign Misstatements of Donald Trump," Politifact, December 21, 2015, https://www.politifact.com/truth-o-meter/article/2015/dec/21/2015-lie-year-donald-trump-campaign-misstatements/. Trump, or his coauthor Tony Schwartz, coined the term to describe one aspect of his deal-making in Donald J. Trump, *The Art of the Deal* (New York: Ballantine Books, 1987), 58.

43. Donald J. Trump, "President Donald J. Trump's State of the Union Address," Whitehouse.gov, February 5, 2019, https://www.whitehouse.gov/briefings-statements/president-donald-j-trumps-state-union-address-2/.

44. "Trump's State of the Union Gave Us the Same Old Polarizing Demagoguery—at Great Length," *Washington Post,* February 5, 2019, https://www.washingtonpost.com/opinions/trumps-state-of-the-union-gave-us-the-same-old-polarizing-demagoguery--at-length/2019/02/05/98fa86a8-29ba-11e9-b011-d8500644dc98_story.html?utm_term=.0a2bf3c86d38; Jennifer Rubin, "The State of the Union Is Boring," *Washington Post,* February 5, 2019, https://www.washingtonpost.com/opinions/2019/02/06/state-union-is-boring/?utm_term=.9306661b6d08; Glenn Kessler, Salvador Rizzo, and Meg Kelly, "Fact-Checking President Trump's 2019 State of the Union Address," *Washington Post,* February 6, 2019, https://www.washingtonpost.com/politics/2019/02/06/fact-checking-president-trumps-state-union-address/?utm_term=.6f6f5f129192.

45. Michael Gerson, "Trump's State of the Union Was Below Average: But There Were Rays of Light," *Washington Post,* February 6, 2019, https://www.washingtonpost.com/opinions/trumps-state-of-the-union-was-below-average-but-there

-were-rays-of-light/2019/02/06/42168298-2a3b-11e9-b2fc-721718903bfc_story
.html?utm_term=.6d2d7a34a629.

46. The most important analysis of the genres of presidential discourse is
Campbell and Jamieson, *Presidents Creating the Presidency.*

47. A Google search of important ceremonial speeches by Trump produced no
references to actual important ceremonial speeches. Most of the references were
to his Inaugural Address, which of course served both ceremonial and policy-
related functions.

48. Donald Trump, "Remarks by President Trump on the 75th Commemora-
tion of D-Day," June 6, 2019, https://www.whitehouse.gov/briefings-statements
/remarks-president-trump-75th-commemoration-d-day.

49. David Jackson and John Fritz, "'He Can Be a Statesman': Trump's Normandy
Speech Well-Received by Critics: Scarborough Says, 'Hope He Means It,'" *USA
Today,* June 6, 2019, https://www.usatoday.com/story/news/politics/2019/06/06
/d-days-takeaways-donald-trump-praises-allies-veterans/1365156001; Alex Ward,
"Trump's D-Day Speech Was Great: He Was the Wrong Man to Give It," Vox, June
7, 2019, https://www.vox.com/2019/6/7/18656265/trump-d-day-france-normandy
-world-war-2; Peter Nicholas, "Trump Delivered a Strong D-Day Speech—but It
Clashed with His Personal Story," *Atlantic,* June 6, 2019, https://www.theatlantic
.com/politics/archive/2019/06/trump-reassuring-d-day-message/591196/.

50. Stephen B. Presser, "Trump's Finest Hour Dawns with His D-Day Speech,"
Newsmax, June 11, 2019, https://www.newsmax.com/stephenbpresser/leviathan
-maga-war/2019/06/11/id/919899/; see also Quin Hillyer, "Trump's Excellent
D-Day Speech Captured Soldiers' Courage," *Washington Examiner,* June 6, 2019,
https://www.washingtonexaminer.com/opinion/trumps-excellent-d-day-speech
-captured-soldiers-courage.

51. "Nationalism and D-Day," *Wall Street Journal,* June 6, 2019, https://www
.wsj.com/articles/nationalism-and-d-day-11559861787.

52. Bret Stephens, "Hailing the Greatest Generation," *New York Times,* June 8,
2019, A23; see also Nicholas, "Trump Delivered a Strong D-Day Speech"; David
Ignatius, "Trump's Words on D-Day Are at Odds with His Actions," *Washington
Post,* June 6, 2019, https://www.washingtonpost.com/opinions/trumps-words-on
-d-day-are-at-odds-with-his-actions/2019/06/06/e7638e1e-888a-11e9-a870-b9
c411dc4312_story.html?utm_term=.aa3e70fb935d.

53. Mark Landler and Maggie Haberman, "Trump Honors D-Day Sacrifices,
with Some Legacies Unspoken," *New York Times,* June 6, 2019, https://www
.nytimes.com/2019/06/06/world/europe/trump-d-day-speech.html; Max Boot,
"Trump's Behavior in Europe was 'Unpresidented'—and He Isn't Getting Any
Better," *Washington Post,* June 7, 2019, https://www.washingtonpost.com/opinions
/2019/06/07/trumps-behavior-europe-was-unpresidented-he-isnt-getting-any
-better/?utm_term=.df3d3804f5fo.

54. See Gary Wills, *Lincoln at Gettysburg: The Words That Remade America* (New York: Simon and Schuster, 1992).

55. "Nationalism and D-Day."

56. Ronald Reagan, "Remarks at a Ceremony Commemorating the 40th Anniversary of the Normandy Invasion, D-Day," June 6, 1984, https://www.reagan foundation.org/media/128809/normandy.pdf.

57. Donald Trump, "Remarks by President Trump at a Salute to America," July 4, 2019, Whitehouse.gov, https://www.whitehouse.gov/briefings-statements /remarks-president-trump-salute-america/.

58. Gillian Brockell, "Trump's Fourth of July History Speech: Turns Out There Weren't Airports Back Then," *Washington Post*, July 5, 2019, https://www.washing tonpost.com/history/2019/07/05/turns-out-there-werent-airports-back-then /?utm_term=.91b033961a55. Brockell was quoting the Twitter posting of Willamette University historian Seth Cotlar. See https://twitter.com/SethCotlar/status /1146920681851875329.

59. Edward Helmore, "'Battle of the Baggage Claim': Trump's 1775 Airport Claim Inspires Parodies," *Guardian*, July 5, 2019, https://www.theguardian.com /us-news/2019/jul/05/trump-revolutionary-war-airport-claim-memes.

60. See Annie Karni, "Trump Uses Mount Rushmore Speech to Deliver Divisive Culture War Message," *New York Times*, July 3, 2020, https://www.nytimes .com/2020/07/03/us/politics/trump-coronavirus-mount-rushmore.html; Donald Trump, "Remarks by President Trump at South Dakota's 2020 Mount Rushmore Fireworks Celebration, Keystone, South Dakota," July 3, 2020, https://www .whitehouse.gov/briefings-statements/remarks-president-trump-south-dakotas -2020-mount-rushmore-fireworks-celebration-keystone-south-dakota/; Annie Karni and Maggie Haberman, "At Mt. Rushmore and the White House, Trump Updates 'American Carnage' Message for 2020," *New York Times*, July 5, 2020, https://www.nytimes.com/2020/07/04/us/politics/trump-mt-rushmore.html ?action=click&module=Top%20Stories&pgtype=Homepage.

61. Ashley Parker, "President Non Grata: Trump Often Unwelcome and Unwilling to Perform Basic Rituals of the Office," *Washington Post*, August 28, 2018, https://www.washingtonpost.com/politics/president-non-grata-trump-often -unwelcome-and-unwilling-to-perform-basic-rituals-of-the-office/2018/08/28 /302b60ee-aa16-11e8-a8d7-0f63ab8b1370_story.html?utm_term=.0c6b52a7e9.

62. Phillip Rucker, "Bush Funeral: Trump Sits with Fellow Presidents but Still Stands Alone," *Washington Post*, December 5, 2018, https://www.washingtonpost .com/politics/bush-funeral-trump-sits-with-fellow-presidents-but-still-stands -alone/2018/12/05/fdc6663a-f8a3-11e8-8d64-4e79db33382f_story.html?no redirect=on&utm_term=.6ab2561f85f6.

63. Dana Milbank, "George H. W. Bush's Funeral Was a Powerful Renunciation of Trump," *Washington Post*, December 5, 2018, https://www.washingtonpost

.com/opinions/george-hw-bushs-funeral-was-a-powerful-renunciation-of
-trump/2018/12/05/e8c2a8a0-f8d2-11e8-8c9a-860ce2a8148f_story.html?utm_term
=.7168a83c9e7; Greg Jaffe, "At George H. W. Bush's Funeral, a Magisterial Presidency Meets One Diminished by Division," *Washington Post*, December 5,
2018, https://www.washingtonpost.com/politics/at-george-hw-bushs-funeral-a
-magisterial-presidency-meets-one-diminished-by-division/2018/12/05/9595a
982-f8ac-11e8-8c9a-860ce2a8148f_story.html?utm_term=.a80c3e239486.

64. Barack Obama, "Remarks by the President to a Joint Session of Congress
on Health Care," September 9, 2009, https://obamawhitehouse.archives.gov/the
-press-office/remarks-president-a-joint-session-congress-health-care.

CHAPTER 5. TRUMP RALLIES THE BASE WITH A NEVER-ENDING CAMPAIGN OF NATIONALIST POPULISM

1. Maggie Koerth, "Donald Trump Incites His Crowds—and His Crowds Incite Him," FiveThirtyEight, March 15, 2016, https://fivethirtyeight.com/features
/donald-trump-incites-his-crowds-and-his-crowds-incite-him/.

2. See Jenna Johnson and Seung Min Kim, "A Rambling Trump Tosses Out
the Script—Literally—in W.Va.," *Washington Post*, April 5, 2018, https://www
.washingtonpost.com/politics/a-rambling-trump-tosses-out-the-script
--literally--in-w-va/2018/04/05/c8d86c72-38e9-11e8-acd5-35eac230e514_story
.html; Donald Trump, "Remarks: Donald Trump Hosts a Roundtable in West
Virginia on Tax Reform—April 5, 2018," Factbase, https://factba.se/transcript
/donald-trump-remarks-tax-roundtable-west-virginia-april-5-2018.

3. See Louis Jacobson, "Donald Trump Says the Unemployment Rate May
Be 42 Percent," Politifact, September 30, 2015, https://www.politifact.com/truth
-o-meter/statements/2015/sep/30/donald-trump/donald-trump-says-unemploy
ment-rate-may-be-42-perc/.

4. See Donald J. Trump, "'I Can Be More Presidential Than Any President':
Read Trump's Ohio Rally Speech," *Time*, July 26, 2017, http://time.com/4874161
/donald-trump-transcript-youngstown-ohio/; "President Trump Ranted for 77
Minutes in Phoenix: Here's What He Said," *Time*, August 23, 2017, http://time
.com/4912055/donald-trump-phoenix-arizona-transcript/; Donald J. Trump,
"Speech: Donald Trump Speaks at a Make America Great Again Rally in Pennsylvania—March 10, 2018," Factbase, March 10, 2018, https://factba.se/transcript
/donald-trump-speech-rally-saccone-pennsylvania-march-10-2018; Donald J.
Trump, "Speech: Donald Trump Holds a Political Rally in Wilkes-Barre, Pa.—
August 2, 2018," Factbase, August 2, 2018, https://factba.se/transcript/donald
-trump-speech-maga-wilkes-barre-pa-august-2-2018. I reviewed a number of
other rally speeches and found them broadly representative of his presidential rallies. See also Donald J. Trump, "Read: Full Transcript of Trump's Rally
Speech in Florida," February 18, 2017, https://www.ajc.com/news/national/read

NOTES TO PAGES 90–96 [203]

-full-transcript-trump-rally-speech-florida/DeDCp0NEKLQmWcIKndWBoM; Donald J. Trump, "Speech: Donald Trump Holds a Make America Great Again Rally in Duluth, Minnesota—June 20, 2018," Factbase, June 20, 2018, https://factba.se/transcript/donald-trump-speech-political-rally-duluth-minnesota-june-20-2018; Donald J. Trump, "Speech: Donald Trump Holds a Political Rally in Houston," October 22, 2018, Factbase, https://factba.se/transcript/donald-trump-speech-maga-rally-houston-tx-october-22-2018; Donald J. Trump, "Remarks by President Trump at the 2019 Conservative Political Action Conference [CPAC]," Whitehouse.gov, March 3, 2019, https://www.whitehouse.gov/briefings-statements/remarks-president-trump-2019-conservative-political-action-conference/. The CPAC speech is so long that I will reference it by paragraph number.

5. Jacey Fortin, "Has Trump 'Watched ICE Liberate Towns from the Grasp of MS-13'? No," *New York Times,* July 1, 2018, https://www.nytimes.com/2018/07/01/us/trump-ms13-immigration-fact-check.html.

6. Michael D. Shear and Maggie Haberman, "Trump Defends Initial Remarks on Charlottesville; Again Blames 'Both Sides,'" *New York Times*, August 16, 2017, A1.

7. For the role of the United States in the founding of MS-13, see Lisa Ling, "How the US Helped Create Trump's 'Violent Animals,'" CNN, September 9, 2018, https://www.cnn.com/2018/09/19/opinions/ms-13-trump-america-ice-salvador/index.html.

8. Christina Caron, "Trump, Answering Rebuke in TV Interview, Mocks James's Intelligence," *New York Times,* August 5, 2018, SP5.

9. The title of the *Time* transcript was "President Trump Ranted for 77 Minutes in Phoenix: Here's What He Said."

10. Greg Sargent, "Trump Takes an Old Republican Lie and Makes It Even Worse," *Washington Post,* October 23, 2018, https://www.washingtonpost.com/blogs/plum-line/wp/2018/10/23/trump-takes-an-old-republican-lie-and-makes-it-even-worse/?utm_term=.44938adcf3c; Dana Milbank, "What Hath Trump Wrought?" *Washington Post,* October 24, 2018, https://www.washingtonpost.com/opinions/stop-the-mob-mr-president/2018/10/24/7a8fe2fa-d7c9-11e8-aeb7-ddcad4a0a54e_story.html?utm_term=.58976aeb3fd9.

11. Paul Waldman, "Yes, Elizabeth Warren Has Native Ancestry: No, That Won't Stop Trump's Racist Attacks," *Washington Post,* October 15, 2018, https://www.washingtonpost.com/blogs/plum-line/wp/2018/10/15/yes-elizabeth-warren-has-native-ancestry-no-that-wont-stop-trumps-racist-attacks/?utm_term=.79197a9e4513.

12. Glenn Kessler, "A Witches' Brew of Over-the-Top Trump Attacks," *Washington Post*, October 24, 2018, https://www.washingtonpost.com/politics/2018/10/24/president-trumps-witchs-brew-over-the-top-attacks/?utm_term=.ca20ff7a709f.

13. Michael Gerson, "Trump Boldly Asserts That He Has Learned Nothing These Past Two Years," *Washington Post*, March 4, 2019, https://www.washington post.com/opinions/trump-boldly-asserts-that-he-has-learned-nothing-these -past-two-years/2019/03/04/e85aa238-3eb8-11e9-922c-64d6b7840b82_story.html ?utm_term=.5e6304164078.

14. Amanda Sakuma, "The 7 Most Bizarre Moments from Trump's Long-Winded CPAC Rant," Vox, March 2, 2019, https://www.vox.com/2019/3/2/18247712 /trump-cpac-bizarre-rant; Tal Axelrod, "The Top 9 Moments from Trump's Two-Hour CPAC Speech," *Hill*, March 2, 2019, https://thehill.com/homenews/admin istration/432341-the-top-9-moments-from-trumps-freewheeling-cpac-speech; Chris Cilliza, "The 67 Most Stunning Lines from Donald Trump's Epic 2-hour CPAC Speech," CNN, March 4, 2019, https://www.cnn.com/2019/03/04/politics /donald-trump-cpac-speech/index.html.

15. Glenn Kessler, Salvador Rizzo, and Meg Kelly, "President Trump Has Made 9,014 False or Misleading Claims over 773 Days," *Washington Post*, March 4, 2019, https://www.washingtonpost.com/politics/2019/03/04/president-trump-has -made-false-or-misleading-claims-over-days/?utm_term=.8ff120545c2a.

16. Axelrod, "Top 9 Moments from Trump's Two-Hour CPAC Speech"; Robert Costa, "'We're Not Going to Turn on Our Own': Republicans Rally Around Trump as Threats Mount," *Washington Post*, March 2, 2019, https://www.washingtonpost .com/politics/were-not-going-to-turn-on-our-own-republicans-rally-around -trump-as-threats-mount/2019/03/02/6b9786ac-3bb2-11e9-aaae-69364b2ed137 _story.html?utm_term=.232b6c7e96dd; Elizabeth Bruenig, "Trump's Love May Be Why He's Maintained a Strong Grasp of His Base," *Washington Post*, March 5, 2019, https://www.washingtonpost.com/opinions/trumps-cpac-speech-was -full-of-love-its-been-a-successful-formula-for-him/2019/03/05/6047df16-3f7e -11e9-9361-301ffb5bd5e6_story.html?utm_term=.9d17cd6816a3.

17. Glenn Kessler, "Spicer Earns Four Pinocchios for a Series of False Claims on Inauguration Crowd Size," *Washington Post*, January 22, 2017, https://www .washingtonpost.com/news/fact-checker/wp/2017/01/22/spicer-earns-four -pinocchios-for-a-series-of-false-claims-on-inauguration-crowd-size.

18. Kat Devlin, "International Relations Experts and U.S. Public Agree: America Is Less Respected Globally," Pew Research Center, December 17, 2018, https://www.pewresearch.org/fact-tank/2018/12/17/international-relations -experts-and-u-s-public-agree-america-is-less-respected-globally/; John Gram-lich and Kat Devlin, "More People Around the World See U.S. Power and Influ-ence as a 'Major Threat' to Their Country," Pew Research Center, February 14, 2019, https://www.pewresearch.org/fact-tank/2019/02/14/more-people-around -the-world-see-u-s-power-and-influence-as-a-major-threat-to-their-country/.

19. "Donald Trump Speech Transcript at North Carolina Rally 'MAGA' Event," Rev, July 17, 2019, https://www.rev.com/blog/donald-trump-maga-event-speech -transcript-north-carolina-rally.

20. Donald J. Trump, TrumpTwitterArchive, July 14, 2019, https://twitter.com/realdonaldtrump/status/1150381395078000643.

21. Katie Rogers and Nicholas Fandos, "In Twitter Rant, Trump Goes after Rogue Democrats," *New York Times,* July 15, 2019, A1; Julie Hirschfeld Davis, Maggie Haberman, and Michael Crowley, "Pressed by G.O.P., Trump Disavows 'Send Her Back,'" *New York Times,* July 19, 2019, A1; Annie Karni, "From the Attack to the Retreat and Back Again," *New York Times,* July 20, 2019, A12; Julie Hirschfeld Davis, "After Fiery Fray, House Condemns Trump's Tweets," *New York Times,* July 17, 2019, A1.

22. Jeremy W. Peters, Maggie Haberman, and Annie Karni, "Divisive Words Nod to Strategy for Re-Election," *New York Times,* July 17, 2019, A1, A14; Daniel Dale and Tara Subramaniam, "Trump Made 20 False Claims at His North Carolina Rally," CNN, July 18, 2019, https://www.cnn.com/2019/07/18/politics/trump-false-claims-in-greenville-north-carolina-rally/index.html.

23. Adrienne Dunn, "Fact Check: Trump Did Host Rallies, Play Golf as COVID-19 Outbreak Ramped Up," *USA Today,* April 17, 2020, https://www.usatoday.com/story/news/factcheck/2020/04/17/fact-check-trump-had-rallies-golfed-covid-19-outbreak-grew/5126918002/; Linda Qiu, Bill Marsh, and Jon Huang, "The President vs. the Experts: How Trump Downplayed the Coronavirus," *New York Times,* March 20, 2020, A13.

24. Greg Miller and Ellen Nakashima, "President's Intelligence Briefing Book Repeatedly Cited Virus Threat," *Washington Post,* April 27, 2020, https://www.washingtonpost.com/national-security/presidents-intelligence-briefing-book-repeatedly-cited-virus-threat/2020/04/27/ca66949a-8885-11ea-ac8a-fe9b8088e101_story.html; Michael Morell and Kristin Wood, "The Tragedy Is That We Knew This Was Coming," *Washington Post,* March 27, 2020, https://www.washingtonpost.com/opinions/2020/03/27/tragedy-is-that-we-knew-this-was-coming/.

25. Peter Baker, "Trump Stays Quiet on Toll as U.S. Nears a Milestone," *New York Times,* May 25, 2020, A1.

26. See Philip Rucker, Josh Dawsey, Yasmeen Abutaleb, Robert Costa, and Lena H. Sun, "34 Days of Pandemic: Inside Trump's Desperate Attempts to Reopen America," *Washington Post,* May 2, 2020, https://www.washingtonpost.com/politics/34-days-of-pandemic-inside-trumps-desperate-attempts-to-reopen-america/2020/05/02/e99911f4-8b54-11ea-9dfd-990f9dcc71fc_story.html.

27. See Michael Gerson, "The Moment When Trump's Schtick Finally Failed," *Washington Post,* May 4, 2020, https://www.washingtonpost.com/opinions/as-coronavirus-deaths-continue-the-trump-show-gets-even-more-surreal/2020/05/04/387fb6c0-8e29-11ea-a9c0-73b93422d691_story.html.

28. See Eric Lipton, David E. Sanger, Maggie Haberman, Michael D. Shear, Mark Mazzetti, and Julian E. Barnes, "Despite Timely Alerts, Trump Was Slow to Act," *New York Times,* April 12, 2020, A1, A13–A15.

29. One study by an epidemiologist at Columbia University found that if the United States had implemented a shutdown on March 1, 2020, rather than two weeks later, "about 54,000 fewer people would have died by early May." See James Glanz and Campbell Robertson, "Lockdown Delays Cost at Least 36,000 Lives, Data Show," *New York Times*, May 21, 2020, A1, A8. Nicholas Kristof found that "if the United States had the coronavirus death rate of the average female-led country, 102,000 American lives would have been saved out of the 114,000 lost" in mid-June 2020. The point is that the policies implemented by leaders such as Angela Merkel in Germany worked to produce a much lower death rate than in the United States (11 deaths per 100,000 people in Germany versus 35 in the United States). See "Nations May Be Safer under Women," *New York Times*, June 14, 2020, SR 9; "Coronavirus Map: Tracking the Global Outbreak," *New York Times*, June 15, 2020, https://www .nytimes.com/interactive/2020/world/coronavirus-maps.html#countries.

30. Fareed Zakaria, "It's Easy to Blame Trump for This Fiasco: But There's a Much Larger Story," *Washington Post*, March 26, 2020, https://www.washington post.com/opinions/the-us-is-still-exceptional--but-now-for-its-incompetence /2020/03/26/4d6d1ade-6f9b-11ea-a3ec-70d7479d83f0_story.html.

31. Dana Milbank, "Other Countries Are Winning Against the Virus: We Are Quitting," *Washington Post*, May 8, 2020, https://www.washingtonpost.com /opinions/2020/05/08/other-countries-are-winning-against-virus-we-are -quitting/. For a comprehensive analysis of the administration's failures through the end of March 2020, see Amber Phillips, "What Exactly Has Trump Done— or Not Done—to Receive Such Harsh Criticism for His Coronavirus Re- sponse?," *Washington Post*, March 27, 2020, https://www.washingtonpost.com /politics/2020/03/27/what-exactly-has-trump-done-or-not-done-receive-such -harsh-criticism-his-coronavirus-response/.

32. Jeanna Smialek, "Recovery Path Is Uncertain, Fed Warns," *New York Times*, June 13, 2020, B3.

33. In an in-depth analysis, the *Washington Post* reported on how the Trump administration left testing, contact tracing, and other crisis responses to the states. See Rucker, Dawsey, Abutaleb et al., "34 Days of Pandemic." Greg Sargent describes how the administration essentially transferred "responsibility to states" to orga- nize a public health response. See Sargent, "Trump's War on Reality Just Got a Lot More Dangerous," *Washington Post*, May 26, 2020, https://www.washingtonpost .com/opinions/2020/05/26/trumps-war-reality-just-got-lot-more-dangerous/.

34. See, for example, Nell Greenfieldboyce, "As the Coronavirus Crisis Heats Up, Why Isn't America Hearing from the CDC?" NPR, March 25, 2020, https:// www.npr.org/sections/health-shots/2020/03/25/821009072/as-the-coronavirus -crisis-heats-up-why-arent-we-hearing-from-the-cdc.

35. Margaret Sullivan, "The Trump Administration Is Muzzling Government Scientists: It's Essential to Let Them Speak Candidly to the Press Again," *Wash-*

ington Post, April 17, 2020, https://www.washingtonpost.com/lifestyle/media/the
-trump-administration-is-muzzling-government-scientists-its-essential-to-let
-them-speak-candidly-to-the-press-again/2020/04/17/1d934c0e-80a6-11ea-a3ee
-13e1ae0a3571_story.html.

36. Carolyn Y. Johnson and William Wan, "Trump Is Breaking Every Rule
in the CDC's 450-Page Playbook for Health Crisis," *Washington Post,* March 14,
2020, https://www.washingtonpost.com/health/2020/03/14/cdc-manual-crisis
-coronavirus-trump/.

37. Giovanni Russonello, "Voters Agree on Threat Posed by Virus, but Split
over Trump's Response," *New York Times,* March 29, 2020, A22.

38. Philip Bump and Ashley Parker, "13 Hours of Trump: The President Fills
Briefings with Attacks and Boasts, but Little Empathy," *Washington Post,* April
25, 2020, https://www.washingtonpost.com/politics/13-hours-of-trump-the
-president-fills-briefings-with-attacks-and-boasts-but-little-empathy/2020/04
/25/7eec5ab0-8590-11ea-a3eb-e9fc93160703_story.html; E. J. Dionne Jr., "The Presidency Is Now Just a Daily Talk Show," *Washington Post,* March 25, 2020, https://
www.washingtonpost.com/opinions/the-government-that-works-vs-the-man-in
-the-white-house/2020/03/25/694f4770-6ecb-11ea-aa80-c2470c6b2034_story.html.

39. Jeremy W. Peters, Elaina Plott, and Maggie Haberman, "260,000 Words,
Full of Self-Praise, from Trump on the Virus," *New York Times,* April 26, 2020,
https://www.nytimes.com/interactive/2020/04/26/us/politics/trump-corona
virusbriefings-analyzed.html.

40. Paul Waldman, "A National Crisis and a President Incapable of Empathy,"
Washington Post, March 20, 2020, https://www.washingtonpost.com/opinions
/2020/03/20/national-crisis-president-incapable-empathy/.

41. "Remarks by President Trump, Vice President Pence, and Members of the
Coronavirus Task Force in Press Conference," Whitehouse.gov, March 13, 2020,
https://www.whitehouse.gov/briefings-statements/remarks-president-trump
-vice-president-pence-members-coronavirus-task-force-press-conference-3/.

42. "Remarks by President Trump, Vice President Pence, and Members of
the Coronavirus Task Force in Press Briefing," Whitehouse.gov, March 16, 2020,
https://www.whitehouse.gov/briefings-statements/remarks-president-trump
-vice-president-pence-members-coronavirus-task-force-press-briefing-3.

43. "Remarks by President Trump, Vice President Pence, and Members of
the Coronavirus Task Force in Press Briefing," Whitehouse.gov, March 19, 2020,
https://www.whitehouse.gov/briefings-statements/remarks-president-trump
-vice-president-pence-members-coronavirus-task-force-press-briefing-6/;
see also Allison Chiu, "Trump Has No Qualms about Calling Coronavirus the
'Chinese Virus': That's a Dangerous Attitude, Experts Say," *Washington Post,*
March 20, 2020, https://www.washingtonpost.com/nation/2020/03/20/corona
virus-trump-chinese-virus/.

44. For representative examples, see "Remarks by President Trump, Vice President Pence, and Members of the Coronavirus Task Force in Press Briefing," Whitehouse.gov, March 17, 2020, https://www.whitehouse.gov/briefings -statements/remarks-president-trump-vice-president-pence-members-corona virus-task-force-press-briefing-4"; Remarks by President Trump, Vice President Pence, and Members of the Coronavirus Task Force in Press Briefing," Whitehouse.gov, March 21, 2020, https://www.whitehouse.gov/briefings-state ments/remarks-president-trump-vice-president-pence-members-coronavirus -task-force-press-briefing-7; "Remarks by President Trump, Vice President Pence, and Members of the Coronavirus Task Force in Press Briefing," Whitehouse .gov, March 25, 2020, https://www.whitehouse.gov/briefings-statements/remarks -president-trump-vice-president-pence-members-coronavirus-task-force-press -briefing-11/.

45. Mark Landler, "A Fumbled Global Response to the Virus in a Leadership Void," *New York Times,* March 12, 2020, A18.

46. Michael D. Shear and Donald G. McNeil Jr., "Trump, Seeing Poll Numbers Drop, Blames W.H.O. for Virus Mistakes," *New York Times,* April 15, 2020, A7.

47. Jeremy W. Peters, "Pro-Trump Media's Virus Pivot: From Alarm to Denial to Blame," *New York Times,* April 2, 2020, A1, A9.

48. "Remarks by President Trump, Vice President Pence, and Members of the Coronavirus Task Force in Press Briefing," Whitehouse.gov, April 6, 2020, https:// www.whitehouse.gov/briefings-statements/remarks-president-trump-vice -president-pence-members-coronavirus-task-force-press-briefing-20/.

49. Aaron Blake, "FDA's Hydroxychloroquine Reversal Raises Even Bigger Questions about Trump's Role in Pushing for the Drug," *Washington Post,* June 15, 2020, https://www.washingtonpost.com/politics/2020/06/15/fdas-hydroxychloro quine-reversal-raises-even-bigger-questions-about-trumps-role-pushing-drug/.

50. See Ariana Eunjung Cha and Laurie McGinley, "Antimalarial Drug Touted by President Trump Is Linked to Increased Risk of Death in Coronavirus Patients, Study Says," *Washington Post,* May 22, 2020, https://www.washingtonpost.com /health/2020/05/22/hydroxychloroquine-coronavirus-study/; Tara Haelle, "Man Dead from Taking Chloroquine Product after Trump Touts Drug for Coronavi-rus," *Forbes,* March 23, 2020, https://www.forbes.com/sites/tarahaelle/2020/03/23 /man-dead-from-taking-chloroquine-after-trump-touts-drug-for-coronavirus /#50e6c2b72e91.

51. Shear and McNeil, "Trump, Seeing Poll Numbers Drop, Blames W.H.O. for Virus Mistakes," A7.

52. Aaron Blake, "Trump Ties Coronavirus Decisions to Personal Grievances," *Washington Post,* March 27, 2020, https://www.washingtonpost.com/politics /2020/03/27/trump-suggests-personal-grievances-factor-into-his-coronavirus -decisions/.

53. Peter Baker, "As Numbers Sink In, New Reality Confronts a More Somber Trump," *New York Times*, April 2, 2020, A7.

54. See for example, Aaron Blake, "Trump's Eruption at an NBC Reporter Says It All about His Alternate Reality on Coronavirus," *Washington Post*, March 20, 2020, https://www.washingtonpost.com/politics/2020/03/20/trumps-eruption -an-nbc-reporter-says-it-all-about-his-alternate-reality-coronavirus/; Manuel Roig-Franzia and Sarah Ellison, "A History of the Trump War on Media—the Obsession Not Even Coronavirus Could Stop," *Washington Post*, March 28, 2020, https://www.washingtonpost.com/lifestyle/media/a-history-of-the-trump -war-on-media--the-obsession-not-even-coronavirus-could-stop/2020/03/28 /71bb21d0-f433-11e9-8cf0-4cc99f74d127_story.html.

55. Erik Wemple, "Trump Called the Media 'the Enemy of the People': He Means It," *Washington Post*, March 20, 2020, https://www.washingtonpost.com /opinions/2020/03/20/trump-called-media-enemy-people-he-means-it/.

56. Peter Baker and Maggie Haberman, "Crisis Easing, Trump Leaps to Call Shots, Setting Up Standoff with Governors," *New York Times*, April 14, 2020, A18.

57. "Remarks by President Trump, Vice President Pence, and Members of the Coronavirus Task Force in Press Briefing," Whitehouse.gov, April 14, 2020, https://www.whitehouse.gov/briefings-statements/remarks-president-trump -vice-president-pence-members-coronavirus-task-force-press-briefing-25/.

58. "Remarks by President Trump, Vice President Pence, and Members of the Coronavirus Task Force in Press Conference," Whitehouse.gov, March 13, 2020.

59. "Remarks by President Trump, Vice President Pence, and Members of the Coronavirus Task Force in Press Briefing," Whitehouse.gov, March 16, 2020.

60. Michael Gerson, "Trump's Unhinged Tweets Are an Attempt to Divert At- tention away from a Historic Fiasco," *Washington Post*, May 11, 2020, https://www .washingtonpost.com/opinions/trumps-tweets-are-a-strategy-of-distraction -to-obscure-a-policy-of-abdication/2020/05/11/720d00f6-93b4-11ea-91d7-cf 4423d47683_story.html; E. J. Dionne Jr., "Trump's Signal Is His Noise: Stop Try- ing to Distinguish Between the Two," *Washington Post*, May 20, 2020, https:// www.washingtonpost.com/opinions/trumps-signal-is-his-noise-stop-trying-to -distinguish-between-the-two/2020/05/20/c8764552-9ad4-11ea-89fd-28fb 313d1886_story.html; Paul Waldman, "Can We Stop Pretending Trump Is Fit to Be President?," *Washington Post*, May 25, 2020, https://www.washingtonpost.com /opinions/2020/05/25/can-we-stop-pretending-trump-is-fit-be-president/.

61. Peter Baker, "Trump and Kushner Boast of Success in Recasting Adminis- tration's Response," *New York Times*, April 30, 2020, A8.

62. Annie Karni, Nate Schweber, and Christina Capecchi, "Briefings Draw Viewers but Fail to Change Views," *New York Times*, April 13, 2020, A10.

63. "Remarks by President Trump, Vice President Pence, and Members of the Coronavirus Task Force in Press Briefing," Whitehouse.gov, April 23, 2020,

https://www.whitehouse.gov/briefings-statements/remarks-president-trump
-vice-president-pence-members-coronavirus-task-force-press-briefing-31/.

64. Keith Collins, "Coronavirus Testing Needs to Triple Before the U.S. Can
Reopen, Experts Say," *New York Times*, April 18, 2020, https://www.nytimes.com
/interactive/2020/04/17/us/coronavirus-testing-states.html.

65. Matt Flegenheimer, "Trump's Disinfectant Remark Raises a Question
about the 'Very Stable Genius,'" *New York Times*, April 27, 2020, A1, A10; Allyson
Chiu, Katie Shepherd, Brittany Shammas, and Colby Itkowitz, "Trump Claims
Controversial Comment about Injecting Disinfectants Was 'Sarcastic,'" *Washington Post*, April 24, 2020, https://www.washingtonpost.com/nation/2020/04/24
/disinfectant-injection-coronavirus-trump/.

66. Christine Hauser and Alan Yuhas, "Science Fires Back Loudly on Trump's
Cure-All," *New York Times*, April 25, 2020, A1, A5; Chiu, Shepherd, and Shammas
et al., "Trump Claims Controversial Comment about Injecting Disinfectants Was
'Sarcastic.'"

67. See, for example, Adrian Horton, "Trevor Noah: 'There's No Way Trump
Even Understands What Bleach Is,'" *Guardian*, April 28, 2020, https://www.the
guardian.com/culture/2020/apr/28/trevor-noah-trump-bleach-stephen-colbert
-seth-meyers-jimmy-kimmel.

68. Gerson, "Moment When Trump's Schtick Finally Failed."

69. See Michael Gerson, "Trump Has Taken Up Residence in an Alternate Political Reality," *Washington Post*, July 9, 2020, https://www.washingtonpost.com
/opinions/trump-is-our-boy-in-the-bubble--a-right-wing-information-bubble
/2020/07/09/9aad6b18-c20d-11ea-9fdd-b7ac6b051dc8_story.html.

70. Donald J. Trump, "Donald Trump Tulsa, Oklahoma, Rally Speech Transcript," June 20, 2020, https://www.rev.com/blog/transcripts/donald-trump-tulsa
-oklahoma-rally-speech-transcript; Ruth Marcus, "Trump's Problem in Tulsa
Wasn't Just Empty Seats: It Was Empty Rhetoric," *Washington Post*, June 21, 2020,
https://www.washingtonpost.com/opinions/2020/06/21/trumps-problem-tulsa
-wasnt-just-empty-seats-it-was-empty-rhetoric; Jose A. Del Real, "With 'Kung
Flu,' 'Thugs,' and 'Our Heritage,' Trump Leans on Racial Grievance as He Reaches
for a Campaign Reset," *Washington Post*, June 21, 2020, https://www.washington
post.com/politics/with-kung-flu-thugs-and-our-heritage-trump-leans-on
-racial-grievance-as-he-reaches-for-a-campaign-reset/2020/06/21/945d7a1e
-b3df-11ea-a510-55bf26485c93_story.html.

71. Astead W. Herndon, "A Safe Space for Believers," *New York Times*, June 22,
2020, A18.

72. David Nakamura and Josh Dawsey, "Few Masks, Little Distancing: Trump
Celebrates at Crowded White House Party Largely Devoid of Coronavirus Precautions," *Washington Post*, August 27, 2020, https://www.washingtonpost.com

/politics/white-house-convention-covid-testing/2020/08/27/44b53cda-e8c4-11ea
-bc79-834454439a44_story.html.

73. Donald J. Trump, "Full Transcript: President Trump's Republican National Convention Speech," *New York Times*, August 28, 2020, https://www.nytimes .com/2020/08/28/us/politics/trump-rnc-speech-transcript.html.

74. Several commentators noted that the speech described an "alternate re- ality." See Michelle Cottle, "Classic Moves at the G.O.P. Convention," *New York Times*, August 29, 2020, A26. Timothy Egan called the speech an "ALT REALITY Show" that functioned as part of the "master con of Trumpism." See "Trump Can't Avoid Reality Forever," *New York Times*, August 29, 2020, A26.

75. See Frank Bruni, "We're Here and They're Not," *New York Times*, August 30, 2020, SR 3; Maureen Dowd, "The Princess vs. the Portrait," *New York Times*, August 30, 2020, SR 2; Michael Gerson, "Trump's Speech Was Nasty, Brutish, and Interminable," *Washington Post*, August 28, 2020, https://www.washingtonpost .com/opinions/trumps-speech-was-nasty-brutish-and-interminable/2020/08 /28/d3a0ff96-e947-11ea-97e0-94d2e46e759b_story.html.

76. Annie Karni and Maggie Haberman, "Hoarse President Addresses Un- masked Florida Crowd," *New York Times*, October 13, 2020, A17.

77. Glenn Thrush, "New Outcry as Trump Rebukes Charlottesville Racists 2 Days Later," *New York Times*, August 14, 2017, https://www.nytimes.com/2017/08 /14/us/politics/trump-charlottesville-protest.html.

78. Perry Bacon Jr. and Dhrumil Mehta, "A 'Great' and 'Excellent' Economy Isn't Making Trump Popular," FiveThirtyEight.com, June 8, 2018, https://five thirtyeight.com/features/trump-might-be-more-popular-if-he-werent-so -trumpy.

79. See David A. Graham, "Corruption in the Trump Administration Is Spread- ing," *Atlantic*, June 22, 2018, https://www.theatlantic.com/politics/archive/2018/06 /wilbur-ross-navigator-trump-pruitt/563441.

80. See Conor Friedersdorf, "Trump Has Filled, Not Drained, the Swamp," *Atlantic*, September 21, 2017, https://www.theatlantic.com/politics/archive/2017 /09/meet-the-new-swamp/540540/.

81. Peter Sullivan, "Poll: Obamacare Favorability Reaches All-Time High," *Hill*, March 1, 2018, http://thehill.com/policy/healthcare/376210-poll-obamacare -favorability-reaches-all-time-high.

82. Phillip Bump, "Real Wages Are Down over the Year—but Republican Sat- isfaction Is Spiking," *Washington Post*, August 15, 2018, https://www.washington post.com/news/politics/wp/2018/08/15/real-wages-are-down-over-the-year-but -republican-satisfaction-is-spiking/?utm_term=.8f3ac9fab80a; also see Jim Tan- kersley, "White House Crafts Yardstick to Show Wage Growth," *New York Times*, September 6, 2018, B4.

83. Ben Casselman and Jim Tankersley, "Booming Economy May Be Little Felt as Voters Decide," *New York Times,* August 17, 2018, B2; Gideon Resnick, "Republicans Largely Abandon Running on Trump's Tax Cuts," *Daily Beast,* July 25, 2018, https://www.thedailybeast.com/republicans-largely-abandon-running-on-trumps-tax-cuts.

84. Natalie Kitroeff and Ben Casselman, "Trade War Worries Iowa Republicans in a Close House Race," *New York Times,* August 17, 2018, https://www.nytimes.com/2018/08/17/business/economy/iowa-trade-midterms.html.

85. For descriptions of these crises in Trump's first term, see Michael Wolfe, *Fire and Fury: Inside the Trump White House* (New York: Henry Holt, 2018); David Frum, *Trumpocracy: The Corruption of the American Republic* (New York: HarperCollins, 2018); Bob Woodward, *Fear: Trump in the White House* (New York: Simon and Schuster, 2018).

86. Amina Dunn, "Trump Approval Ratings So Far Are Unusually Stable—and Deeply Partisan," Pew Research Center, August 1, 2018, http://www.pewresearch.org/fact-tank/2018/08/01/trumps-approval-ratings-so-far-are-unusually-stable-and-deeply-partisan/.

87. Peter Baker, "Trump Seeks to Shadow Nixon but Echoes Wallace in 1968," *New York Times,* June 10, 2020, A18.

88. Max Boot, "This Is the Presidency George Wallace Never Had," *Washington Post,* May 29, 2020, https://www.washingtonpost.com/opinions/2020/05/29/george-wallace-was-too-extreme-gop-now-trump-channels-him/.

89. Donald J. Trump, "Statement by the President," June 1, 2020, https://www.whitehouse.gov/briefings-statements/statement-by-the-president-39/. Trump eventually backed down on his threat to send in the US military across the country but ordered federal law enforcement and National Guard forces to clear Lafayette Park across from the White House in Washington of nonviolent protesters so that he could hold a photo op with a bible at a nearby historic church, an action widely criticized. His rhetoric and actions were so outrageous that they produced major backlash from high-ranking former military officers and leaders of the Department of Defense. See Campbell Robertson, Rick Rojas, and Kate Taylor, "Protests in 140 Cities Bring 5 Deaths and Thousands of Arrests," *New York Times,* June 2, 2020, A1, A16; "89 former Defense Officials: The Military Must Never Be Used to Violate Constitutional Rights," *Washington Post,* June 5, 2020, https://www.washingtonpost.com/opinions/2020/06/05/89-former-defense-officials-military-must-never-be-used-violate-constitutional-rights; James Mattis, "In Union There Is Strength," NPR, June 4, 2020, https://www.npr.org/2020/06/04/869262728/read-the-full-statement-from-jim-mattis.

90. See Kenneth Burke, *Language as Symbolic Action: Essays on Life, Literature, and Method* (Los Angeles: University of California Press, 1966), 16–20; Burke, *A Rhetoric of Motives* (Berkeley: University of California Press, 1950), 14. The dan-

gers of entelechialization are described in Robert C. Rowland and David A. Frank, *Shared Land/Conflicting Identity: Trajectories of Israeli and Palestinian Symbol Use* (East Lansing: Michigan State University Press, 2002), 32–33, 299–300, 303–306.

91. Michelle Goldberg, "Democracy Grief Is Real," *New York Times*, December 15, 2019, SR 5.

92. Emily Stewart, "Watch John McCain Defend Barack Obama Against a Racist Voter in 2008," Vox, August 25, 2018, https://www.vox.com/policy-and-politics /2018/8/25/17782572/john-mccain-barack-obama-statement-2008 video.

93. Karen Tumulty, "Trump Is Building His Reelection Campaign on a Foundation of Racism," *Washington Post*, July 18, 2019, https://www.washingtonpost .com/opinions/trump-is-building-his-reelection-campaign-on-a-foundation -of-racism/2019/07/18/3a5b2608-a975-11e9-9214-246e594de5d5_story.html?utm _term=.63b211101100.

94. Miriam Beard, "The Tune Hitlerism Beats for Germany," *New York Times*, June 7, 1931, 117, 124.

CHAPTER 6. TRUMP'S DYSTOPIAN TWITTERVERSE

1. The argument that Trump's message particularly fit the technological and social nature of Twitter is developed in a fine book: Brian L. Ott and Greg Dickinson, *The Twitter Presidency: Donald J. Trump and the Politics of White Rage* (New York: Routledge, 2019).

2. Shontavia Johnson, "Donald Trump Tweeted Himself into the White House," Conversation, November 10, 2016, https://theconversation.com/donald -trump-tweeted-himself-into-the-white-house-68561.

3. Astead W. Herndon and Jennifer Medina, "Democrats Recalibrate as Trump Exploits Race," *New York Times*, July 22, 2019, A12.

4. For a similar argument about how Trump created a sense of authenticity on Twitter, see Ramona Kreis, "The 'Tweet Politics' of President Trump," *Journal of Language and Politics* 16 (2017): 615.

5. Brian L. Ott applies "media ecology" to argue that Trump's rhetoric on Twitter is defined by simplicity, impulsivity, and incivility. See Ott, "The Age of Twitter: Donald J. Trump and the Politics of Debasement," *Critical Studies in Media Communication* 34 (2017): 59–68.

6. Chaim Perelman and L. Olbrechts-Tyteca, *The New Rhetoric: A Treatise on Argumentation*, trans. J. Wilkinson and P. Weaver (Notre Dame, IN: Notre Dame University Press, 1969), 116, 118.

7. For a similar argument, see Galen Stolee and Steve Caton, "Twitter, Trump, and the Base: A Shift to a New Form of Presidential Talk?," *Signs and Society* 6 (2018): 161.

8. Perelman and Olbrechts-Tyteca, *New Rhetoric*, 142, 144, 147.

9. Adam Ozimek, "Reminder That Deep Trump Country Has Very Few Immigrants," *Forbes*, April 28, 2018, https://www.forbes.com/sites/modeledbehavior

/2018/04/28/reminder-that-deep-trump-country-has-very-few-immigrants/#3955b22f5024.

10. Christopher Ingraham, "Two Charts Demolish the Notion That Immigrants Here Illegally Commit More Crime," *Washington Post*, June 19, 2018, https://www.washingtonpost.com/news/wonk/wp/2018/06/19/two-charts-demolish-the-notion-that-immigrants-here-illegally-commit-more-crime/?utm_term=.f4addd7febce.

11. Chaim Perelman, *The Realm of Rhetoric*, trans. W. Kluback (Notre Dame, IN: Notre Dame University Press, 1982), 37.

12. Thomas F. Mader, "On Presence in Rhetoric," *College Composition and Communication* 24 (1973): 376, 377.

13. David Smith, "How Trump Uses Twitter Storms to Make the Political Weather," *Guardian*, December 2, 2017, https://www.theguardian.com/us-news/2017/dec/02/how-trump-uses-twitter-storms-to-make-the-political-weather; also see Ott and Dickinson, *Twitter Presidency*, 81.

14. Maggie Haberman, Glenn Thrush, and Peter Baker, "Inside Trump's Hour-by-Hour Battle for Self-Preservation," *New York Times*, December 10, 2017, A1.

15. Robert C. Rowland, "The Battle for Health Care Reform and the Liberal Public Sphere," in *Exploring Argumentative Contexts*, ed. Frans H. van Eemeren and Bart Garssen (Amsterdam: John Benjamin, 2012), 269–288.

16. Kevin Quealey, "The People, Places, and Things Trump Has Praised on Twitter: A Complete List," *New York Times*, February 14, 2018, https://www.nytimes.com/interactive/2018/02/14/upshot/trump-compliments-list.html, "Our Updated List Now Includes 547 People, Places, and Things President Trump Has Insulted on Twitter," *New York Times*, November 21, 2018, https://twitter.com/nytimes/status/1065253533979684869?lang=en; "All the People, Places, and Things President Trump Insulted on Twitter in 2018," *New York Times*, December 30, 2018, F12, F13; Trump Twitter Archive, http://www.trumptwitterarchive.com/. I have not provided a cite for each tweet because they are available by date on the Trump Twitter Archive.

17. See Paul Krugman, "A Racist Stuck in the Past," *New York Times*, July 30, 2019, A26.

18. Ott and Dickinson, *Twitter Presidency*, 83.

19. Chaim Perelman, *The New Rhetoric and the Humanities: Essays on Rhetoric and Its Applications*, trans. William Kluback (Dordrecht, Holland: D. Reidel, 1979), 20. For the power of definition, also see David Zarefsky, "Definitions," in *Argument in a Time of Change: Definitions, Frameworks, and Critiques*, ed. James F. Klumpp (Annandale, VA: National Communication Association, 1988), 1–11; Zarefsky, "Presidential Rhetoric and the Power of Definition," *Presidential Studies Quarterly* 34 (2004): 607–619; David Zarefsky, Carol Miller-Tutzauer, and Frank Tutzauer, "Reagan's Safety Net for the Truly Needy: The Rhetorical Uses

of Definition," *Central States Speech Journal* 35 (Summer 1984): 113–119; Robert C. Rowland and John M. Jones, "Reagan's Farewell Address: Redefining the American Dream," *Rhetoric and Public Affairs* 20 (2017): 635–665; Robert C. Rowland and John M. Jones, "Reagan's Strategy for the Cold War and the Evil Empire Address," *Rhetoric and Public Affairs* 19 (2016): 427–464.

20. Donald J. Trump, Trump Twitter Archive, June 25, 2018, https://twitter.com/realdonaldtrump/status/1011295779422695424.

21. Donald J. Trump, Trump Twitter Archive, July 14, 2019, https://twitter.com/realdonaldtrump/status/1150381395078000643.

22. Donald J. Trump, Trump Twitter Archive, July 22, 2019, https://twitter.com/realdonaldtrump/status/1153315875476463616.

23. Erik Wemple, "To Discredit and to Demean: Trump Bragged about His Media-Bashing Strategy," *Washington Post,* May 22, 2018, https://www.washingtonpost.com/blogs/erik-wemple/wp/2018/05/22/to-discredit-and-to-demean-trump-bragged-about-his-media-bashing-strategy/?utm_term=.b4f441cf446e.

24. Max Boot, "Trump Just Proved He Doesn't Even Know the Meaning of America," *Washington Post,* June 29, 2019, https://www.washingtonpost.com/opinions/2019/06/29/trump-just-proved-he-doesnt-even-know-meaning-america/?utm_term=.ed6a284b66db.

25. The Trump Twitter Archive includes more than 280 tweets between May 2017 and November 11, 2019, denying collusion.

26. Jennifer Rubin, "Trump Stonewalls, and a Court Slaps Him Down," *Washington Post,* May 21, 2019, https://www.washingtonpost.com/opinions/2019/05/21/trump-stonewalls-court-slaps-him-down/?utm_term=.336ad48a01a1.

27. Donald J. Trump, Trump Twitter Archive, May 12, 2019, https://twitter.com/realdonaldtrump/status/1127745216088367106.

28. Donald J. Trump," Trump Twitter Archive, June 16, 2019, https://twitter.com/realdonaldtrump/status/1140252529428717568; Chris Cillizza, "Donald Trump Just Keeps 'Joking' about Serving More Than 2 Terms as President," CNN, June 18, 2019, https://www.cnn.com/2019/06/18/politics/donald-trump-term-limit/index.html; Felecia Sonmez, "Trump Says Supporters Might 'Demand' That He Serve More Than Two Terms as President," *Washington Post,* June 16, 2019, https://www.washingtonpost.com/politics/trump-says-supporters-might-demand-that-he-serve-more-than-two-terms-as-president/2019/06/16/4b6b9ae2-9041-11e9-b570-6416efdc0803_story.html?utm_term=.36dae41c0260.

29. Darren Samuelsohn, "Poll Shows Mueller's Public Image at All-Time Low," *Politico,* June 13, 2018, https://www.politico.com/story/2018/06/13/mueller-investigation-trump-poll-643491.

30. Amelia Thomson-DeVeaux, "Will Hearing from Mueller Really Change Americans' Minds about His Report?" FiveThirtyEight.com, July 23, 2019, https

://fivethirtyeight.com/features/will-hearing-from-mueller-really-change-americans-minds-about-his-report/.

31. Jo Becker, Adam Goldman, and Matt Apuzzo, "Emails Disclose Trump Son's Glee at Russian Offer," *New York Times*, July 12, 2017, A1.

32. Jennifer Rubin, "What the Latest Russia Revelations Mean," *Washington Post*, May 16, 2018, https://www.washingtonpost.com/blogs/right-turn/wp/2018/05/16/what-the-latest-russia-revelations-mean/?utm_term=.deac64ef64e2; see also Michael Gerson, "Don't All Campaigns Try to Work with Hostile States and Porn Stars? No. They Don't," *Washington Post*, August 6, 2018, https://www.washingtonpost.com/opinions/dont-all-campaigns-try-to-work-with-hostile-states-and-porn-stars-no-they-dont/2018/08/06/7302115e-99b0-11e8-b60b-1c897f17e185_story.html?utm_term=.6e36ec1e8405.

33. "Statement by Former Federal Prosecutors," Medium, May 6, 2019, https://medium.com/@dojalumni/statement-by-former-federal-prosecutors-8ab7691c2aa1.

34. Jennifer Rubin, "The Smoking Quid Pro Quo," *Washington Post*, October 23, 2019, https://www.washingtonpost.com/opinions/2019/10/23/smoking-quid-pro-quo/.

35. Eugene Robinson, "Trump Is a Putin Fanboy: Someday We'll Know Why," *Washington Post*, July 16, 2018, https://www.washingtonpost.com/opinions/trump-is-a-putin-fanboy-someday-well-know-why/2018/07/16/f2b1ef66-892d-11e8-85ae-511bc1146b0b_story.html?utm_term=.799f72152cc1.

36. For the partial transcript of the call released by the White House, see https://www.whitehouse.gov/wp-content/uploads/2019/09/Unclassified09.2019.pdf.

37. Marc A. Thiessen, "The Clinton Campaign Sought Dirt on Trump from Russian Officials: Where's the Outrage?" *Washington Post*, August 2, 2018, https://www.washingtonpost.com/opinions/the-clinton-campaign-sought-dirt-on-trump-from-russian-officials-wheres-the-outrage/2018/08/02/dee4be12-9672-11e8-810c-5fa705927d54_story.html?utm_term=.cd938c39434e.

38. Brooke Seipel, "Trump: 'Make America Great Again' Slogan 'Was Made Up by Me,'" *Hill*, April 2, 2019, https://thehill.com/homenews/administration/437070-trump-make-america-great-again-slogan-was-made-up-by-me.

39. Donald J. Trump, Trump Twitter Archive, May 13, 2019, https://twitter.com/realdonaldtrump/status/1127878614761050112.

40. Glenn Kessler, "Trump's Claim That He Imposed the First 'China Ban,'" *Washington Post*, April 7, 2020, https://www.washingtonpost.com/politics/2020/04/07/trumps-claim-that-he-imposed-first-china-ban/.

41. See Eric Lipton, David E. Sanger, Maggie Haberman, Michael D. Shear, Mark Mazzetti, and Julian E. Barnes, "He Could Have Seen What Was Coming: Behind Trump's Failure on the Virus," *New York Times*, April 12, 2020, A1, A13.

42. Michael Gerson, "The Horrendous Reality at the Heart of Trump's Pandemic Response," *Washington Post,* April 13, 2020, https://www.washingtonpost .com/opinions/2020/04/13/trumps-deadly-negligence-is-now-demonstrated -beyond-reasonable-doubt/.

43. Nolan D. McCaskill, "Trump Credits Social Media for His Election," *Politico,* October 20, 2017, https://www.politico.com/story/2017/10/20/trump-social -media-election-244009; Ashley Parker, "'Like a Rocket': Trump Revels in His Love-Hate Relationship with Twitter," *Washington Post,* July 11, 2019, https://www .washingtonpost.com/politics/like-a-rocket-trump-revels-in-his-love-hate -relationship-with-twitter/2019/07/11/421391a4-a41c-11e9-bd56-eac6bb02d01d _story.html?utm_term=.a3a43a3efe2a.

44. See, for example, Ryan Teague Beckwith, "Here Are the 10 Donald Trump Tweets Americans Hate the Most," *Time,* January 24, 2018, https://time.com /5116461/donald-trump-twitter-tweets-poll-yougov/.

45. Andrew Buncombe, "Donald Trump One Year On: How the Twitter President Changed Social Media and the Country's Top Office," *Independent,* January 17, 2018, https://www.independent.co.uk/news/world/americas/us-politics /the-twitter-president-how-potus-changed-social-media-and-the-presidency -a8164161.html.

46. Nicholas Carr, "Why Trump Tweets (and Why We Listen)," *Politico,* January 26, 2018, https://www.politico.com/magazine/story/2018/01/26/donald-trump -twitter-addiction-216530.

47. David Folkenflik, "Analysis: In Trump's Twitter Feed, a Tale of Sound and Fury," NPR, April 7, 2018, https://www.npr.org/2018/04/07/600138358/analysis-in -trumps-twitter-feed-a-tale-of-sound-and-fury.

48. Matthew Ingram, "The 140 Character President," *Columbia Journalism Review* (Fall 2017), https://www.cjr.org/special_report/trump-twitter-tweets -president.php.

49. See Gunn Enli, "Twitter as Arena for the Authentic Outsider: Exploring the Social Media Campaigns of Trump and Clinton in the 2016 US Presidential Election," *European Journal of Communication* 32 (2017): 50–61.

50. Alan Gross, "Presence as Argument in the Public Sphere," *Rhetoric Society Quarterly* 35 (2005): 19.

CHAPTER 7. THE RESONANCE OF
NATIONALIST POPULISM

1. Binyamin Appelbaum, "Grim View of the Economy Is at Odds with Reality," *New York Times,* January 21, 2017, A21. Wage growth was the weakest economic indicator for Obama, but in his second term, wages grew 1.3 percent per year, substantially faster than during Trump's first two years in office. See Daniel Griswold, "Trump vs. Obama: The Economic Tale of the Tape," *Hill,* October 24, 2018,

https://thehill.com/opinion/finance/412904-trump-vs-obama-the-economic -tale-of-the-tape.

2. Maureen Dowd, "Trump's Pile of Rubble," *New York Times*, August 11, 2019, SR 9.

3. Will Wilkinson, "A Tale of Two Moralities, Part One: Regional Inequality and Moral Persuasion," Niskanen Center, Princeton, January 19, 2017, https://niskanen center.org/blog/tale-two-moralities-part-one-regional-inequality-moral-polar ization/.

4. Diana C. Mutz, "Status Threat, Not Economic Hardship, Explains the 2016 Presidential Vote," PNAS, May 8, 2018, 4, www.pnas.org/cgi/doi/10.1073/pnas .1718155115.

5. Thomas B. Edsall, "The Peculiar Populism of Donald Trump," *New York Times*, February 2, 2017, https://www.nytimes.com/2017/02/02/opinion/the-pe culiar-populism-of-donald-trump.html. Also see Wilkinson, "Tale of Two Mo-ralities"; Amanda Taub, "Trump's Victory and the Rise of White Populism," *New York Times*, November 10, 2016, https://www.nytimes.com/2016/11/10/world /americas/trump-white-populism-europe-united-states.html.

6. Princeton professors Anne Case and Angus Deaton are quoted in Joel Achenbach and Dan Keating, "New Research Identifies a 'Sea of Despair' among White, Working-Class Americans," *Washington Post*, March 22, 2017, https:// www.washingtonpost.com/national/health-science/new-research-identifies-a -sea-of-despair-among-white-working-class-americans/2017/03/22/c777ab6e -0da6-11e7-9b0d-d27c98455440_story.html; also see Taub, "Trump's Victory and the Rise of White Populism."

7. Mutz, "Status Threat, Not Economic Hardship, Explains the 2016 Presiden-tial Vote," 2.

8. Emma Green, "It Was Cultural Anxiety That Drove White, Working-Class Voters to Trump," *Atlantic*, May 9, 2017, https://www.theatlantic.com/politics /archive/2017/05/white-working-class-trump-cultural-anxiety/525771/; see also Mutz, "Status Threat, Not Economic Hardship, Explains the 2016 Presidential Vote," 5.

9. Daniel Cox, Rachel Lienesch, and Robert P. Jones, *Beyond Economics: Fears of Cultural Displacement Pushed the White Working Class to Trump*, PRRI, May 9, 2017, https://www.prri.org/research/white-working-class-attitudes-economy-.

10. See E. J. Dionne Jr., Norman J. Ornstein, and Thomas E. Mann, *One Nation after Trump: A Guide for the Perplexed, the Disillusioned, the Desperate, and the Not-Yet Deported* (New York: St. Martin's, 2017), 153.

11. See Marc J. Hetherington and Jonathan D. Weiler, *Authoritarianism and Polarization in American Politics* (Cambridge, UK: Cambridge University Press, 2009), 205–210.

12. Cox, Lienesch, and Jones, *Beyond Economics*.

13. Karen Stenner, *The Authoritarian Dynamic* (Cambridge, UK: Cambridge University Press, 2005), 27.

14. Andrew J. Cherlin, "Money and Culture Are Inseparable," *New York Times*, May 8, 2018, A25.

15. Stenner, *Authoritarian Dynamic*, 32.

16. Amanda Taub, "The Rise of American Authoritarianism," Vox, March 1, 2016, https://www.vox.com/2016/3/1/11127424/trump-authoritarianism.

17. Mutz, "Status Threat, Not Economic Hardship, Explains the 2016 Presidential Vote," 2,

18. Thomas B. Edsall, "The Contract with Authoritarianism," *New York Times*, April 5, 2018, https://www.nytimes.com/2018/04/05/opinion/trump-authoritarianism-republicans-contract.html.

19. Edsall, "Contract with Authoritarianism"; see also Matt Grossmann and Daniel Thaler, "Mass-Elite Divides in Aversion to Social Change and Support for Donald Trump," *American Politics Research* 46 (2018): 2, 3.

20. Denise Bostdorff makes a similar observation; see Bostdorff, "Obama, Trump, and Reflections on the Rhetoric of Political Change," *Rhetoric and Public Affairs* 20 (2017): 700.

21. Leonie Huddy, Stanley Feldman, and Erin Cassese, "On the Distinct Political Effects of Anger," in *The Affect Effect: Dynamics of Emotion in Political Thinking and Behavior*, ed. W. Russell Neuman, George E. Marcus, Ann N. Crigler, and Michael Mackuen (Chicago: University of Chicago Press, 2007), 213, 228, 229.

22. Huddy, Feldman, and Cassese, "On the Distinct Political Effects of Anger," 229.

23. See Mutz, "Status Threat, Not Economic Hardship, Explains the 2016 Presidential Vote," 1.

24. Cox, Lienesch, and Jones, *Beyond Economics*.

25. Cox, Lienesch, and Jones, *Beyond Economics*.

26. Cox, Lienesch, and Jones, *Beyond Economics*.

27. Thomas B. Edsall, "Donald Trump's Identity Politics," *New York Times*, August 24, 2017, https://www.nytimes.com/2017/08/24/opinion/donald-trump-identity-politics.html; also see Ta-Nehisi Coates, "The First White President," *Atlantic*, October 2017, https://www.theatlantic.com/magazine/archive/2017/10/the-first-white-president-ta-nehisi-coates/537909/.

28. Coates, "First White President"; Eduardo Porter, "Democrats Have More Than Wages to Focus On," *New York Times*, August 16, 2017, B4.

29. Nate Cohn, "A Closer Look at Voters Who Backed Obama, Then Trump," *New York Times*, August 17, 2017, A18. See also Carol Anderson, "The Policies of White Resentment," *New York Times*, August 6, 2017, SR 1; Edsall, "Peculiar Populism of Donald Trump."

30. Quoted in Edsall, "Peculiar Populism of Donald Trump."

31. Taub, "Rise of American Authoritarianism."

32. David Brooks, "The Alienated Mind," *New York Times*, May 23, 2017, A25.

33. Green, "It Was Cultural Anxiety."

34. Olga Khazan, "People Voted for Trump Because They Were Anxious, Not Poor," *Atlantic*, April 23, 2018, https://www.theatlantic.com/science/archive/2018/04/existential-anxiety-not-poverty-motivates-trump-support/5.

35. Stenner, *Authoritarian Dynamic*, 32.

36. Stenner, 284.

37. Stenner, 33.

38. Marc J. Heatherington and Elizabeth Suhay, "Authoritarianism, Threat, and Americans' Support for the War on Terror," *American Journal of Political Science* 55 (July 2011): 547.

39. Amanda Taub, "Partisanship as Tribal Identity: Voting Against One's Economic Interests," *New York Times*, April 13, 2017, A10.

40. Taub, "Rise of American Authoritarianism."

41. Hetherington and Weiler, *Authoritarianism and Polarization in American Politics*, 139. Also see Peter Baker, "A Divider, Not a Uniter: The President Widens the Breach," *New York Times*, September 25, 2017, A15; Chip Berlet, "'Trumping' Democracy: Right-Wing Populism, Fascism, and the Case for Action," Political Research Associates, December 12, 2015, 3, http://www.politicalresearch.org/2015/12/12/trumping-democracy-right-wing-populism-fascism-and-the-case-for-action/#sthash.7Lk503sn.dpbs, 5; David Neiwert, "Trump and Right-Wing Populism: A Long Time Coming," Political Research Associates, June 21, 2016, https://www.politicalresearch.org/2016/06/21/trump-and-right-wing-populism-a-long-time-coming; Mabel Berezin, "Donald Trump Is a Uniquely American Populist," *New Republic*, December 20, 2016, https://newrepublic.com/article/139434/donald-trump-uniquely-ameri.

42. Khazan, "People Voted for Trump Because They Were Anxious, Not Poor."

43. Kristin Kobes Do Mez, *Jesus and John Wayne: How White Evangelicals Corrupted a Faith and Fractured a Nation* (New York: Liveright, 2020), 3, 13, 271.

44. James Hohmann, "The Daily 202: Trump Voters Stay Loyal Because They Feel Disrespected," *Washington Post*, May 14, 2018, https://www.washingtonpost.com/news/powerpost/paloma/daily-202/2018/05/14/daily-202-trump-voters-stay-loyal-because-they-feel-disrespected/5af8aac530fb0425887994cc.

45. Greg Sargent, "Why Did Trump Win? New Research by Democrats Offers a Worrisome Answer," *Washington Post*, May 1, 2017, https://www.washingtonpost.com/blogs/plum-line/wp/2017/05/01/why-did-trump-win-new-research-by-democrats-offers-a-worrisome-answer/.

46. Michael Gerson, "'Trump Forces' and the Smashing of GOP Orthodoxy," *Washington Post*, August 31, 2017, https://www.washingtonpost.com/opinions/trump-forces-and-the-smashing-of-gop-orthodoxy/2017/08/31/de5f440e-8e89-11e7-91d5-ab4e4bb76a3a_story.html.

47. Jeremy Engels, *The Politics of Resentment: A Genealogy* (University Park: Pennsylvania State University Press, 2015), 12.

48. Engels, *Politics of Resentment*, 19.

49. Engels, 87, 150.

50. See Mark Shields, "Our Last Liberal President," *Washington Post*, August 4, 1996, https://www.washingtonpost.com/archive/opinions/1996/08/04/our-last -liberal-president/cec55416-5f85-4872-9fde-2a93eaa49b88/; Eduardo Porter, "G.O.P. Shift Moves Center Far to Right," *New York Times*, September 5, 2012, B1.

51. Amanda Taub, "In a Cozy Berlin Suburb, Understanding the Rise of the Far Right," *New York Times*, March 21, 2017, A4.

52. Mary Stuckey draws a similar conclusion. See "American Elections and the Rhetoric of Political Change: Hyperbole, Anger, and Hope in U.S. Politics," *Rhetoric and Public Affairs* 20, no. 4 (Winter 2017): 679.

53. Sabrina Tavernise, "Trump's Tumultuous Week? To Supporters, It Went Well," *New York Times*, August 20, 2017, A17.

54. Eduardo Porter, "Diagnosis? On Target. The Cure? Misguided," *New York Times*, March 29, 2017, B1.

55. Cox, Lienesch, and Jones, *Beyond Economics*.

56. Hetherington and Weiler, *Authoritarianism and Polarization in American Politics*, 34, 41.

57. Emma Roller, "Donald Trump's Fear Factor," *New York Times*, June 14, 2016, https://www.nytimes.com/2016/06/14/opinion/campaign-stops/donald-trumps -fear-factor.html; Nicholas Lemann, "On the Election III," *New York Review of Books*, November 10, 2016, 35; Ronald Inglehart and Pippa Norris, "Trump, Brexit, and the Rise of Populism: Economic Have-Nots and Cultural Backlash," HKS Faculty Research Working Paper Series RWP16-026, August 2016, 28, 29, https://www.hks.harvard.edu/publications/trump-brexit-and-rise-populism -economic-have-nots-and-cultural-backlash.

58. Edsall, "Contract with Authoritarianism."

59. Jonathan Raban, "Telling It Like It Is, and Winning," *New York Times*, January 8, 2017, SR 7.

60. Michael Gerson, "Trump's Rhetorical Schizophrenia Is Easy to See Through," *Washington Post*, August 24, 2017, https://www.washingtonpost.com /opinions/trumps-rhetorical-schizophrenia-is-easy-to-see-through/2017/08/24 /2163ab42-88f3-11e7-a50f-e0d4e6ec070a_story.html.

61. Joshua Green, *Devil's Bargain: Steve Bannon, Donald Trump, and the Nationalist Uprising* (New York: Penguin, 2017), 180.

62. Jan-Werner Müller, *What Is Populism?* (Philadelphia: University of Pennsylvania Press, 2016), 4.

63. Jeremy W. Peters, "In a Backlash to the Backlash, Republican Voters Embrace Trump," *New York Times*, June 24, 2018, A1.

64. Phillip Bump, "The Freewheeling, Uncontainable Nature of Trump's Anti-Elite Get-Togethers," *Washington Post*, August 16, 2019, https://www.washington post.com/politics/2019/08/16/freewheeling-uncontainable-nature-trumps-anti -elite-get-togethers/; see also Maggie Haberman and Annie Karni, "2016 All Over Again," *New York Times*, June 18, 2019, https://www.nytimes.com/2019/06/18/us /politics/orlando-rally-trump-campaign.html?searchResultPosition=18.

65. Quoted in Phillip Rucker, "Staring Down Impeachment, Trump Sees Himself as a Victim of Historic Proportions," *Washington Post*, September 28, 2019, https://www.washingtonpost.com/politics/staring-down-impeachment-trump -sees-himself-as-a-victim-of-historic-proportions/2019/09/28/815fbbea-e14c -11e9-b199-f638bf2c340f_story.html.

66. Phillip Bump, "Trump Embraces the 'Reverse Racism' Feared by His Supporters in a New 'Squad' Attack," *Washington Post*, July 22, 2019, https://www .washingtonpost.com/politics/2019/07/22/trump-embraces-reverse-racism -feared-by-his-supporters-new-squad-attack/. The poll results are found in "Sharp Rise in the Share of Americans Saying Jews Face Discrimination," Pew Research Center, April 15, 2019, https://www.people-press.org/2019/04/15/sharp -rise-in-the-share-of-americans-saying-jews-face-discrimination/.

67. Katie Rogers, "The Trump Rally: A Play in Three Acts," *New York Times*, October 14, 2018, A18–20.

68. See Aaron Blake, "Trump and the GOP Are Sneaking a Trojan Horse into the 2020 Dialogue," *Washington Post*, July 19, 2019, https://www.washingtonpost .com/politics/2019/07/19/trump-gop-are-sneaking-trojan-horse-into-dialogue/. Blake quotes multiple members of the House and Senate, including Senator Lindsay Graham, Representative Steve Scalise, and Republican National Committee chair Ronna McDaniel.

69. Arlie Russell Hochschild, *Strangers in Their Own Land: Anger and Mourning on the American Right* (New York: New Press, 2016), 218, 221.

70. Hochschild, *Strangers in Their Own Land*, 243, 256.

71. Hochschild, 226.

72. Hochschild, 224, 225, emphasis in original.

73. Hetherington and Weiler, *Authoritarianism and Polarization in American Politics*, 39–40.

74. Stenner, *Authoritarian Dynamic*, 327.

75. Stenner, 327.

76. "Super Tuesday State Results," *Washington Post*, March 1, 2016, https://www .washingtonpost.com/2016-election-results/super-tuesday/?utm_term=.af4257 c19117.

77. Thomas B. Edsall, "Trump Says Jump: His Supporters Ask, How High?" *New York Times*, September 14, 2017, https://www.nytimes.com/2017/09/14/opinion /trump-republicans.html; see also Edsall, "Contract with Authoritarianism."

78. Lilliana Mason, "Ideologues Without Issues: The Polarizing Consequences of Ideological Identities," *Public Opinion Quarterly* 82 (2018): 885.

79. Taub, "Rise of American Authoritarianism"; see also Edsall, "Contract with Authoritarianism."

80. Matt Viser and Robert Costa, "'An Angry Mob': Republicans Work to Recast Democratic Protests as Out-of-Control Anarchy," *Washington Post*, October 8, 2018, https://www.washingtonpost.com/politics/an-angry-mob-republicans-work-to-recast-democratic-protests-as-out-of-control-anarchy/2018/10/08/c8648e8a-cb13-11e8-a3e6-44daa3d35ede_story.html?utm_term=.e35bf46ea047.

81. Michael Gerson, "Democrats Are Playing with Fire," *Washington Post*, October 11, 2018, https://www.washingtonpost.com/opinions/democrats-are-playing-with-fire/2018/10/11/0dd5b7a2-cd79-11e8-920f-dd52e1ae4570_story.html?utm_term=.e504fe4ae3ff.

82. Ashley Parker, Phillip Rucker, and Josh Dawsey, "Trump and Republicans Settle on Fear—and Falsehoods—as a Midterm Strategy," *Washington Post*, October 22, 2018, https://www.washingtonpost.com/politics/trump-and-republicans-settle-on-fear--and-falsehoods--as-a-midterm-strategy/2018/10/22/1ebbf222-d614-11e8-a10f-b51546b10756_story.html?utm_term=.b1fdb4125bbe; see also Alexander Burns and Astead W. Herndon, "Trump Escalates Use of Migrants as Election Ploy," *New York Times*, October 23, 2018, A1.

83. Greg Sargent, "Why Is the Mob Angry? Because Trump Is Ripping Us apart with Bigotry and Hatred," *Washington Post*, October 12, 2018, https://www.washingtonpost.com/blogs/plum-line/wp/2018/10/12/why-is-the-mob-angry-because-trump-is-ripping-us-apart-with-bigotry-and-hatred/?utm_term=.22acca4428c1.

84. Taub, "Rise of American Authoritarianism."

85. Heatherington and Suhay, "Authoritarianism, Threat, and Americans' Support for the War on Terror," 549.

86. Sabrina Tavernise and Robert Gebelhoff, "They Voted for Obama, Then Went for Trump: Can Democrats Win Them Back?" *New York Times*, May 6, 2018, A18; Steven L. Morgan and Jiwon Lee, "Trump Voters and the White Working Class," *Sociological Science* 5 (2018): 236, https://sociologicalscience.com/articles-v5-10-234/.

87. Mutz, "Status Threat, Not Economic Hardship, Explains the 2016 Presidential Vote," 2.

88. Hetherington and Weiler, *Authoritarianism and Polarization in American Politics*, 109.

89. Stenner, *Authoritarian Dynamic*, 286.

90. Stenner, 309.

91. Stenner, 328–329, 330.

92. Barack Obama, "A More Perfect Union," March 18, 2008, https://www.nytimes.com/2008/03/18/us/politics/18text-obama.html.

93. Barack Obama, "Reclaiming the Promise to the People," *Vital Speeches of the Day* 70 (2004): 625. See the discussion of these two speeches in Robert C. Rowland and John Jones, "One Dream: Barack Obama, Race, and the American Dream," *Rhetoric and Public Affairs* 14 (2011): 125–154; Robert C. Rowland and John Jones, "Recasting the American Dream and American Politics: Barack Obama's Keynote Address to the 2004 Democratic National Convention," *Quarterly Journal of Speech* 93 (2007): 425–448.

94. Grossmann and Thaler, "Mass-Elite Divides in Aversion to Social Change and Support for Donald Trump."

95. Stenner, *Authoritarian Dynamic*, 330.

CHAPTER 8. NATIONALIST POPULISM AND
THE THREAT TO AMERICAN DEMOCRACY

1. Kathleen Hall Jamieson and Doron Taussig referred to Trump's "norm-shattering rhetoric," which involved "spontaneity laced with Manichean, evidence-flouting, accountability-dodging, and institution-disdaining claims as his 'rhetorical signature.'" See Jamieson and Taussig, "Disruption, Demonization, Deliverance, and Norm Destruction: The Rhetorical Signature of Donald J. Trump," *Political Science Quarterly* 132 (2017–2018): 619, 620.

2. Michael Gerson, "Trump's Failing Presidency Has the GOP in a Free Fall," *Washington Post*, March 30, 2017, https://www.washingtonpost.com/opinions/trumps-failing-presidency-has-the-gop-in-a-free-fall/2017/03/30/e0882d62-1581-11e7-adao-1489b735b3a3_story.html.

3. Michael Kazin, *The Populist Persuasion: An American History*, rev. ed. (Ithaca, NY: Cornell University Press, 1998), 288.

4. Kevin Roose, "'Phony Phil'? 'Sleeping Joe'? Candidates Adopt Trump's Art of the Insult," *New York Times*, October 23, 2018, A14.

5. See Robert C. Rowland and John Jones, "Reagan's Farewell Address: Redefining the American Dream," *Rhetoric and Public Affairs* 20 (2017): 635–665; John Jones and Robert C. Rowland, "Redefining the Proper Role of Government: Ultimate Definition in Reagan's First Inaugural," *Rhetoric and Public Affairs* 18 (2015): 691–718.

6. R. R. Reno, "The New Party of 'America First,'" *New York Times*, April 30, 2017, SR 1, 6.

7. Ronald Reagan, "Farewell Address to the Nation," January 11, 1989, para. 34, https://www.reaganlibrary.gov/research/speeches/011189i.

8. E. J. Dionne Jr., "Where Are the Conservatives We Need?" *Washington Post*, April 22, 2018, https://www.washingtonpost.com/opinions/where-are-the-conservatives-we-need/2018/04/22/7a036e76-44e2-11e8-ad8f-27a8c409298b_story.html?utm_term=.46567151536b.

9. Corey Robin, "The G.O.P.'s Existential Crisis," *New York Times*, March 26, 2017, SR 1, 3.

10. Michael Gerson, "Will the GOP Become the Party of White Backlash?" *Washington Post*, July 2, 2018, https://www.washingtonpost.com/opinions/trumpism -a-whites-only-ideology/2018/07/02/82abd142-7e28-11e8-b660-4d0f9f0351f1 _story.html.

11. David Brooks, "Republican or Conservative, You Have to Choose," *New York Times*, June 26, 2018, A27.

12. "The Cult of Trump," *New York Times*, June 8, 2018, A24.

13. Max Boot, "I Left the Republican Party: Now I Want Democrats to Take Over," *Washington Post*, July 3, 2018, https://www.washingtonpost.com/opinions /i-left-the-republican-party-now-i-want-democrats-to-take-over/2018/07/03 /54a4007a-7e38-11e8-boef-fffcabeff946_story.html. Boehner is quoted in "The Cult of Trump," A24. Boot's comment became literally true when the Republican Party failed to adopt a platform at the 2020 convention, creating a situation in which the party's agenda was "anything President Donald Trump wished at the moment." See Michael Gerson, "The Three Plans of Trump's GOP," *Lawrence Journal-World*, October 20, 2020, 7A.

14. George F. Will, "Vote Against the GOP This November," *Washington Post*, June 22, 2018, https://www.washingtonpost.com/opinions/vote-against-the-gop -this-november/2018/06/22/a6378306-7575-11e8-b4b7-308400242c2e_story.html.

15. David Neiwert, "Trump and Right-Wing Populism: A Long Time Coming," Political Research Associates, June 21, 2016, https://www.politicalresearch .org/2016/06/21/trump-and-right-wing-populism-a-long-time-coming.

16. Michael Barbaro, Ashley Parker, and Trip Gabriel, "Donald Trump's Heated Words Were Destined to Stir Violence, Opponents Say," *New York Times*, March 13, 2016, A22.

17. Mabel Berezin, "Donald Trump Is a Uniquely American Populist," *New Republic*, December 20, 2016, https://newrepublic.com/article/139434/donald -trump-uniquely-american-populist.

18. For a summary of the argumentative content of the debate, see Robert C. Rowland, "Donald Trump and the Rejection of the Norms of American Politics and Rhetoric," in *An Unprecedented Election: Campaign Coverage, Communication, and Citizens Divided*, ed. Benjamin R. Warner, Dianne G. Bystrom, Mitchell S. McKinney, and Mary C. Banwart (Santa Barbara, CA: ABC-Clio, 2018), 189–205.

19. Polling and other reports on the outcome of the 2016 debates are summarized in Robert C. Rowland, "Implicit Standards of Public Argument in Presidential Debates: What the 2016 Debates Reveal about Public Deliberation," *Argumentation and Advocacy* 54 (2018): 76–94. A similar pattern was evident in response to the debates in 2020. See Philip Bump, "Reliable Polls Show That Biden Won the Debate—So Those Aren't What Trump's Allies Are Highlighting," *Washington Post*, September 30, 2020, https://www.washingtonpost.com/politics/2020/09/30

/reliable-polls-show-that-biden-won-debate-so-those-arent-what-trumps-allies
-are-highlighting; Jennifer Agiesta, "CNN Poll: Biden Wins Final Presidential
Debate," CNN, October 23, 2020, https://www.cnn.com/2020/10/22/politics/cnn
-poll-final-presidential-debate/index.html.

20. Christopher R. Browning, "The Suffocation of Democracy," *New York Review of Books*, October 25, 2018, 16.

21. Marc J. Hetherington and Jonathan D. Weiler, *Authoritarianism and Polarization in American Politics* (Cambridge, UK: Cambridge University Press, 2009), 41.

22. Stephen Reicher and Alexander Haslam, "What Psychology Can Teach Us about Trump's Victory—and What Trump's Victory Can Teach Us about Psychology," European Association of Social Psychology, June 6, 2017, https://www.easp.eu/news/itm/-452.html.

23. Hetherington and Weiler, *Authoritarianism and Polarization in American Politics*, 45.

24. Hetherington and Weiler, 61.

25. David Friend, "The '90s Gave Us the Trump Teens," *New York Times*, September 3, 2017, SR 10.

26. James Pniewozik, "A Hollywood Snub to a Celebrity in Chief," *New York Times*, August 4, 2017, A16.

27. Paul Krugman, "Politicians, Promises, and Getting Real," *New York Times*, September 15, 2017, A25.

28. Brian Ott and Greg Dickinson also argue that Trump threatens US democracy. See Ott and Dickinson, *The Twitter Presidency: Donald J. Trump and the Politics of White Rage* (New York: Routledge, 2019), 95.

29. See Mark Danner, "What He Could Do," *New York Review of Books*, March 23, 2017, 4.

30. Peter Baker and Jeremy W. Peters, "Call for Unity Quickly Fades into Acrimony," *New York Times*, October 26, 2018, A1.

31. Max Boot, "America Will Need Years to Clean Up the Toxins Trump Has Released," *Washington Post*, November 14, 2018, https://www.washingtonpost.com/opinions/global-opinions/america-will-need-years-to-clean-up-the-toxins-trump-has-released/2018/11/14/3474b816-e833-11e8-bbdb-72fdbf9d4fed_story.html. For an argument that Trump's rhetoric functioned as a form of demagoguery based in toxic masculinity, see Paul Elliott Johnson, "The Art of Masculine Victimhood: Donald Trump's Demagoguery," *Women's Studies in Communication* 20 (2017): 229–250.

32. Jan-Werner Müller quoted in Francis Wilkinson, "Why Donald Trump Really Is a Populist," *Bloomberg*, February 16, 2017, https://www.bloomberg.com/opinion/articles/2017-02-16/why-donald-trump-really-is-a-populist.

33. Quoted in Barbaro, Parker, and Gabriel, "Donald Trump's Heated Words Were Destined to Stir Violence," A22.

34. Frank Bruni, "I'm O.K.—You're Pure Evil," *New York Times*, June 18, 2017, SR 3; Michael Gerson, "America Is Riding a Carousel of Hate," *Washington Post*, June 15, 2017, https://www.washingtonpost.com/opinions/america-is-riding-a-carousel-of-hate/2017/06/15/c85caabc-520b-11e7-91eb-9611861a988f_story.html. See also Bret Stephens, "The Trump Presidency: 'No Guardrails,'" *New York Times*, July 29, 2017, A25; Thomas L. Friedman, "The American Civil War, Part II," *New York Times*, October 3, 2018, A26.

35. Frank Bruni, "This Is Eloquence: Remember That?" *New York Times*, May 24, 2017, A24.

36. David Leonhardt, "All the President's Lies," *New York Times*, March 21, 2017, A25.

37. David Leonhardt and Stuart A. Thompson, "Trump's Lies," *New York Times*, June 25, 2017, SR 10.

38. Glenn Kessler and Michelle Ye Hee Lee, "President Trump's First 100 Days: The Fact Check Tally," *Washington Post*, May 1, 2017, https://www.washingtonpost.com/news/fact-checker/wp/2017/05/01/president-trumps-first-100-days-the-fact-check-tally/; Glenn Kessler, Michelle Ye Hee Lee, and Meg Kelly, "President Trump's List of False and Misleading Claims Tops 1,000," *Washington Post*, August 22, 2017, https://www.washingtonpost.com/news/fact-checker/wp/2017/08/22/president-trumps-list-of-false-and-misleading-claims-tops-1000.

39. Glenn Kessler, "Meet the Bottomless Pinocchio, a New Rating for a False Claim Repeated over and over Again," *Washington Post*, December 10, 2018, https://www.washingtonpost.com/politics/2018/12/10/meet-bottomless-pinocchio-new-rating-false-claim-repeated-over-over-again/?utm_term=.a99171f14145.

40. E. J. Dionne Jr., "Trump's Greatest Single Achievement Almost Never Gets Mentioned," *Washington Post*, April 26, 2017, https://www.washingtonpost.com/opinions/trumps-greatest-single-achievement-almost-never-gets-mentioned/2017/04/26/6465447e-2aab-11e7-b605-33413c691853_story.html.

41. Sheryl Gay Stolberg, "Many Politicians Lie, but Trump Has Elevated the Art of Fabrication," *New York Times*, August 8, 2017, A16.

42. Glenn Kessler noted, "His rhetoric is fundamentally based on making statements that are not true." See Kessler, "How Trump Bobs and Weaves to Avoid the Truth," *Washington Post*, October 16, 2018, https://www.washingtonpost.com/politics/2018/10/16/how-trump-bobs-weaves-avoid-truth/?utm_term=.11abe118ficf.

43. Greg Sargent, "Trump Has Nothing but Contempt for Facts and Reality-Based Policy: Now It's Backfiring," *Washington Post*, March 30, 2017, https://www.washingtonpost.com/blogs/plum-line/wp/2017/03/30/trump-has-nothing-but-contempt-for-facts-and-reality-based-policy-now-its-backfiring/.

44. Michael Tackett, "Shrugging at a Tax Cut That Might Buy a Fill-Up," *New York Times*, March 8, 2018, A19.

45. Linda Qui, "Claims about Tax Plan, Deducting for Dishonesty," *New York Times*, November 30, 2017, A18.

46. Leonard Pitts Jr., "Intellectual Dishonesty Now Rules," *Lawrence Journal-World*, May 25, 2017, 5A; also see Jennifer Rubin, "Something Is Seriously off about This President," *Washington Post*, September 4, 2017, https://www.washingtonpost.com/blogs/right-turn/wp/2017/09/04/something-seriously-off-about-this-president/?utm_term=.aa6204b7ccce.

47. Roger Cohen, "Trump 2020 Is No Joke: Nor Are the Head-Spinning Distractions," *New York Times*, June 24, 2017, A18; Rubin, "Something Is Seriously off about This President."

48. E. J. Dionne Jr., Norman J. Ornstein, and Thomas E. Mann, *One Nation after Trump: A Guide for the Perplexed, the Disillusioned, the Desperate, and the Not-Yet Deported* (New York: St. Martin's, 2017), 286.

49. Charles M. Blow, "In Defense of the Truth," *New York Times*, September 4, 2017, A21; Michelle Goldberg, "Democracy Grief Is Real," *New York Times*, December 15, 2019, SR 4.

50. Glenn Kessler and Salvador Rizzo, "President Trump Has Made 4,229 False or Misleading Claims in 558 Days," *Washington Post*, August 1, 2018, https://www.washingtonpost.com/news/fact-checker/wp/2018/08/01/president-trump-has-made-4229-false-or-misleading-claims-in-558-days/?utm_term=.5c01849eed7e.

51. Glenn Kessler, Salvador Rizzo, and Meg Kelly, "President Trump Has Made 13,435 False or Misleading Claims over 993 Days," *Washington Post*, October 14, 2019, https://www.washingtonpost.com/politics/2019/10/14/president-trump-has-made-false-or-misleading-claims-over-days/.

52. James Madison, *Writings* (New York: Library of America, 1999), 167, 230.

53. Michael Gerson, "Republicans Are Defining Lunacy Down," *Washington Post*, March 13, 2017, https://www.washingtonpost.com/opinions/republicans-are-defining-lunacy-down/2017/03/13/7f505ba4-0821-11e7-b77c-0047d15a24e0_story.html. See also Catherine Rampell, "The Trump Administration Dons a Tinfoil Hat," *Washington Post*, March 13, 2017, https://www.washingtonpost.com/opinions/the-trump-administration-dons-a-tinfoil-hat/2017/03/13/597d65d0-082a-11e7-93dc-00f9bdd74ed1_story.html.

54. See Abigail Tracy, "The Department of Justice Is a Hydra: Trump's Witch Hunt Drives the Deep State Underground," *Vanity Fair*, September 13, 2018, https://www.vanityfair.com/news/2018/09/trumps-witch-hunt-drives-the-deep-state-underground; Brett Samuels, "Trump Hits the 'Deep State,' the 'Left,' and the Media in Wake of Anonymous Op-Ed," *Hill*, September 6, 2018, https://thehill.com/homenews/administration/405297-trump-hits-the-deep-state-the-left-and-the-media-in-aftermath-of.

55. The deep state allegation became a focus of conservative commentary after the *New York Times* published an anonymous op-ed from a senior Trump

administration official critical of the president. Fox commentator Steve Hilton wrote, "Members of the arrogant ruling class in Washington, furious that a populist interloper was elected by the people to dismantle the elitist policies that have hurt working Americans for decades, are fighting back." See Anonymous, "The Quiet Resistance Inside the Trump Administration," *New York Times*, September 6, 2018, A21; Steve Hilton, "Unmask the Anti-Trump Deep State Working Against America's Best Interests," *Fox News*, September 9, 2018, http://www.foxnews.com/opinion/2018/09/09/steve-hilton-unmask-anti-trump-deep-state-working-against-america-s-best-interests.html.

56. Jan-Werner Müller, *What Is Populism?* (Philadelphia: University of Pennsylvania Press, 2016), 32.

57. Katie Rogers, "As Impeachment Moves Forward, Trump's Language Turns Darker," *New York Times*, October 2, 2019, A13.

58. Between mid-June 2018 and August 30, 2018, Trump sent out ten tweets attacking the press as the "enemy of the people." See Trump Twitter Archive, http://www.trumptwitterarchive.com/.

59. Trump is quoted in John Wagner and Felicia Sonmez, "About 80 Percent of the Media Are 'the Enemy of the People' Trump Says," *Washington Post*, August 22, 2018, https://www.washingtonpost.com/politics/about-80-percent-of-the-media-are-the-enemy-of-the-people-trump-says/2018/08/22/d7d5710c-a635-11e8-a656-943eefab5daf_story.html?utm_term=.39654bdb8a6b.

60. Greg Sargent, "Trump Is Leading a 'Hate Movement' Against the Media," *Washington Post*, August 1, 2018, https://www.washingtonpost.com/blogs/plum-line/wp/2018/08/01/trump-is-leading-a-hate-movement-against-the-media/?utm_term=.9eae2ca3496b.

61. David Frum, *Trumpocracy: The Corruption of the American Republic* (New York: HarperCollins, 2018), 122.

62. Eugene Robinson, "Trump's Rally Rhetoric Is Going to Get Somebody Killed," *Washington Post*, August 6, 2018, https://www.washingtonpost.com/opinions/trumps-rally-rhetoric-is-going-to-get-somebody-killed/2018/08/06/d3bccad8-99ac-11e8-b60b-1c897f17e185_story.html?utm_term=.cd6dc4ac5d4b.

63. Katie Rogers, "Trump, at Charlotte Rally, Tries to Rebuild Political 'Momentum' by Reviving Old Attacks," *New York Times*, October 27, 2018, A12.

64. Frum, *Trumpocracy*, 122.

65. Phillip Bump, "Half of Republicans Say the News Media Should Be Described as the Enemy of the American People," *Washington Post*, April 26, 2018, https://www.washingtonpost.com/news/politics/wp/2018/04/26/half-of-republicans-say-the-news-media-should-be-described-as-the-enemy-of-the-american-people/?utm_term=.e145bd59eb61; Phillip Bump, "Three-Quarters of Republicans Trust Trump over the Media," *Washington Post*, July 25, 2018, https://www.washingtonpost.com/news/politics/wp/2018/07/25/three-quarters-of

-republicans-trust-trump-over-the-media/?utm_term=.7f035f877cb. In both cases, Bump cited a Quinnipiac University poll.

66. "No News Is Bad News for Hungary," *New York Times*, December 4, 2018, A24.

67. Hetherington and Weiler, *Authoritarianism and Polarization in American Politics*, 154, 159, 194.

68. Nate Cohn, "In Affirmative Action, an Example of How Polls Can Mislead," *New York Times*, August 5, 2017, A11.

69. Amanda Taub and Brendan Nyhan, "Why Objectively False Things Continue to Be Believed," *New York Times*, March 22, 2017, A18.

70. Sabrina Tavernise, "One Country, Two Tribes," *New York Times*, January 29, 2017, SR 4.

71. Jennifer Rubin, "The Judiciary Committee Votes to Impeach, and Trump Is on His Way to His One Line in History," *Washington Post*, December 13, 2019, https://www.washingtonpost.com/opinions/2019/12/13/judiciary-committee-votes-impeach-trump-is-his-way-his-one-line-history/; Amber Phillips, "6 Takeaways from the Marathon Impeachment Vote in the Judiciary Committee," *Washington Post*, December 13, 2019, https://www.washingtonpost.com/politics/2019/12/12/takeaways-impeachment-articles-markup/.

72. Lilliana Mason, "Ideologues Without Issues: The Polarizing Consequences of Ideological Identities," *Public Opinion Quarterly* 82 (2018): 884.

73. Stuart M. Butler, *A Policy Maker's Guide to the Health Care Crisis, Part II: The Heritage Consumer Choice Health Plan* (Washington, DC: Heritage Foundation, 1992).

74. See Robert C. Rowland, "Barack Obama and the Revitalization of Public Reason," *Rhetoric and Public Affairs* 14 (2011): 693–725.

75. Nicholas Bakalar, "28.6 Million," *New York Times*, May 23, 2017, D6.

76. Dionne, Ornstein, and Mann, *One Nation after Trump*, 276–277.

77. Quoted in Greg Sargent, "Trump's Lies Are Working Brilliantly: This New Poll Proves It," *Washington Post*, April 27, 2017, https://www.washingtonpost.com/blogs/plum-line/wp/2017/04/27/trumps-lies-are-working-brilliantly-this-new-poll-proves-it.

78. Davey Alba and Nick Corasaniti, "False 'Coup' Claims by Trump Echo as Unifying Theme Against Impeachment," *New York Times*, October 3, 2019, A19.

79. Peter Wehner, "Full-Spectrum Corruption," *New York Times*, August 26, 2018, SR 9.

80. Dionne, Ornstein, and Mann, *One Nation after Trump*, 109.

81. Marc J. Heatherington and Elizabeth Suhay, "Authoritarianism, Threat, and Americans' Support for the War on Terror," *American Journal of Political Science* 55 (2011): 552, 556, 557; see also Amanda Taub, "The Rise of American Authoritarianism," Vox, March 1, 2016, https://www.vox.com/2016/3/1/11127424/trump-authoritarianism.

82. Hetherington and Suhay, "Authoritarianism, Threat, and Americans' Support for the War on Terror," 547.

83. See Brittany Lyte, "Americans Have Grown More Supportive of Torture," FiveThirtyEight.com, December 9, 2014, https://fivethirtyeight.com/features/senate-torture-report-public-opinion/; Rupert Stone, "Science Shows That Torture Doesn't Work and Is Counterproductive," *Newsweek*, May 8, 2016, https://www.newsweek.com/2016/05/20/science-shows-torture-doesnt-work-456854.html. See also Steven Levitsky and Daniel Ziblatt, *How Democracies Die* (New York: Crown, 2018), 94.

84. Karen Stenner, *The Authoritarian Dynamic* (Cambridge, UK: Cambridge University Press, 2005), 323–324.

85. John Judis, *The Populist Explosion: How the Great Recession Transformed American and European Politics* (New York: Columbia Global Reports, 2016), 16.

86. Cas Mudde and Cristóbal Rovira Kaltwasser, *Populism: A Very Short Introduction* (New York: Oxford University Press, 2017), 91; Müller, *What Is Populism?*, 103.

87. Matthew N. Lyons, "Ctrl-Alt-Delete: The Origins and Ideology of the Alternative Right," Political Research Associates, January 20, 2017, https://www.politicalresearch.org/2017/01/20/ctrl-alt-delete-report-on-the-alternative-right, 2.

88. Dionne, Ornstein, and Mann, *One Nation after Trump*, 146.

89. Rosie Gray, "Trump Defends White-Nationalist Protesters: 'Some Very Fine People on Both Sides,'" *Atlantic*, August 15, 2017, https://www.theatlantic.com/politics/archive/2017/08/trump-defends-white-nationalist-protesters-some-very-fine-people-on-both-sides/537012/; Michael D. Shear and Maggie Haberman, "Trump Defends Initial Remarks on Charlottesville; Again Blames 'Both Sides,'" *New York Times*, August 15, 2017, https://www.nytimes.com/2017/08/15/us/politics/trump-press-conference-charlottesville.html.

90. Shear and Haberman, "Trump Defends Initial Remarks on Charlottesville; Again Blames 'Both Sides.'"

91. Associated Press, "Victimized Family Visited by Reagan," *New York Times*, May 4, 1982, B8.

92. On Ronald Reagan's civil rights record, see Pedro Noguera and Robert Cohen, "Remembering Reagan's Record on Civil Rights and the South African Freedom Struggle," *Nation*, February 11, 2011, https://www.thenation.com/article/remembering-reagans-record-civil-rights-and-south-african-freedom-struggle/.

93. Mary E. Stuckey, "American Elections and the Rhetoric of Political Change: Hyperbole, Anger, and Hope in U.S. Politics," *Rhetoric and Public Affairs* 20, no. 4 (Winter 2017): 687; Max Boot, "President Trump Is Normalizing Racism," *Washington Post*, May 30, 2018, https://www.washingtonpost.com/opinions/global

-opinions/president-trump-is-normalizing-racism/2018/05/30/7d5f726e-6417
-11e8-a768-ed043e33f1dc_story.html?utm_term=.c16f1a32e68d.

94. Berezin, "Donald Trump Is a Uniquely American Populist"; see also Paul Krugman, "How Republics End," *New York Times*, December 19, 2016, A21.

95. Chip Berlet, "'Trumping' Democracy: Right-Wing Populism, Fascism, and the Case for Action," Political Research Associates, December 12, 2015, 3, http://www.politicalresearch.org/2015/12/12/trumping-democracy-right-wing -populism-fascism-and-the-case-for-action/#sthash.7Lk503sn.dpbs; see also Dionne, Ornstein, and Mann, *One Nation after Trump*, 96; Jeff Shesol, "Dark Rhetoric in Washington," *New York Times*, January 21, 2017, A27; Steve Coll, "The Strongman Problem, from Modi to Trump," *New Yorker*, January 18, 2017, https://www .newyorker.com/news/daily-comment/the-strongman-problem-from-modi-to -trump.

96. Max Fisher and Amanda Taub, "How Does Democracy Erode? Venezuela Is a Case in Point," *New York Times*, April 2, 2017, A8.

97. Ruth Marcus, "Authoritarianism Creeps Up on You: This Is How," *Washington Post*, June 29, 2017, https://www.washingtonpost.com/opinions/the -creeping-authoritarianism-of-trumps-attacks-on-the-free-press/2017/06/29 /81e92ca6-5cea-11e7-9fc6-c7ef4bc58d13_story.html.

98. Ariel Malka and Yphtach Leikes, "In a New Poll, Half of Republicans Say They Would Support Postponing the 2020 Election If Trump Proposed It," *Washington Post*, August 10, 2017, https://www.washingtonpost.com/news /monkey-cage/wp/2017/08/10/in-a-new-poll-half-of-republicans-say-they -would-support-postponing-the-2020-election-if-trump-proposed-it/; see also Frum, *Trumpocracy*, 231.

99. See E. J. Dionne Jr., "Are Republicans Abandoning Democracy?" *Washington Post*, December 9, 2018, https://www.washingtonpost.com/opinions/are -republicans-abandoning-democracy/2018/12/09/8ad0b278-fa62-11e8-8c9a-860 ce2a8148f_story.html?utm_term=.bbbd323d70c; Max Boot, "America Now Has a Party of Authoritarianism—It's the GOP," *Washington Post*, December 11, 2018, https://www.washingtonpost.com/opinions/2018/12/11/america-now-has-party -authoritarianism-its-gop/?utm_term=.0b7b3ea176b2. The quotation is from Boot.

100. Hetherington and Suhay, "Authoritarianism, Threat, and Americans' Support for the War on Terror," 557.

101. Stenner, *Authoritarian Dynamic*, 331, 333.

102. Taub, "Rise of American Authoritarianism."

103. Ashley Parker, "'Totally Dishonest': Trump Asserts *Only* He Can Be Trusted over Opponents and 'Fake News,'" *Washington Post*, August 30, 2018, https://www.washingtonpost.com/politics/trump-pushes-a-reality-where -opponents-are-peddling-false-facts-and-only-he-can-be-trusted/2018/08/30

/d7ac7c38-ac62-11e8-b1da-ff7faa680710_story.html?utm_term=.5242e4a72166; Felicia Sonmez, "Critics Fear Trump's Attacks Are Doing Lasting Damage to the Justice System," *Washington Post*, August 23, 2018, https://www.washington post.com/politics/critics-fear-trumps-attacks-are-doing-lasting-damage-to -the-justice-system/2018/08/23/67410ad4-a6fb-11e8-97ce-cc9042272f07_story .html?utm_term=.5b02370f5b4b.

104. Michael Gerson, "This Is the New GOP: Angry and Afraid," *Washington Post*, August 30, 2018, https://www.washingtonpost.com/opinions/the gop -must-take-a-stand--if-it-still-has-legs/2018/08/30/a992dd8e-ac7f-11e8-b1da-f f7faa680710_story.html?utm_term=.e7cc4e1af5d8.

105. Trump Twitter Archive, http://www.trumptwitterarchive.com/, September 3, 2018.

106. Trump Twitter Archive, http://www.trumptwitterarchive.com/, June 4, 2018; Maggie Haberman and Michael Crowley, "Trump Pushes Attorney General to 'Act' Against Biden Before Election," *New York Times*, October 21, 2020, A19.

107. Felicia Sonmez, "Trump Suggests That Protesting Should Be Illegal," *Washington Post*, September 4, 2018, https://www.washingtonpost.com/politics /trump-suggests-protesting-should-be-illegal/2018/09/04/11cfd9be-b0a0-11e8 -aed9-001309990777_story.html?utm_term=.3b67374b88b2.

108. Ashley Parker, Seung Min Kim, and Robert Costa, "'I'm Not Going There': As Trump Hurls Racial Invective, Most Republicans Stay Silent," *Washington Post*, August 18, 2018, https://www.washingtonpost.com/politics/im-not-going -there-as-trump-hurls-racial-invective-most-republicans-stay-silent/2018/08/18 /aab7fd8a-a189-11e8-83d2-70203b8d7b44_story.html?utm_term=.1a3fd6974ad3.

109. Phillip Bump, "By a 3-to-1 Margin, Trump Supporters Embrace His Personality over His Policies," *Washington Post*, August 23, 2018, https://www .washingtonpost.com/news/politics/wp/2018/08/23/by-a-3-to-1-margin-trump -supporters-embrace-his-personality-over-his-policies/?utm_term=.24a0c 5277523.

110. Paul Krugman, "A Quisling and His Enablers," *New York Times*, June 12, 2018, A22.

111. Levitsky and Ziblatt, *How Democracies Die*, 5.

112. Levitsky and Ziblatt, 5, 7.

113. Levitsky and Ziblatt, 23–24, 61–67, 176–187.

114. Levitsky and Ziblatt, 23–24.

115. Peter Baker and Katie Rogers, "In Trump's America, the Conversation Turns Ugly and Angry, Starting at the Top," *New York Times*, June 30, 2018, A1; Karen Tumulty, "Trump Spreads Racism with a Fighter Pilot's Precision," *Washington Post*, August 14, 2018, https://www.washingtonpost.com/opinions/trump -is-plenty-racist-without-the-n-word/2018/08/14/69d35c78-9fcd-11e8-93e3 -24d1703d2a7a_story.html?utm_term=.3ec138e1a9b5.

116. Michael Gerson, "Trump Doesn't Just Fail a Moral Standard: He Enables Cruelty and Abuse," *Washington Post*, May 31, 2018, https://www.washington post.com/opinions/trump-doesnt-just-fail-a-moral-standard-he-enables -cruelty-and-abuse/2018/05/31/31a8bdfe-6506-11e8-99d2-0d678ec08c2f_story .html?utm_term=.69f18cbfc778.

117. Ronald Reagan, "Speech of the Former President at the 1992 Republican Convention," August 17, 1992, American History, http://www.let.rug.nl/usa /presidents/ronald-wilson-reagan/speech-of-the-former-president-at-the-1992 -republican-convention.php.

118. Barack Obama, "Remarks by the President in State of the Union Address," January 24, 2012, https://obamawhitehouse.archives.gov/the-press-office /2012/01/24/remarks-president-state-union-address.

119. See Michael Gerson, "What Does Ascendance of Trump Mean about U.S.?" *Lawrence Journal-World*, October 20, 2018, 11.

120. Jonathan Chait, "How Hitler's Rise to Power Explains Why Republicans Accept Donald Trump," *New York Magazine*, July 7, 2016, http://nymag.com /daily/intelligencer/2016/07/donald-trump-and-hitlers-rise-to-power.html; E. J. Dionne Jr., "The Path to Autocracy Is All Too Familiar," *Washington Post*, August 8, 2018, https://www.washingtonpost.com/opinions/the-path-to-autocracy -is-all-too-familiar/2018/08/08/6f3602f8-9b25-11e8-b60b-1c897f17e185_story .html?utm_term=.87c45e6dd12a.

121. Patrick Kingsley, "As West Fears the Rise of Autocrats, Hungary Shows What's Possible," *New York Times*, February 10, 2018, https://www.nytimes.com /2018/02/10/world/europe/hungary-orban-democracy-far-right.html.

122. Frum, *Trumpocracy*, 154; Jackson Diehl, "Trump's Most Political Export," *Washington Post*, September 2, 2018, https://www.washingtonpost.com/opinions /global-opinions/trumps-most-potent-political-export/2018/09/02/aba0bf92 -ac66-11e8-8a0c-70b618c98d3c_story.html?utm_term=.3ed4b63b70e7.

123. Thomas B. Edsall, "The Contract with Authoritarianism," *New York Times*, April 5, 2018, https://www.nytimes.com/2018/04/05/opinion/trump -authoritarianism-republicans-contract.html.

124. Bertram Gross, *Friendly Fascism: The New Face of Power in America* (Montreal: Black Rose, 1980), see especially xii–xvii.

125. See Ronald Reagan, "Address to Members of the British Parliament," June 8, 1982, https://www.reaganlibrary.gov/research/speeches/60882a; also see Robert C. Rowland and John M. Jones, *Reagan at Westminster: Foreshadowing the End of the Cold War* (College Station: Texas A&M University Press, 2010).

126. Barack Obama, "Barack Obama's New Hampshire Primary Speech," *New York Times*, January 8, 2008, http://www.nytimes.com/2008/01/08/us/politics /08text-obama.html?mcubz=3.

127. Derek Thompson, "Trump's Populism Is a Fiction," *Atlantic*, January 20, 2017, https://www.theatlantic.com/business/archive/2017/01/trumps-populism-is-a-fiction/513989/.

128. Dionne, Ornstein, and Mann, *One Nation after Trump*, 129, 133.

129. John Adams, "Speech by John Adams at the Boston Massacre Trial," December 3, 1770, http://www.bostonmassacre.net/trial/acct-adams2.htm.

I list here only sources central to the argument developed in the book. In particular, I focus on key sources related to Trump's rhetoric of nationalist populism with an outsider and then strongman persona. I cited sources that document the background or influence of particular works of Trump's rhetoric in the notes in each chapter. The sources I cite here are central to understanding Trump's norm-breaking use of rhetoric.

Beasley, Vanessa. *You, the People: American National Identity in Presidential Rhetoric.* College Station: Texas A&M University Press, 2004.

Berlet, Chip. "'Trumping' Democracy: Right-Wing Populism, Fascism, and the Case for Action." Political Research Associates, December 12, 2015. http://www.politicalresearch.org/2015/12/12/trumping-democracy-right-wing-populism-fascism-and-the-case-for-action/#sthash.7Lk503sn.dpbs.

Bostdorff, Denise. "Obama, Trump, and Reflections on the Rhetoric of Political Change." *Rhetoric and Public Affairs* 20 (2017): 695–706.

Buncombe, Andrew. "Donald Trump One Year On: How the Twitter President Changed Social Media and the Country's Top Office." *Independent,* January 17, 2018. https://www.independent.co.uk/news/world/americas/us-politics/the-twitter-president-how-potus-changed-social-media-and-the-presidency-a8164161.html.

Burke, Kenneth. *Language as Symbolic Action: Essays on Life, Literature, and Method.* Los Angeles: University of California Press, 1966.

———. *A Rhetoric of Motives.* Berkeley: University of California Press, 1950.

Campbell, Karlyn Kohrs, and Kathleen Hall Jamieson. *Presidents Creating the Presidency: Deeds Done in Words.* Chicago: University of Chicago Press, 2008.

Carr, Nicholas. "Why Trump Tweets (and Why We Listen)." *Politico,* January 26, 2018. https://www.politico.com/magazine/story/2018/01/26/donald-trump-twitter-addiction-216530.

Cox, Daniel, Rachel Lienesch, and Robert P. Jones. *Beyond Economics: Fears of Cultural Displacement Pushed the White Working Class to Trump,* PRRI, May 9, 2017, https://www.prri.org/research/white-working-class-attitudes-economy-.

Dionne, E. J. Jr., Norman J. Ornstein, and Thomas E. Mann. *One Nation after Trump: A Guide for the Perplexed, the Disillusioned, the Desperate, and the Not-Yet Deported.* New York: St. Martin's, 2017.

Edsall, Thomas B. "The Contract with Authoritarianism," *New York Times,* April 5, 2018. https://www.nytimes.com/2018/04/05/opinion/trump-authori tarianism-republicans-contract.html.

———. "The Peculiar Populism of Donald Trump." *New York Times,* February 2, 2017. https://www.nytimes.com/2017/02/02/opinion/the-peculiar-populism -of-donald-trump.html.

Engels, Jeremy. *The Politics of Resentment: A Genealogy.* University Park: Pennsyl-vania State University Press, 2015.

Folkenflik, David. "Analysis: In Trump's Twitter Feed, a Tale of Sound and Fury." NPR, April 7, 2018. https://www.npr.org/2018/04/017/600138538/analysis-in -trumps-twitter._

Frum, David. *Trumpocracy: The Corruption of the American Republic.* New York: HarperCollins, 2018.

Green, Emma. "It Was Cultural Anxiety That Drove White, Working-Class Vot-ers to Trump." *Atlantic,* May 9, 2017. https://www.theatlantic.com/politics /archive/2017/05/white-working-class-trump-cultural-anxiety/525771.

Green, Joshua. *Devil's Bargain: Steve Bannon, Donald Trump, and the Nationalist Uprising.* New York: Penguin, 2017.

Guilford, Gwynn. "Inside the Trump Machine: The Bizarre Psychology of Amer-ica's Newest Political Movement." Quartz, April 1, 2016. https://qz.com/645345 /inside-the-trump-machine-the-bizarre-psychology-of-americas-newest -political-movement/.

Hart, Roderick P. *Campaign Talk: Why Elections Are Good for Us.* Princeton, NJ: Princeton University Press, 2000.

Hetherington, Marc J., and Jonathan D. Weiler. *Authoritarianism and Polariza-tion in American Politics.* Cambridge, UK: Cambridge University Press, 2009.

Hogan, J. Michael, ed. *Rhetoric and Reform in the Progressive Era: A Rhetorical History of the United States,* vol. 6. East Lansing: Michigan State University Press, 2003.

Homans, Charles. "The Post-Campaign Campaign of Donald Trump." *New York Times Magazine,* April 9, 2018. https://www.nytimes.com/2018/04/09 /magazine/donald-trump-rallies-campaigning-president.html.

Huddy, Leonie, Stanley Feldman, and Erin Cassese. "On the Distinct Political Effects of Anger." In *The Affect Effect: Dynamics of Emotion in Political Think-ing and Behavior,* edited by W. Russell Neuman, George E. Marcus, Ann N. Crigler, and Michael Mackuen. Chicago: University of Chicago Press, 2007.

Jamieson, Kathleen Hall, and Doron Taussig. "Disruption, Demonization, De-liverance, and Norm Destruction: The Rhetorical Signature of Donald J. Trump." *Political Science Quarterly* 132 (2017–2018): 619–650.

Johnson, Paul Elliott. "The Art of Masculine Victimhood: Donald Trump's Dem-agoguery." *Women's Studies in Communication* 20 (2017): 229–250.

Judis, John. *The Populist Explosion: How the Great Recession Transformed American and European Politics.* New York: Columbia Global Reports, 2016.

Kazin, Michael. *The Populist Persuasion: An American History,* rev. ed. Ithaca, NY: Cornell University Press, 1998.

Kellner, Douglas. *American Nightmare: Donald Trump, Media Spectacle, and Authoritarian Populism.* Rotterdam: Sense Publishers, 2016.

Khazan, Olga. "People Voted for Trump Because They Were Anxious, Not Poor." *Atlantic,* April 23, 2018. https://www.theatlantic.com/science/archive/2018/04/existential-anxiety-not-poverty-motivates-trump-support/558674/.

Koerth, Maggie. "Donald Trump Incites His Crowds—and His Crowds Incite Him." FiveThirtyEight, March 15, 2016. https://fivethirtyeight.com/features/donald-trump-incites-his-crowds-and-his-crowds-incite-him/.

Levitsky, Steven, and Daniel Ziblatt. *How Democracies Die.* New York: Crown, 2018.

Mercieca, Jennifer R. "Afterword: Trump as Anarchist and Sun King." In *Faking the News: What Rhetoric Can Teach Us about Donald J. Trump,* edited by Ryan Skinnell. Exeter, UK: Imprint Academic, 2018.

Mudde, Cas, and Cristóbal Rovira Kaltwasser. *Populism: A Very Short Introduction.* New York: Oxford University Press, 2017.

Müller, Jan-Werner. *What Is Populism?* Philadelphia: University of Pennsylvania Press, 2016.

Mutz, Diana C. "Status Threat, Not Economic Hardship, Explains the 2016 Presidential Vote." *PNAS* (May 8, 2018). www.pnas.org/cgi/doi/10.1073/pnas.1718155115.

Neiwert, David. "Trump and Right-Wing Populism: A Long Time Coming." Political Research Associates, June 21, 2016, https://www.politicalresearch.org/2016/06/21/trump-and-right-wing-populism-a-long-time-coming.

Norris, Pippa. "It's Not Just Trump: Authoritarian Populism Is Rising Across the West—Here's Why." *Washington Post,* March 11, 2016. https://www.washingtonpost.com/news/monkey-cage/wp/2016/03/11/its-not-just-trump-authoritarian-populism-is-rising-across-the-west-heres-why/.

Ott, Brian L. "The Age of Twitter: Donald J. Trump and the Politics of Debasement." *Critical Studies in Media Communication* 34 (2017): 59–68.

Ott, Brian L., and Greg Dickinson. *The Twitter Presidency: Donald J. Trump and the Politics of White Rage.* New York: Routledge, 2019.

Peters, Jeremy W., Elaina Plott, and Maggie Haberman. "260,000 Words, Full of Self-Praise, from Trump on the Virus." *New York Times,* April 26, 2020. https://www.nytimes.com/interactive/2020/04/26/us/politics/trump-coronavirus-briefings-analyzed.html.

Reicher, Stephen, and Alexander Haslam. "What Psychology Can Teach Us about Trump's Victory—and What Trump's Victory Can Teach Us about Psychology."

European Association of Social Psychology (June 6, 2017), https://www.easp
.eu/news/itm/-452.html.

———. "Trump's Appeal: What Psychology Tells Us." *Scientific American*,
March 1, 2017. https://www.scientificamerican.com/article/trump-rsquo-s
-appeal-what-psychology-tells-us.

Roig-Franzia, Manuel, and Sarah Ellison. "A History of the Trump War on Media—the Obsession Not Even Coronavirus Could Stop." *Washington Post*,
March 28, 2020. https://www.washingtonpost.com/lifestyle/media/a-history
-of-the-trump-war-on-media--the-obsession-not-even-coronavirus-could
-stop/2020/03/28/71bb21d0-f433-11e9-8cf0-4cc99f74d127_story.html.

Rolfe, Mark. *The Reinvention of Populist Rhetoric in the Digital Age: Insiders and
Outsiders in Democratic Politics*. London: Palgrave Macmillan, 2016.

Rowland, Robert C. "The 2016 Presidential Debates as Public Argument." In
Televised Presidential Debates in a Changing Media Environment, vol. 1: *The
Candidates Make Their Case*, edited by Edward A. Hinck. Santa Barbara, CA:
Praeger, 2019.

———. "Donald Trump and the Rejection of the Norms of American Politics
and Rhetoric." In *An Unprecedented Election: Campaign Coverage, Communication, and Citizens Divided*, edited by Benjamin R. Warner, Dianne G.
Bystrom, Mitchell S. McKinney, and Mary C. Banwart. Santa Barbara, CA:
ABC-Clio, 2018.

———. "Implicit Standards of Public Argument in Presidential Debates: What
the 2016 Debates Reveal about Public Deliberation." *Argumentation and Advocacy* 54 (2018): 76–94.

———. "The Populist and Nationalist Roots of Trump's Rhetoric." *Rhetoric and
Public Affairs* 22 (2019): 343–388.

Smith, David. "How Trump Uses Twitter Storms to Make the Political Weather."
Guardian, December 2, 2017. https://www.theguardian.com/us-news/2017
/dec/02/how-trump-uses-twitter-storms-to-make-the-political-weather.

Stenner, Karen. *The Authoritarian Dynamic*. Cambridge, UK: Cambridge University Press, 2005.

Stuckey, Mary E. "American Elections and the Rhetoric of Political Change: Hyperbole, Anger, and Hope in U.S. Politics." *Rhetoric and Public Affairs* 20, no.
4 (Winter 2017): 667–694.

Taub, Amanda. "The Rise of American Authoritarianism." Vox, March 1, 2016.
https://www.vox.com/2016/3/1/11127424/trump-authoritarianism.

———. "Trump's Victory and the Rise of White Populism." *New York Times*, November 10, 2016. https://www.nytimes.com/2016/11/10/world/americas/trump
-white-populism-europe-united-states.html.

Tulis, Jeffrey K. *The Rhetorical Presidency*. Princeton, NJ: Princeton University
Press, 1987.

Tur, Katy. *Unbelievable: My Front-Row Seat to the Craziest Campaign in American History*. New York: HarperCollins, 2017.

Woodward, Bob. *Fear: Trump in the White House*. New York: Simon and Schuster, 2018.

Zarefsky, David. "Presidential Rhetoric and the Power of Definition." *Presidential Studies Quarterly* 34 (2004): 607–619.

INDEX

ACA. *See* Affordable Care Act
Access Hollywood tape, 14
Adams, John, 180
affective genre: nationalist
  populism as, 4, 12, 13, 16–17,
  20–21
Affordable Care Act (ACA), xiv,
  23, 63, 132; alternative to, 65;
  case for, 120; opposition to, 38,
  64; repeal of, 65, 75, 113, 170–171
agendas, 65, 87, 135; coherent, 76;
  conservative, 31; corporate,
  180; domestic, 147; economic,
  139, 140; governing, 159;
  ideological, 53; immigration,
  94; policy, 38, 55, 58, 111;
  positive, 59; progressive, 53;
  rhetorical, 64
al-Badawi, Jamal, 122
al-Qaeda, 12, 122
Altman, Alex, 50
alt right, 17, 91, 93, 115, 174
America First, 35, 36, 57–58, 59,
  159
"American carnage," xii, 56, 57, 58,
  69, 139, 148, 160, 161, 164, 166
American dream, 24, 36, 39, 97,
  179; dystopian variant of, 51;
  protecting, 50; retelling, 139;
  vision of, 178
American dystopia, 22, 25, 29–32,
  38, 39, 40–41, 51, 53, 55, 56, 59,
  111, 119, 121, 123, 139–140, 164,
  170
American Revolution, 84
anger, 2, 90, 118, 150, 163; stoking,
  30, 80, 112, 142, 159, 167

antitrust laws, 10
Apprentice, The, 93
Aristotle, 2
Art of the Deal, The (Trump), 23
Atlantic, 47, 143
authoritarianism, 11–20, 13, 115,
  142, 144–145, 146, 151, 152,
  161–162, 169, 172, 179; creeping,
  175–176; disposition toward,
  141, 156; intolerance and, 156;
  normative worldview of, 14;
  Republicans and, 176; strength
  of, 180; Trump and, 173–174;
  white working class and, 148;
  women and, 154
authoritarian mind-set, 13, 20, 55,
  91, 140, 141, 142, 157
authoritarian personality, 13, 14,
  20, 141, 145, 148, 152, 154, 157,
  158, 173, 174, 176
authoritarian voters, 14, 18, 20, 21,
  164; appealing to, 142; female,
  154; role of, 155–156

Bacon, Perry, Jr., 112
Baier, Bret, 48
Baker, Peter, 55, 102, 115, 120
Bannon, Steve, 34, 35, 36
Barr, William P., 177
base. *See* core supporters
Battle of the Baggage Chain, 84
Beard, Miriam, 116–117
Beasley, Vanessa, 62
behavior, xiii, 112; authoritarian,
  178; personal, 82; presidential,
  177
Berezin, Mabel, 175